Easy Grammar®: Grade 3

Wanda C. Phillips, Ed.D.

Published by Easy Grammar Systems Inc.

7717 E. Greenway Road

Scottsdale, AZ 85260

Printed in the United States of America

www.easygrammar.com

Printed in the United States of America

A student workbook entitled **Easy Grammar Grade 3 Student Workbook** is available. This workbook does not include an answer key or strategies for effective teaching. In addition, tests are not included.

Easy Grammar Grade 3 Student Test Booklet is now available; this contains a pre-assessment test, all unit tests and cumulative tests, and a post-assessment test.

Correlation pages for **Easy Grammar: Grade 3** and **Easy Grammar Grade 3 Student Workbook** have been placed throughout this textbook. Also, a correlation of teacher edition pages and workbook pages has been placed at the back of this text.

TABLE OF CONTENTS

NOUNS   185

ADJECTIVES   243

TO THE TEACHER: *Please read!*

Each **TO THE TEACHER** page is helpful. Please read the entire page. Also, on occasion, I have placed **Note to Teacher** information on answer key pages. Please read the answer key *before* you have your students do the page.

Familiarize yourself with the text. If you have not spent time perusing it, I suggest that you do so. Do the lessons in a time frame that facilitates learning. (In other words, adapt it to your students' needs and your style of teaching.)

As in all good teaching, use what is appropriate for your students. For example, within the preposition unit, I have placed numerous activities that will help children to learn their prepositions. You may decide that students need not do every activity.

Students need to **memorize** the prepositions. (Only 28 prepositions have been listed in this text.) In addition to the activities, **I recommend that you ask students to be able to write or to say the entire list**. (Some teachers choose to set the prepositions to music, e.g. a familiar song like "Yankee Doodle.") In order to make learning the prepositions an easy process, I advise asking students to be able to write the prepositions that begin with *a*. When they can do that successfully, assign the *b* prepositions. Then, ask students to list all of column one. Column two should be learned in a similar manner. Give students ample time to do the activities and to learn the list. If the list is learned at **automaticity**, the rest of the preposition unit and the other parts of grammar will prove to be very **easy**.

I have placed a bingo game on pages 14 and 15. An explanation is offered on page 14. A reproducible bingo card has been provided on page 15. Some teachers prefer to ask students to write whichever prepositions they choose on a card. Other teachers choose to play the bingo card on construction paper, write in the prepositions, and laminate each card. These, then, can be used from year to year. As mentioned earlier, do whatever fits your style of teaching and your students' needs.

The **capitalization and punctuation** units are located at the end of this text. You may choose to teach these units at the end of the year. However, I have found that teaching them at the beginning of the year and using **Daily Grams: Grade 3** review each days helps children to master these concepts. The first 10 *Daily Grams: Grade 3* lessons have been provided for you. I highly recommend that you do Day 1 the first day of school, Day 2 on the second day, etc. If you find them as valuable as I think you will, you may order the *Daily Grams: Grade 3* text. Do one *gram* a day at the beginning of each class period. More information is provided before the *Daily Grams* section which is located after the writing unit and before the index.

Please be enthusiastic in your teaching of English. We want students to become interested and excited about learning!

Why should I use <u>Easy Grammar: Grade 3</u>?

Easy Grammar: Grade 3 uses a unique approach. Students memorize and learn prepositions first. Many "fun" pages that will help students to learn and to identify prepositions are included at the beginning of this book. Reading the remainder of this introduction will help you to understand how the approach works. You may encounter concepts on this page (and the next) that may make you doubtful about your own knowledge. Let me assure you that *Easy Grammar* is as the name implies---*EASY!*

1. In a step-by-step manner, students learn to identify prepositional phrases and to delete them from the sentence.

2. After a prepositional phrase is crossed out, the student no longer needs to be concerned with it. **The subject and verb won't be in a prepositional phrase.*** This makes it very easy to determine subject and verb of a sentence.

3. **Example:** In the following sentence, students who do not use this approach may respond that the subject is *child* or *park.*

A mother with her child ran across the park.

The prepositional approach eliminates the guessing. Prepositional phrases are crossed out. Therefore, the subject and verb of a sentence are readily determined.

A <u>mother</u> ~~with her child~~ <u>ran</u> ~~across the park.~~

4. In using this process, students are actively engaged in learning. They love the "hands-on" process, and using it helps them to be successful.

*most of the time

i

5. This approach is used periodically throughout the text in order for students to understand other concepts: direct objects, subject/verb agreement, etc.

✺✺✺✺✺✺✺✺✺✺✺✺✺✺✺✺✺✺✺✺✺✺✺✺✺✺✺✺✺✺✺✺✺✺✺✺

Another important difference of *Easy Grammar* texts is that concepts are **introduced and reviewed throughout the school year**. In addition, **reviews and cumulative reviews** are provided along the way to help insure mastery learning.

✺✺✺✺✺✺✺✺✺✺✺✺✺✺✺✺✺✺✺✺✺✺✺✺✺✺✺✺✺✺✺✺✺✺✺✺

IMPORTANT QUESTIONS:

How may prepositions are introduced in *Easy Grammar: Grade 3*?

✺ *Easy Grammar: Grade 3* includes only **28** prepositions for students to learn. Games have been included, and concepts are presented in a way that third graders will understand easily.

Should I use *Daily Grams: Guided Review Aiding Mastery Skills – Grade 3* along with this text?

✺Yes! In fact, you will find the first **10** pages of *Daily Grams: Grade 3* in the last section for you to introduce to your students. Copy each *Daily Grams* lesson (day) for your students to do at the beginning of each class. It should take only about ten minutes for students to complete it *and* for you to discuss it with them. *Daily Grams: Grade 3* is especially effective for reinforcing capitalization, punctuation, grammar usage, sentence combining for improved writing skills, and various other concepts.

Does this text have a writing section?

✺Yes! A section regarding writing sentences begins after the pronoun unit. Students will learn to write sentences containing items in a series and appositives.

TO THE TEACHER: Information Regarding Student Test Booklet

The student test booklet begins with a pre-assessment and ends with an identical post-assessment. The pre-assessment is found on pages 1 – 5; the post-assessment appears on pages 39 – 43.

The test booklet has been designed with teachers in mind. Tests are arranged so that students can remove each test without affecting other tests in the booklet. Obviously, the test booklet can be used in a multitude of ways. Use it in the manner that works best for you and your students.

Test Booklet Pages Correlated with Teacher Edition Answer Key Pages:

	BOOKLET PAGES	TEACHER ED. PAGES
Grade 3 **PRE-ASSESSMENT**	1-5	522-526
Preposition Test	7	66
Verb Test	9-11	178, 180, 182
Noun Test	13	224
Cumulative Test (End of Noun Unit)	15-16	238, 240
Adjective Test	17	270
Cumulative Test (End of Adjective Unit)	19-22	288, 290, 292, 294
Adverb Test	23	330
Pronoun Test	25	366
Cumulative Test (End of Pronoun Unit)	27-29 30-31 32-33	392, 394, 396 398, 400 402, 404
Capitalization Test	35	434
Punctuation Test	37	468
Grade 3 **Post-ASSESSMENT**	39-43	522-526

TO THE TEACHER: *Assessment Test Information*

An assessment test is provided on the next five pages.

Go to page 522 for answers to the assessment test.

1. Please allow students to take this test before beginning any lessons. Although the assessment may seem lengthy, it should not take students long to complete. For the pretest, you may want to tell students to leave an answer blank if they don't know.   (This usually places students at ease.)

2. Score the test and review it for information regarding the level of each student's understanding.

(I recommend that you do not share the pretest results with students. If the score is low, a child may feel deflated before he begins this approach to grammar and usage. Students' scores on last year's standardized tests may be reviewed to determine areas of strengths and weaknesses, also.)

3. After scoring the test, please store it somewhere to be retrieved **after** the student takes it as a posttest. After you have scored the posttest, share both the pretest and posttest results with students so that they can see their increase in understanding. This is positive in that students can see the product of their work and can **internalize success**. (Consider *individual conferences* to discuss the pre and post tests' results.)

SCORING: I have provided one method of scoring. Feel free to create your own by determining which areas you consider most important. However, be sure that you use the same method of scoring for **both** the pretest and the posttest.

Note: Deletion of prepositional phrases has been suggested (not graded) on the assessment test. I suggest that you use this process all year so that it becomes an automatic tool.

A. Sentence Types:
Directions: Place the letter of the sentence type in the blank.

1. _____ Put the cereal away.   A. declarative

2. _____ Yeah! I'm finished!   B. exclamatory

3. _____ Where's your dog?   C. imperative

4. _____ Kim ate a few grapes.   D. interrogative

B. Capitalization:
Directions: Place a capital letter above any word that should be capitalized.

1. on monday, i am going to kaw lake near ponca city.

2. jake asked, "who lives on dale lane?"

3. dear liz,

    is uncle bo driving to long beach on memorial

  day this spring?

                your buddy,

                tate

C. Punctuation:
Directions: Place punctuation where needed (commas, colons, question marks, exclamation points, underlining, and quotation marks).

1. Emily may I help you

2. No we cant leave before 4 00

3. Yikes Im late

4. We met Mr J Cobb on Dec 24 2004

v

D. Subjects and Verbs:
   Directions: Underline the subject once and the verb or verb phrase twice.
   Note: Crossing out prepositional phrases will help you.

1. Our aunt visits at the end of every summer.

2. After lunch, two boys sat under a tree and talked.

3. My sister and big brother camp in a state park.

4. The shed behind the big barn was struck by a car.

E. Contractions:
   Directions: Write the contraction.

1. are not - _____   3. we are - _____   5. here is - _____

2. who is - _____   4. have not - _____   6. were not - _____

F. Subject-Verb Agreement:
   Directions: Underline the subject once. Underline the verb that agrees twice.
   (Crossing out prepositional phrases will help you.)

1. On the weekends, their dad (bake, bakes).

2. The pastor and his wife (plays, play) tennis.

3. Farmers in that dry area (hope, hopes) for rain.

G. Irregular Verbs:
   Directions: Underline the subject once and the correct verb phrase twice.

1. That team has (chose, chosen) uniforms.

2. He must have (flown, flew) home.

3. A check could be (wrote, written).

4. Pears were (ate, eaten) for a snack.

5. Have you ever (saw, seen) a rattler?

6. The river had (rose, risen) two feet.

7. Lanzo should have (took, taken) his father's advice.

H. Tenses:
    Directions: Underline the subject once and the verb or verb phrase twice. Write the tense in the blank.

1. _____ Berry tarts are our dessert.

2. _____ The bell will ring soon.

3. _____ My sister sneezed.

I. Common and Proper Nouns:
    Directions: Circle the common nouns.

1. EMMA   2. DOG   3. POODLE   4. CITY

J. Singular and Plural Nouns:
    Directions: Write the plural of each noun.

1. zebra - _____   5. deer - _____

2. ruby - _____   6. tray - _____

3. mix - _____   7. watch - _____

4. child - _____   8. calf - _____

K. Possessive Nouns:
    Directions: Write the possessive in each blank.

1. a drum that belongs to Ben - _____

2. a corral used by many horses - _____

3. computer belonging to children - _____

L. Identifying Nouns:
   Directions: Circle any nouns.

1. We need to take this shovel, a sleeping bag, two tents, and some strong rope.

M. Conjunctions and Interjections:
   Directions: Draw a box around a conjunction. Circle an interjection.

1. Wow! Jacy won!

2. Give your ticket to my friend or me.

N. Identifying Adjectives:
   Directions: Circle any adjective.

1. Many dirty rags lay on the new carpet.

2. We ordered orange juice and French toast.

O. Degrees of Adjectives:
   Directions: Circle the correct answer.

1. The second pail of water was (sudsier, sudsiest) than the first.

2. Of the five kittens, the gray one is (more playful, most playful).

3. My left foot is (longer, longest) than my right one.

P. Adverbs:
   Directions: Circle adverbs.

1. One child stood up quietly.

2. Peter always goes there with his family.

Q. Degrees of Adverbs:
   Directions: Circle the correct answer.

1. Of the four friends, Tate swims (better, best).

2. Lisa rides her bike (oftener, more often) than her brother.

3. He held the second rope (more tightly, most tightly) than the first rope.

R. Pronouns:
    Directions: Circle the correct answer.

1. (She, Her) likes shepherd's pie.

2. Will a bellman take (we, us) to our room?

3. Jacy and (him, he) played checkers.

4. Today, (me and my friend, my friend and me, my friend and I) rode in a taxi.

5. These shells are for (them, they).

6. Mr. Bonds chose (we, us) to hand out posters.

S. Usage:
    Directions: Circle the correct answer.

1. I don't feel (good, well).

2. Marco doesn't know (nothing, anything) about it.

3. Do you want to go to the zoo to see (an, a) elephant?

4. The eagles soared high above (its, their) nest.

5. (Your, You're) a great skater!

T. Other Items:

1. Circle the direct object: A boy threw a stone into the stream.

2. Circle the object of the preposition: That man in the dark blue suit is my uncle.

3. Write a regular verb: _____

4. Write an irregular verb: _____

TO THE TEACHER:

A dictionary definition of a preposition is on the next page. It is obviously too difficult for this level.   It, perhaps, will suffice to say that a preposition is the main part of a prepositional phrase. Prepositional phrases are used in our language to add more meaning to sentences.

      Example: A boy ran fast.

                 A boy **in a red checkered shirt** ran fast **down the tree-lined street.**

Again, **please** have students memorize the list of prepositions. Your goal is for students to have a successful learning experience.

DEFINITION

A preposition is "a relation or function word...that connects a lexical word, usually a noun or pronoun, or a syntactic construction to another element of the sentence, as a verb, to a noun, or to an adjective..."

- Webster's New World Dictionary

PREPOSITIONS

above	from
across	in
after	inside
around	into
at	of
before	off
behind	on
below	out
beside	over
between	through
by	to
down	under
during	up
for	with

WORKBOOK PAGE 2
Date_____

Note to teacher: Be sure to discuss that words that rhyme don't have to end with the same letter. You may wish to write student responses on the board to demonstrate this.

A.   Rhyming: Words that rhyme have the same sound at the end.
          Examples: top / pop   red / head

1.   Write a preposition that rhymes with *clown*.   _____**down**_____

2.   Write a preposition that rhymes with *clover*.   _____**over**_____

3.   Write a preposition that rhymes with *thunder*.   _____**under**_____

4.   Write a preposition that rhymes with *drum*.   _____**from**_____

5.   Write six words that rhyme with the preposition, *at*.
          ANSWERS WILL VARY/REPRESENTATIVE ANSWERS:

     bat   cat   fat   hat   mat   pat   rat   sat

     brat   flat   gnat

B.   Our language is interesting. We use definite words to be more exact.
Example: *To look* means to set eyes on something in order to see.

          If we want to be more specific, we can use words like *glance* or
          stare.

          To glance means to look at something for a very short time.
          To stare means to look at something for a long time.

Use three of your rhyming words for *at* to complete each sentence.
          ANSWERS WILL VARY.

1.   I looked at the _____**rat**_____.

2.   I glanced at the _____**cat**_____.

3.   I stared at the _____**bat**_____.

2

Name_____ **PREPOSITIONS**

Date_____

A. Rhyming: Words that rhyme have the same sound at the end.

Examples: top / pop   red / head

1. Write a preposition that rhymes with *clown.* _____

2. Write a preposition that rhymes with *clover.* _____

3. Write a preposition that rhymes with *thunder.* _____

4. Write a preposition that rhymes with *drum.* _____

5. Write six words that rhyme with the preposition, *at.*

_____   _____

_____   _____

_____   _____

B. Our language is interesting. We use definite words to be more exact.

Example: *To look* means to set eyes on something in order to see.

If we want to be more specific, we can use words like *glance* or *stare.*

To glance means to look at something for a very short time.
To stare means to look at something for a long time.

Use three of your rhyming words for *at* to complete each sentence.

1. I looked at the _____.

2. I glanced at the _____.

3. I stared at the _____.

A.   Write the prepositions that have only two letters.

     a <u>t</u>   b <u>y</u>   i <u>n</u>   o <u>f</u>

     o <u>n</u>   t <u>o</u>   u <u>p</u>

B.   Write the prepositions that have three letters.

     f <u>o</u> <u>r</u>   o <u>f</u> <u>f</u>   o <u>u</u> <u>t</u>

C.   Write the following prepositions in alphabetical order.

Remember: **Look at the first letter. Find the boldfaced letter that comes first in the alphabet. Write that word on the first line. Find the letter that comes next in the alphabet. Write that word second. Use this method to write your list.**

     through   **i**nside   **d**uring   **w**ith

     _____**during**_____

     _____**inside**_____

     _____**through**_____

     _____**with**_____

Name_____   **PREPOSITIONS**

Date_____

A. Write the prepositions that have only two letters.

    a _   b _   i _   o _

    o _   t _   u _

B. Write the prepositions that have three letters.

    f _ _   o _ _   o _ _

C. Write the following prepositions in alphabetical order.

Remember: **Look at the first letter. Find the boldfaced letter that comes first in the alphabet. Write that word on the first line. Find the letter that comes next in the alphabet. Write that word second. Use this method to write your list.**

    through   **inside**   **during**   **with**

    _____

    _____

    _____

    _____

Name_____

WORKBOOK PAGE 4

Date_____

A. Write the prepositions that begin with *be*.

      be **<u>l o w</u>**   be **<u>f o r e</u>**   be **<u>h i n d</u>**

      be **<u>s i d e</u>**   be **<u>t w e e n</u>**

Which preposition begins with *b* but not with *be*? ____**by**_____

B. Two prepositions end with *side*. Write those prepositions.

_____**beside**_____

_____**inside**_____

C. Write these prepositions that begin with *a* in alphabetical order.

Remember: When the first letter is the same, you look at the second letter.

    after   across   above   at   around

1. ____**above**_____

2. ____**across**_____

3. ____**after**_____

4. ____**around**_____

5. ____**at**_____

6

Name_____   **PREPOSITIONS**

Date_____

A. Write the prepositions that begin with *be*.

be _ _ _   be _ _ _ _   be _ _ _ _

be _ _ _ _   be _ _ _ _ _

Which preposition begins with *b* but not with *be*? _____

B. Two prepositions end with *side*. Write those prepositions.

_____

_____

C. Write these prepositions that begin with *a* in alphabetical order.

**Remember: When the first letter is the same, you look at the
             second letter.**

after   across   above   at   around

1. _____

2. _____

3. _____

4. _____

5. _____

A. Look at the picture. Then, fill in the blank with a preposition that fits.

1.

The sun is ____**behind**____ the hill.

2.

The sun is ____**above/over**____ the hill.

B. Draw a picture and write a sentence:

1. Draw a hill. Then, draw something **beside** the hill.

APPROPRIATE PICTURE

Write a sentence to tell what is **beside** the hill.
ANSWERS WILL VARY.

2. Draw a hill. Then, draw something going **down** the hill.

APPROPRIATE PICTURE

Write a sentence to tell what is going **down** the hill.
ANSWERS WILL VARY.

Name_____   **PREPOSITIONS**

Date_____

A. Look at the picture. Then, fill in the blank with a preposition that fits.

1.

The sun is _____ the hill.

2.

The sun is _____ the hill.

B. Draw a picture and write a sentence:

1. Draw a hill. Then, draw something **beside** the hill.

Write a sentence to tell what is **beside** the hill.

_____

2. Draw a hill. Then, draw something going **down** the hill.

Write a sentence to tell what is going **down** the hill.

_____

WORKBOOK PAGE 6
Date_____
Note to teacher: Be sure to review that words that rhyme don't have to end with the same letter.

A. Rhyming: Write nine words that rhyme with the preposition, *by*:

**Remember: Words that rhyme end in the same sound.
ANSWERS WILL VARY.**

my	**fly**	**guy**
sky	**pie**	**sigh**
hi	**rye**	**why**

B. Homonyms: Homonyms are words that sound the same but have different meanings.

     Example: tea / tee

          Tea is a drink. *Tee* is the item on which a golf ball is placed. *Tea* and *tee* are both pronounced *tē*.

Write a preposition for the following homonyms:

1. four - _____**for**_____   3. inn - _____**in**_____

2. two - _____**to**_____   4. threw - _____**through**_____

C. Draw a tree. Draw something **in** the tree.

   APPROPRIATE PICTURE

     Write a sentence to tell what is **in** the tree.
     ANSWERS WILL VARY.

Name_____   **PREPOSITIONS**

Date_____

A. Rhyming: Write nine words that rhyme with the preposition, *by.*

Remember: Words that rhyme end in the same sound.

_____   _____   _____

_____   _____   _____

_____   _____   _____

B. Homonyms: Homonyms are words that sound the same but have
            different meanings.

      Example: tea / tee
            Tea is a drink. *Tee* is the item on which a golf ball is
            placed. *Tea* and *tee* are both pronounced *tē*.

Write a preposition for the following homonyms:

1. four - _____   3. inn - _____

2. two - _____   4. threw - _____

C. Draw a tree.   Draw something **in** the tree.

      Write a sentence to tell what is **in** the tree.

_____

A.   Write the following prepositions in alphabetical order.

Remember: **Look at the first letter. Find the boldfaced letter that comes first in the alphabet. Write that word on the first line. Find the letter that comes next in the alphabet. Write that word second. Use this method to write your list.**

under   between   into   around   off   during

1.   **around**   4.   **into**

2.   **between**   5.   **off**

3.   **during**   6.   **under**

B.   Draw a hill.   Draw something going up the hill.

APPROPRIATE PICTURE

Write a sentence to tell what is going **up** the hill.
ANSWERS WILL VARY.

_____

C.   Write the prepositions that contain six or more letters:

1.   i<u>nsid</u>e   3.   a<u>roun</u>d   5.   b<u>efore</u>   7.   b<u>ehind</u>

2.   b<u>eside</u>   4.   a<u>cross</u>   6.   b<u>etween</u>   8.   t<u>hrough</u>

12

A. Write the following prepositions in alphabetical order.

Remember: **Look at the first letter. Find the boldfaced letter that comes first in the alphabet. Write that word on the first line. Find the letter that comes next in the alphabet. Write that word second. Use this method to write your list.**

under **b**etween **i**nto **a**round **o**ff **d**uring

1. _____ 4. _____

2. _____ 5. _____

3. _____ 6. _____

B. Draw a hill. Draw something going up the hill.

  Write a sentence to tell what is going **up** the hill.

_____

C. Write the prepositions that contain six or more letters:

1. i _ _ _ _ _   3. a _ _ _ _ _   5. b _ _ _ _ _   7. b _ _ _ _ _

2. b _ _ _ _ _   4. a _ _ _ _ _   6. b _ _ _ _ _ _   8. t _ _ _ _ _ _

BINGO

Below is a diminutive bingo card. Its purpose is to depict how each square needs to be filled. Because there are 24 blank squares per card and 28 prepositions on the list, students will use all but four prepositions. Encourage students to **write prepositions in a random fashion**.

Before the game, duplicate the list of prepositions. Place the list on a piece of construction paper and laminate it. Then, cut the prepositions into small squares and place in a small box or bag. (You may choose to cut the pieces first and laminate each small square; this reduces eventual tearing.)

To play the game, students use their completed bingo cards. Use small pieces of paper or other appropriate items for covering squares. (If you are using small paper pieces, pass the trash at the end of the games. Otherwise, your floor may become littered.)

1. To begin, pull out a square. Say the preposition.

    Example: **for**

2. Use the preposition in a phrase. (At this point, phrases have not been introduced. However, this is great preparation for their forthcoming introduction.)

    Example: **for Mary**

3. Use the prepositional phrase in a sentence.

    Example: The gift was **for Mary.**

with	during	above	past	between
by	down	along	before	near
toward	out	FREE	to	under
across	from	beside	behind	on
below	around	into	until	through

4. Place the prepositions that have been called on a flat surface.

5. Proceed in this manner until someone obtains bingo. Standard bingo, I believe, is usually a vertical column, a horizontal column, a diagonal row, or four corners. (You may wish to investigate other possibilities.)

6. Ascertain that the student has bingo. Because your squares are lying before you, this process should be quick and easy.

7. Offer a reward that is in line with your philosophy. (You may choose not to offer one.)

PAGE 15 = WORKBOOK PAGE 8

		FREE		

PAGE 17 = WORKBOOK PAGE 9

PREPOSITIONAL PHRASES

A **phrase** is a group of words.

two words:	for you
three words:	out the door
four words:	in a candy store
five or more words:	with my mom and dad

A **prepositional phrase** starts with a preposition and ends with a noun or pronoun. To make it easy, let's say that a prepositional phrase usually ends with something you can see.

Examples: **on** the **table**

behind a **chair**

with Tom

Sometimes, **describing words** are included in a prepositional phrase.

Examples: **on** the kitchen **table**

behind a red **chair**

A. Directions: Write words to complete each prepositional phrase.
ANSWERS WILL VARY.

1. down **the steps** _____

2. under **a cherry tree** _____

3. across **the street** _____

4. with **my father** _____

5. in **an attic** _____

6. to **a frozen pond** _____

🐢 🐢 🐢 🐢 🐢 🐢 🐢 🐢 🐢 🐢 🐢 🐢 🐢 🐢 🐢 🐢 🐢 🐢 🐢

B. Directions: Unscramble the following prepositional phrases:

1. picnic on a - **on a picnic** _____

2. old inside an shed - **inside an old shed** _____

3. tunnel the through - **through the tunnel** _____

4. by car that yellow - **by that yellow car** _____

5. the diving off board - **off the diving board** _____

6. a baseball after game - **after a baseball game** _____

7. water into cold the - **into the cold water** _____

18

A. Directions: Write words to complete each prepositional phrase.

1. <u>down</u> _____

2. <u>under</u> _____

3. <u>across</u> _____

4. <u>with</u> _____

5. <u>in</u> _____

6. <u>to</u> _____

🐢 🐢 🐢 🐢 🐢 🐢 🐢 🐢 🐢 🐢 🐢 🐢 🐢 🐢 🐢 🐢 🐢

B. Directions: Unscramble the following prepositional phrases:

1. <u>picnic on a -</u> _____

2. <u>old inside an shed -</u> _____

3. <u>tunnel the through -</u> _____

4. <u>by car that yellow -</u> _____

5. <u>the diving off board -</u> _____

6. <u>a baseball after game -</u> _____

7. <u>water into cold the -</u> _____

<u>**Note to Teacher:**   **Be sure to stress that more than one word can be used.**</u>

Directions: Fill in the blank with a word (or words) that makes sense. Then, write the prepositional phrase on the line.

Example: Rod walked **around** a ____lake_____.

prepositional phrase: __around a lake__

ANSWERS WILL VARY/REPRESENTATIVE ANSWERS:

1. Our cat is lying **by** the ____door_____.

prepositional phrase: __by the door__

2. They stopped **at** a __department store_____.

prepositional phrase: __at a department store__

3. **Before** __lunch_____, we played a game.

prepositional phrase: __Before lunch__

4. This box is made **of** ____wood_____.

prepositional phrase: __of wood__

5. Jane ran **for** the ____car_____.

prepositional phrase: __for the car__

6. **During** a __birthday party__, Mom served cake.

prepositional phrase: __During a birthday party__

7. We rode **on** a ___wagon_____.

prepositional phrase: __on a wagon__

Name_____

Date_____

Directions: Fill in the blank with a word (or words) that makes sense. Then, write the prepositional phrase on the line.

Example: Rod walked **around** a _____lake_____.

prepositional phrase: ___around a lake____

1. Our cat is lying **by** the _____.

    prepositional phrase: _____

2. They stopped **at** a _____.

    prepositional phrase: _____

3. **Before** _____, we played a game.

    prepositional phrase: _____

4. This box is made **of** _____.

    prepositional phrase: _____

5. Jane ran **for** the _____.

    prepositional phrase: _____

6. **During** a _____, Mom served cake.

    prepositional phrase: _____

7. We rode **on** a _____.

    prepositional phrase: _____   21

A. Directions: Fill in the blank with a word (or words) that makes sense.
Then, write the prepositional phrase on the line.

1. Sit **beside** ____me_____ .

prepositional phrase: _____**beside me**_____

2. I ate an apple **after** ___**my basketball practice**___ .

prepositional phrase: _____**after my basketball practice**___

3. He looked **behind** the ___**door**_____for his ball.

prepositional phrase: _____**behind the door**_____

4. This note is **from** ___**their favorite uncle**__ .

prepositional phrase: _____**from their favorite uncle**_____

🐢 🐢 🐢 🐢 🐢 🐢 🐢 🐢 🐢 🐢 🐢 🐢 🐢 🐢 🐢 🐢 🐢 🐢 🐢 🐢

B. Directions: Find the prepositional phrase in the sentence and cross it
out with one horizontal (———) line.

Example: Mr. Lang sat ~~on a park bench~~.

1. The boy rushed ~~out the door.~~

2. Place the picture ~~above this oak table~~.

3. Your skates are ~~in that closet~~.

4. ~~During the program~~, several children sang.

5. The family went ~~inside the old church~~.

22

Name_____

Date_____

A. Directions: Fill in the blank with a word (or words) that makes sense.
Then, write the prepositional phrase on the line.

1. Sit **beside** _____.

   prepositional phrase: _____

2. I ate an apple **after** _____.

   prepositional phrase: _____

3. He looked **behind** the _____ for his ball.

   prepositional phrase: _____

4. This note is **from** _____.

   prepositional phrase: _____

🐢 🐢 🐢 🐢 🐢 🐢 🐢 🐢 🐢 🐢 🐢 🐢 🐢 🐢 🐢 🐢 🐢 🐢

B. Directions: Find the prepositional phrase in the sentence and cross it
out with one horizontal (———) line.

   Example: Mr. Lang sat ~~on a park bench~~.

1. The boy rushed out the door.

2. Place the picture above this oak table.

3. Your skates are in that closet.

4. During the program, several children sang.

5. The family went inside the old church.

23

Object of the Preposition

The object of the preposition is the **last word** in a prepositional phrase.

    Example: to **school**

          School is the object of the preposition.

    Example: with his little **brother**

          Brother is the object of the preposition.

Label the **O**bject of the **P**reposition by writing **O.P.** above it.

                      O.P.
Examples: to school

                     O.P.
           with his brother

A.   Directions: Write an object of the preposition in the blank.
ANSWERS WILL VARY.

1.   She asked **for** a ___**drink**___.

2.   The man stood **in** the ___**rain**___.

3.   Mrs. Bell put the dish **into** the ___**oven**___.

4.   **Before** a ___**movie**___, we always buy popcorn.

5.   Kay lives **by** a large ___**tower**___.

🐢 🐢 🐢 🐢 🐢 🐢 🐢 🐢 🐢 🐢 🐢 🐢 🐢 🐢 🐢 🐢 🐢 🐢 🐢

B.   Directions: Find the prepositional phrase in the sentence and cross it
              out with one horizontal (——) line. Then, write **O.P.**
              above the object of the preposition.

**Remember: The object of the preposition is the last word in a
              prepositional phrase.**

                     O.P.
1.   A bee landed ~~on the flower~~.

                             O.P.
2.   Several dogs barked ~~during the storm~~.

                       O.P.
3.   They often go ~~to the library~~.

                         O.P.
4.   The team ran ~~into the locker room~~.

                  O.P.
5.   Kim fell ~~off her chair~~.

                        O.P.
6.   That horse eats apples ~~from my hand~~.

Name_____

Date_____

A.   Directions: Write an object of the preposition in the blank.

1.   She asked **for** a _____.

2.   The man stood **in** the _____.

3.   Mrs. Bell put the dish **into** the _____.

4.   **Before** a _____, we always buy popcorn.

5.   Kay lives **by** a large _____.

🐢 🐢 🐢 🐢 🐢 🐢 🐢 🐢 🐢 🐢 🐢 🐢 🐢 🐢 🐢 🐢 🐢 🐢 🐢

B.   Directions: Find the prepositional phrase in the sentence and cross it
                    out with one horizontal (———) line. Then, write **O.P.**
                    above the object of the preposition.

Remember: **The object of the preposition is the last word in a**
                prepositional phrase.

1.   A bee landed on the flower.

2.   Several dogs barked during the storm.

3.   They often go to the library.

4.   The team ran into the locker room.

5.   Kim fell off her chair.

6.   That horse eats apples from my hand.

TO THE TEACHER:

In introducing the subject and verb of a sentence, it is imperative that you write examples on the board or overhead. Students need to see the process of deleting prepositional phrases from the sentence and finding the subject and verb. They need to **practice** this process with you. In addition, I recommend that you do the first few worksheets orally with the children. Again, seeing and hearing how simple it is to determine subject and verb will allow students to learn the process with ease.

HOW TO TEACH THE SUBJECT OF A SENTENCE:

You have already taught students to delete prepositional phrases. Teach them that **the subject won't be in a prepositional phrase***. They need not look for the subject in any phrase they have crossed out. Students should read only the words that have not been deleted. (Do this together in the following example.) To find the subject, ask **who** or **what** the sentence is about.

    Example: Their cat sleeps on a pillow.

    Their cat sleeps ~~on a pillow~~.

Be sure to stress that *pillow* cannot be the subject; *pillow* is in a prepositional phrase. About **what** is the sentence talking? *Cat* is the subject. Be careful; some students may say *their* is the subject. Help students to understand that *their* is incorrect. Is the sentence talking about

28   *most of the time

their? No, it is talking about *their cat.* Also, emphasize that students underline only <u>cat.</u> (We shall discuss complete subject and predicate later.) Be sure to model how to underline the subject; leave nothing to chance.

Example: Their <u>cat</u> sleeps ~~on a pillow~~.

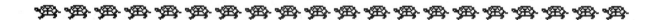

HOW TO TEACH THE VERB OF A SENTENCE:

To determine the verb, decide what **happens** (or happened) or what **is** (or was) in the sentence. **The verb will not be in a prepositional phrase.** Again, show students the **purpose of deleting prepositional phrases**. This process helps to strip the sentence to the bare bones, so to speak. Therefore, we can easily determine subject and verb.

Example: Their <u>cat</u> sleeps ~~on a pillow~~.

We have determined that cat is the subject. What does the cat do? The cat **sleeps**; *sleeps* is the verb. Teach students to place two horizontal lines under the verb.

Example: Their <u>cat</u> <u>sleeps</u> ~~on a pillow~~.

Suggestion: Use these sentences to continue your explanation.
A red car raced down the street. (Be sure to show that red is a describing word and not part of the subject.) **Linda is in a play**. (Be sure to show that this sentence simply states a fact.) **The boy on the diving board is funny.** (This shows a prepositional phrase near the subject.) **During lunch, we sat outside.** (This sentence shows a prepositional phrase at the beginning of a sentence.)

TO THE TEACHER: Please read carefully.

You may wish to skip the explanation on page 31 **if** you have thoroughly introduced the concepts using many examples. Do the worksheet on page 33 orally with the class. That should be enough for the day.   When you return to subject and verb on the ensuing day, have student volunteers read page 31 orally.   Discuss and review the ideas with them. Then, do page 35 orally with the class.   If you feel that students are grasping the concept and enjoying their success, do page 37. However, **always do at least one-third of the sentences on a worksheet with students before allowing them to proceed on their own.** (This is a good teaching practice.) Also, **circulate** and **scan** the children's work as they complete it. **(Do not assign the rest of the page for homework.)** You want to correct errors immediately. When everyone is finished, go over the entire page with your students.* Insist that they correct any mistakes; this is a *learning process*.

*I recommend that you teach children to check their work; this is becoming a "lost art." Also, encourage students to read after they have checked their work. **The more children read, the better readers they become. As students progress to higher reading levels, they internalize more complex sentence structures and higher level vocabulary. These help them to become better writers.** Yes, this is a book to teach grammar; however, writing is very important. Students should also be taught the process of writing.

PAGE 31 = WORKBOOK PAGE 15

FINDING THE SUBJECT AND THE VERB OF A SENTENCE

🐢**Subject:** The subject of a sentence is **who** or **what** a sentence is about.

Good news: **A word in a prepositional phrase will not be the subject of a sentence.**

To find the subject, first cross out each prepositional phrase.

> Example: The duck swam ~~across the pond~~.

Pond cannot be the subject. *Pond* is in a prepositional phrase, and we have crossed it out. To find the subject, read the remaining words.

> The duck swam.

Ask **who** or **what** the sentence is about. The sentence is about a duck. *Duck* is the subject. We place a line under *duck* to show it is the subject.

> The <u>duck</u> swam.

Sometimes, there may be several words in front of the subject.

> The large white <u>duck</u> swam.

We still are only talking about the duck. We underline only *duck*.

🐢**Verb:**

The verb of a sentence is what **happens (or happened)** or what **is (or was)** in a sentence.

Good news: **A word in a prepositional phrase will not be the verb of a sentence.**

To find the verb, first cross out each prepositional phrase. Next, find the subject. Then, ask what is (was) or is happening (happened) in the sentence.

> Example: The <u>duck</u> swam ~~across the pond~~.

What happened in the sentence? What did the duck do? The duck swam. *Swam* is the verb. We underline the verb twice.   The <u>duck</u> <u>swam</u>.   31

Directions: Cross out the prepositional phrase in each sentence. Then, underline the subject once and the verb twice.

Example: Joe played ~~with his friends~~.

1. He sits ~~on a stool~~.

2. I bumped ~~into a door~~.

3. Bob plays ~~in a band~~.

4. A ball rolled ~~behind a table~~.

5. She swam ~~to the steps~~.

6. Butter dripped ~~down his arm~~.

7. We walked ~~by the river~~.

8. Judy laughed ~~at the playful monkey~~.

9. ~~After lunch~~, the baby naps.

10. The child slid ~~under the table~~.

11. That gift is ~~from her brother~~.

12. Peter snacks ~~before dinner~~.

13. The children dashed ~~up the steps~~.

32

Directions: Cross out the prepositional phrase in each sentence. Then, underline the subject once and the verb twice.

Example: Joe played with his friends.

1. He sits on a stool.

2. I bumped into a door.

3. Bob plays in a band.

4. A ball rolled behind a table.

5. She swam to the steps.

6. Butter dripped down his arm.

7. We walked by the river.

8. Judy laughed at the playful monkey.

9. After lunch, the baby naps.

10. The child slid under the table.

11. That gift is from her brother.

12. Peter snacks before dinner.

13. The children dashed up the steps.

Name_____   **PREPOSITIONS**
WORKBOOK PAGE 17   Subject/Verb
Date_____

<u>Note to Teacher:</u>   These sentences contain only one prepositional phrase. Students should be able to determine subject and verb readily. To #14, I have added a direct object. Although direct objects will be introduced later, it may be wise to explain that the object we are washing is *hands*. The hands are not washing! This explanation helps students to determine the subject when a direct object appears in a sentence. Ensuing worksheets will include some sentences that contain a direct object.

Directions: Cross out the prepositional phrase in each sentence. Then, underline the subject once and the verb twice.

Example: Several <u>children</u> <u>skipped</u> ~~to a song~~.

1. <u>Susie</u> <u>lives</u> ~~in a city~~.

2. <u>They</u> <u>hid</u> ~~behind the sofa~~.

3. <u>He</u> <u>went</u> ~~into the garage~~.

4. <u>Sam</u> <u>jumped</u> ~~over a cardboard box~~.

5. Their <u>dog</u> <u>sleeps</u> ~~under their bed~~.

6. <u>Mark</u> <u>sat</u> ~~between his parents~~.

7. A <u>fisherman</u> <u>waded</u> ~~through the water~~.

8. Her <u>cut</u> <u>was</u> ~~below her right knee~~.

9. Some <u>fawns</u> <u>walked</u> ~~across a meadow~~.

10. The <u>package</u> <u>is</u> ~~from Dave's sister~~.

11. His <u>grandmother</u> often <u>sits</u> ~~beside a window~~.

12. The three <u>girls</u> <u>shopped</u> ~~with their aunt~~.

13. A small <u>bee</u> <u>buzzed</u> ~~around the room~~.

14. <u>We</u> <u>wash</u> our hands ~~before every meal~~.

34

Directions: Cross out the prepositional phrase in each sentence. Then, underline the subject once and the verb twice.

Example: Several <u>children</u> <u>skipped</u> ~~to a song~~.

1.   Susie lives in a city.

2.   They hid behind the sofa.

3.   He went into the garage.

4.   Sam jumped over a cardboard box.

5.   Their dog sleeps under their bed.

6.   Mark sat between his parents.

7.   A fisherman waded through the water.

8.   Her cut was below her right knee.

9.   Some fawns walked across a meadow.

10.   The package is from Dave's sister.

11.   His grandmother often sits beside a window.

12.   The three girls shopped with their aunt.

13.   A small bee buzzed around the room.

14.   We wash our hands before every meal.

Name_____   **PREPOSITIONS**
WORKBOOK PAGE 18   Subject/Verb
Date_____

Directions: Cross out **any** prepositional phrase(s) in each sentence. Then,
            underline the subject once and the verb twice.

**Remember: You may have more than one prepositional phrase
            in a sentence.**

                Example: He went ~~up the escalator with his friend~~.

1.   ~~During the spring~~, Jane traveled ~~to Texas~~.

2.   Matt lives ~~by a police station on Birch Street~~.

3.   They waded ~~under the bridge for fifteen minutes~~.

4.   Mr. Hunt went ~~into the building~~ and ~~up the elevator~~.

5.   ~~After the race~~, the girls sat ~~beside their coach~~.

6.   The band marched ~~down the field before a football game~~.

7.   Many bags ~~of groceries~~ lay ~~below the counter~~.

8.   Mrs. Maxwell walked ~~through the door of her office~~.

9.   The letter ~~from Buck~~ fell ~~off the wooden desk~~.

10.   An earthworm crawled ~~across the blade of grass~~.

11.   She placed a star ~~above her name on the paper~~.

12.   Peach yogurt is ~~behind the jam in the refrigerator~~.

36

Directions: Cross out **any** prepositional phrase(s) in each sentence. Then, underline the subject once and the verb twice.

Remember: You may have more than one prepositional phrase in a sentence.

Example: He <u>went</u> ~~up the escalator with his friend~~.

1.   During the spring, Jane traveled to Texas.

2.   Matt lives by a police station on Birch Street.

3.   They waded under the bridge for fifteen minutes.

4.   Mr. Hunt went into the building and up the elevator.

5.   After the race, the girls sat beside their coach.

6.   The band marched down the field before a football game.

7.   Many bags of groceries lay below the counter.

8.   Mrs. Maxwell walked through the door of her office.

9.   The letter from Buck fell off the wooden desk.

10.   An earthworm crawled across the blade of grass.

11.   She placed a star above her name on the paper.

12.   Peach yogurt is behind the jam in the refrigerator.

Name_____   **PREPOSITIONS**
WORKBOOK PAGE 19   **Compound Subject**
Date_____

Sometimes a sentence is talking about two or more people or things. This is called a **compound subject**.

      Example: Her dog and ferret play in her room.

1. Cross out any prepositional phrase(s):

      Her dog and ferret play ~~in her room~~.

2. Look for more than one **who** or **what** in the sentence.

      Her <u>dog</u> and <u>ferret</u> play.

🐢🐢🐢🐢🐢🐢🐢🐢🐢🐢🐢🐢🐢🐢🐢🐢🐢🐢

Directions: Cross out **any** prepositional phrase(s) in each sentence. Then, underline the compound subject once and the verb twice.

Remember: **The subject will not be any word in a prepositional phrase.**

      Example: <u>Jacy</u> and his <u>brother</u> <u><u>are</u></u> ~~in a scout troop~~.

1. <u>Spoons</u> and <u>forks</u> <u><u>are</u></u> ~~beside the napkins~~.

2. <u>Paco</u> or <u>Nikki</u> <u><u>sits</u></u> ~~behind Ama~~.

3. Your <u>shoes</u> and <u>socks</u> <u><u>were</u></u> ~~under the bed~~.

4. Either their <u>mother</u> or <u>father</u> <u><u>reads</u></u> ~~with them~~.

5. ~~In March~~, <u>Lulu</u> and her <u>cousin</u> <u><u>visited</u></u> Pandaland.

6. ~~During the race~~, <u>Dino</u>, <u>Ria</u>, and <u>I</u> <u><u>finished</u></u> ~~at the same time~~.

38

Name_____

Date_____

Sometimes a sentence is talking about two or more people or things. This is called a **compound subject**.

> Example: Her dog and ferret play in her room.

1. Cross out any prepositional phrase(s):

> Her dog and ferret play ~~in her room~~.

2. Look for more than one *who* or *what* in the sentence.

> Her <u>dog</u> and <u>ferret</u> play.

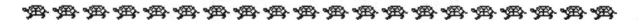

Directions: Cross out **any** prepositional phrase(s) in each sentence. Then, underline the compound subject once and the verb twice.

Remember: **The subject will not be any word in a prepositional phrase.**

> Example: <u>Jacy</u> and his <u>brother</u> <u>are</u> ~~in a scout troop~~.

1. Spoons and forks are beside the napkins.

2. Paco or Nikki sits behind Ama.

3. Your shoes and socks were under the bed.

4. Either their mother or father reads with them.

5. In March, Lulu and her cousin visited Pandaland.

6. During the race, Dino, Ria, and I finished at the same time.

Name_____   **PREPOSITIONS**

WORKBOOK PAGE 20   **Compound Subject**

Date_____

Note to Teacher: Sometimes students become so oriented to finding a prepositional phrase that they become concerned if none is in a sentence.   Please note that two of these sentences have asterisks with a note stating that no prepositional phrases are in them.

Sometimes a sentence is talking about two or more people or things. This is called a **compound subject**.

Look for more than one *who* or *what* in the sentence.

Directions: Cross out **any** prepositional phrase(s) in each sentence. Then, underline the compound subject once and the verb twice.

Example: <u>Tara</u> and her <u>dad</u> <u>swim</u> daily.

1.   New <u>towels</u> and <u>washcloths</u> <u>are</u> ~~in the bathroom~~.

2.   <u>Miss Cortez</u> and her new <u>boyfriend</u> <u>arrived</u> today.*

3.   His <u>brother</u> or <u>sister</u> <u>goes</u> ~~to Colorado~~ ~~during the winter~~.

4.   Her <u>friends</u> and <u>she</u> <u>decorated</u> ~~for the party~~.

5.   <u>Marshmallows</u> and hot <u>dogs</u> <u>are</u> ~~by the fireplace~~.

6.   Several <u>cows</u> and <u>horses</u> <u>rested</u> ~~under some tall trees~~.

7.   <u>Mira</u> and <u>Van</u> <u>walked</u> ~~with Grandma~~ ~~through her flower garden~~.

8.   <u>Mother</u> and <u>I</u> <u>placed</u> pins ~~below the last button of my sweater~~.

9.   <u>Jay</u>, <u>Lali</u>, <u>Kam</u>, and <u>Lana</u> <u>went</u> ~~to the circus~~.

10.   That <u>teacher</u>, the <u>principal</u>, and the <u>secretary</u> <u>meet</u> each Friday.*

*Not all sentences contain prepositional phrases.

40

Name_____

Date_____

Sometimes a sentence is talking about two or more people or things. This is called a **compound subject**.

Look for more than one *who* or *what* in the sentence.

🐢 🐢 🐢 🐢 🐢 🐢 🐢 🐢 🐢 🐢 🐢 🐢 🐢 🐢 🐢 🐢 🐢 🐢

Directions: Cross out **any** prepositional phrase(s) in each sentence. Then, underline the compound subject once and the verb twice.

Example: Tara and her dad swim daily.

1. New towels and washcloths are in the bathroom.

2. Miss Cortez and her new boyfriend arrived today.*

3. His brother or sister goes to Colorado during the winter.

4. Her friends and she decorated for the party.

5. Marshmallows and hot dogs are by the fireplace.

6. Several cows and horses rested under some tall trees.

7. Mira and Van walked with Grandma through her flower garden.

8. Mother and I placed pins below the last button of my sweater.

9. Jay, Lali, Kam, and Lana went to the circus.

10. That teacher, the principal, and the secretary meet each Friday.*

*Not all sentences contain prepositional phrases.

Sometimes more than one thing happens (happened) or is (was) in a sentence. This is called a **compound verb**. Two or more verbs make up a compound verb.

Example: The deer looked at us and ran away.

1.   Cross out any prepositional phrase(s). Underline the subject once.

The <u>deer</u> looked ~~at us~~ and ran away.

2.   Look for more than one thing that happens (happened) or is (was) in the sentence.   What did the deer do?

The <u>deer</u> <u>looked</u> ~~at us~~ and <u>ran</u> away.

The deer did two things. First, he *looked* and then he *ran*.

🐢 🐢 🐢 🐢 🐢 🐢 🐢 🐢 🐢 🐢 🐢 🐢 🐢 🐢 🐢 🐢 🐢 🐢

Directions: Cross out **any** prepositional phrase(s) in each sentence. Then, underline the subject once and the compound verb twice.

Remember: The verb will not be any word in a prepositional phrase.

Example: <u>They</u> <u>sang</u> and <u>clapped</u> ~~to the music~~.

1.   <u>He</u> <u>smiled</u> and <u>waved</u> ~~at us~~.

2.   A glass <u>plate</u> <u>fell</u> and <u>broke</u> ~~into many pieces~~.

3.   A <u>toddler</u> <u>cried</u> and <u>ran</u> ~~to his mother~~.

4.   <u>Jackie</u> <u>laughed</u> and <u>ran</u> ~~across the lawn~~.

5.   A large <u>bug</u> <u>flew</u> ~~to a bush~~ and <u>chewed</u> ~~on a leaf~~.

Sometimes more than one thing happens (happened) or is (was) in a sentence. This is called a **compound verb**. Two or more verbs make up a compound verb.

Example: The deer looked at us and ran away.

1. Cross out any prepositional phrase(s). Underline the subject once.

The <u>deer</u> looked ~~at us~~ and ran away.

2. Look for more than one thing that happens (happened) or is (was) in the sentence.   What did the deer do?

The <u>deer</u> <u>looked</u> ~~at us~~ and <u>ran</u> away.

The deer did two things. First, he *looked* and then he *ran*.

Directions: Cross out **any** prepositional phrase(s) in each sentence. Then, underline the subject once and the compound verb twice.

Remember: The verb will not be any word in a prepositional phrase.

Example: <u>They</u> <u>sang</u> and <u>clapped</u> ~~to the music~~.

1.   He smiled and waved at us.

2.   A glass plate fell and broke into many pieces.

3.   A toddler cried and ran to his mother.

4.   Jackie laughed and ran across the lawn.

5.   A large bug flew to a bush and chewed on a leaf.

Sometimes more than one thing happens (happened) or is (was) in a sentence. This is called a **compound verb**. Two or more verbs make up a compound verb.

> Cross out any prepositional phrase(s). Underline the subject once. Look for more than one thing that happens (happened) or is (was) in a sentence.

> Example: A fire <u>engine</u> <u>roared</u> ~~around the corner~~ and <u>stopped</u>.

> The fire engine did two things. First, it *roared,* and then it *stopped.*

Directions: Cross out **any** prepositional phrase(s) in each sentence. Then, underline the subject once and the compound verb twice.

Remember: The verb will not be any word in a prepositional phrase.

> Example: Her <u>cat</u> <u>lay</u> ~~on the floor~~ and <u>slept</u>.

1. <u>Tad</u> <u>looked</u> ~~at me~~ and <u>laughed</u>.

2. A <u>baby</u> <u>sucked</u> his hand and <u>grinned</u>.

3. Their <u>uncle</u> <u>went</u> ~~to the store~~ and <u>bought</u> chips.

4. That <u>dog</u> <u>looks</u> mean but <u>is</u> very friendly.

5. <u>They</u> <u>drank</u> cola and <u>ate</u> snacks ~~at the party~~.

6. Her <u>cousin</u> <u>sings</u> ~~in a choir~~ and <u>plays</u> the fiddle.

7. A <u>monkey</u> <u>sat</u> ~~on a box~~ and <u>scratched</u> himself.

8. <u>Joan</u> <u>stared</u> ~~in the mirror~~, <u>smiled</u>, and <u>flossed</u> her teeth.

44

Name_____

Date_____

Sometimes more than one thing happens (happened) or is (was) in a sentence. This is called a **compound verb**. Two or more verbs make up a compound verb.

Cross out any prepositional phrase(s). Underline the subject once. Look for more than one thing that happens (happened) or is (was) in a sentence.

Example: A fire <u>engine</u> <u>roared</u> ~~around the corner~~ and <u>stopped</u>.

The fire engine did two things. First, it *roared,* and then it *stopped.*

Directions: Cross out **any** prepositional phrase(s) in each sentence. Then, underline the subject once and the compound verb twice.

Remember: The verb will not be any word in a prepositional phrase.

Example: Her <u>cat</u> <u>lay</u> ~~on the floor~~ and <u>slept</u>.

1. Tad looked at me and laughed.

2. A baby sucked his hand and grinned.

3. Their uncle went to the store and bought chips.

4. That dog looks mean but is very friendly.

5. They drank cola and ate snacks at the party.

6. Her cousin sings in a choir and plays the fiddle.

7. A monkey sat on a box and scratched himself.

8. Joan stared in the mirror, smiled, and flossed her teeth.   45

A. **Compound Subject:** Look for more than one *who* or *what* in a sentence.

Directions: Cross out **any** prepositional phrase(s) in each sentence. Then, underline the compound subject once and the verb twice.

Remember: The subject will not be any word in a prepositional phrase.

Example: Her <u>coat</u> and <u>hat</u> <u>are</u> ~~on the floor~~.

1.   Their <u>aunt</u> and <u>uncle</u> <u>live</u> ~~in Denver~~.

2.   An <u>apple</u> and a <u>banana</u> <u>are</u> ~~on the table~~.

3.   This <u>doll</u> and <u>suitcase</u> <u>were</u> gifts ~~for her birthday~~.

4.   ~~After the storm~~, <u>branches</u> and <u>weeds</u> <u>lay</u> ~~beside the house~~.

5.   <u>Mom</u> and <u>Dad</u> <u>washed</u> our car ~~during the afternoon~~.

🐢 🐢 🐢 🐢 🐢 🐢 🐢 🐢 🐢 🐢 🐢 🐢 🐢 🐢 🐢 🐢 🐢 🐢 🐢

B. **Compound Verb:** Two or more verbs make up a compound verb.

Directions: Cross out **any** prepositional phrase(s) in each sentence. Then, underline the subject once and the compound verb twice.

Remember: The verb will not be any word in a prepositional phrase.

Example: <u>Miss Kent</u> <u>dug</u> ~~in the ground~~ and <u>planted</u> seeds.

1.   <u>Ira</u> <u>stayed</u> and <u>helped</u> ~~with games~~.

2.   The <u>model</u> <u>smiled</u> and <u>looked</u> ~~at the crowd~~.

3.   His <u>friend</u> <u>waters</u> and <u>cuts</u> grass ~~during the summer~~.

4.   <u>Cal</u> <u>rushed</u> ~~into the post office~~ and <u>bought</u> stamps.

5.   A <u>chicken</u> <u>walked</u> ~~around the barnyard~~ and <u>pecked</u> ~~in the dirt~~.

46

Name_____

Date_____

A. **Compound Subject:** Look for more than one *who* or *what* in a sentence.

Directions: Cross out **any** prepositional phrase(s) in each sentence. Then, underline the compound subject once and the verb twice.

Remember: The subject will not be any word in a prepositional phrase.

Example: Her <u>coat</u> and <u>hat</u> <u>are</u> ~~on the floor~~.

1.   Their aunt and uncle live in Denver.

2.   An apple and a banana are on the table.

3.   This doll and suitcase were gifts for her birthday.

4.   After the storm, branches and weeds lay beside the house.

5.   Mom and Dad washed our car during the afternoon.

🐢🐢🐢🐢🐢🐢🐢🐢🐢🐢🐢🐢🐢🐢🐢🐢🐢🐢

B. **Compound Verb:** Two or more verbs make up a compound verb.

Directions: Cross out **any** prepositional phrase(s) in each sentence. Then, underline the subject once and the compound verb twice.

Remember: The verb will not be any word in a prepositional phrase.

Example: <u>Miss Kent</u> <u>dug</u> ~~in the ground~~ and <u>planted</u> seeds.

1.   Ira stayed and helped with games.

2.   The model smiled and looked at the crowd.

3.   His friend waters and cuts grass during the summer.

4.   Cal rushed into the post office and bought stamps.

5.   A chicken walked around the barnyard and pecked in the dirt.   47

An imperative sentence gives a **command**.

> Example: Sit on this chair.

The person writing or speaking the command usually does not include the word, *you*. However, you realize that the person is telling **you** to do something.   We call this *you understood. You understood* is written as (You).

To find subject and verb of an imperative sentence, follow these steps:

1.   Cross out any prepositional phrase(s).   Sit ~~on this chair~~.

2.   Write (You), *you understood*, at the beginning of the sentence.

> (You)   Sit ~~on this chair~~.

3.   Decide the verb by asking what you are being told to do. Underline the verb twice.
> (You)   <u>Sit</u> ~~on this chair~~.

🐢 🐢

Directions: Cross out any prepositional phrase(s).   Underline the subject once and the verb twice.

1.   (You)   <u>Jump</u> ~~into the water~~.

2.   (You)   <u>Hop</u> ~~on one foot~~.

3.   (You)   <u>Smile</u> ~~for the picture~~.

4.   (You)   <u>Stand</u> ~~in line with me~~.

5.   (You)   <u>Place</u> the soap ~~under the sink~~.

6.   (You)   Please <u>pass</u> this pencil ~~to Mike~~.

48

Name_____

Date_____

An imperative sentence gives a **command**.

      Example: Sit on this chair.

The person writing or speaking the command usually does not include the word, *you*. However, you realize that the person is telling **you** to do something. We call this *you understood*. *You understood* is written as (You).

To find subject and verb of an imperative sentence, follow these steps:

1.   Cross out any prepositional phrase(s).   Sit ~~on this chair~~.

2.   Write (You), *you understood*, at the beginning of the sentence.

        (You) Sit ~~on this chair~~.

3.   Decide the verb by asking what you are being told to do. Underline the verb twice.

        (You) <u>Sit</u> ~~on this chair~~.

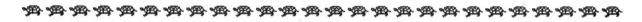

Directions: Cross out any prepositional phrase(s).   Underline the subject once and the verb twice.

1.   Jump into the water.

2.   Hop on one foot.

3.   Smile for the picture.

4.   Stand in line with me.

5.   Place the soap under the sink.

6.   Please pass this pencil to Mike.   49

An imperative sentence gives a **command**.

Example: Sit on this chair.

The person writing or speaking the command usually does not include the word, *you*. However, you realize that the person is telling **you** to do something. We call this *you understood*. *You understood* is written as (You).

To find subject and verb of an imperative sentence, follow these steps:

1. Cross out any prepositional phrase(s).

Please give this ~~to your dad~~.

2. Write (You), *you understood,* at the beginning of the sentence.

(You) Please give this ~~to your dad~~.

3. Decide the verb by asking what you are being told to do. Underline the verb twice.

(You) Please give this ~~to your dad~~.

🐢🐢🐢🐢🐢🐢🐢🐢🐢🐢🐢🐢🐢🐢🐢🐢🐢🐢🐢🐢🐢🐢🐢🐢🐢

Directions: Cross out any prepositional phrase(s). Underline the subject once and the verb twice.

Remember: Not all sentences contain prepositional phrases.

1. (You) Play ~~with me~~.

2. (You) Clean your room.

3. (You) Brush your teeth.

4. (You) Wait ~~for us after school~~.

5. (You) Wash your hands ~~before dinner~~.

6. (You) Throw the ball ~~to first base~~.

50

An imperative sentence gives a **command**.

    Example: Sit on this chair.

The person writing or speaking the command usually does not include the word, *you*. However, you realize that the person is telling **you** to do something. We call this *you understood*. *You understood* is written as (You).

To find subject and verb of an imperative sentence, follow these steps:

1. Cross out any prepositional phrase(s).

        Please give this ~~to your dad~~.

2. Write (You), *you understood,* at the beginning of the sentence.

        (You) Please give this ~~to your dad~~.

3. Decide the verb by asking what you are being told to do. Underline the verb twice.

        (You) Please <u>give</u> this ~~to your dad~~.

🐢🐢🐢🐢🐢🐢🐢🐢🐢🐢🐢🐢🐢🐢🐢🐢🐢🐢🐢🐢🐢🐢🐢🐢

Directions: Cross out any prepositional phrase(s). Underline the subject once and the verb twice.

Remember: **Not all sentences contain prepositional phrases.**

1. Play with me.

2. Clean your room.

3. Brush your teeth.

4. Wait for us after school.

5. Wash your hands before dinner.

6. Throw the ball to first base.

Directions: List the twenty-eight prepositions that you have learned:

1. __**above**__   15. __**from**__

2. __**across**__   16. __**in**__

3. __**after**__   17. __**inside**__

4. __**around**__   18. __**into**__

5. __**at**__   19. __**of**__

6. __**before**__   20. __**off**__

7. __**behind**__   21. __**on**__

8. __**below**__   22. __**out**__

9. __**beside**__   23. __**over**__

10. __**between**__   24. __**through**__

11. __**by**__   25. __**to**__

12. __**down**__   26. __**under**__

13. __**during**__   27. __**up**__

14. __**for**__   28. __**with**__

52

Name_____

Date_____

Directions: List the twenty-eight prepositions that you have learned.

1. _____

2. _____

3. _____

4. _____

5. _____

6. _____

7. _____

8. _____

9. _____

10. _____

11. _____

12. _____

13. _____

14. _____

15. _____

16. _____

17. _____

18. _____

19. _____

20. _____

21. _____

22. _____

23. _____

24. _____

25. _____

26. _____

27. _____

28. _____

53

Name_____   **PREPOSITIONS**
WORKBOOK PAGE 27   Review
Date_____

A.   Directions: Write a prepositional phrase.
ANSWERS WILL VARY.
1.   **between two trees**_____

2.   **under a rock**_____

3.   **for his birthday**_____

B.   Directions: Cross out the prepositional phrase. Then, write O. P. above
                 each object of the preposition.
                                         O.P.
1.   She looked ~~through a~~ **telescope**.
                  O.P.
2.   ~~After~~ **lunch**, they went bowling.
                                        O.P.
3.   Several books are lying ~~on the~~ **sofa**.

C.   Directions: Cross out the prepositional phrase in each sentence.
                   Underline the subject once and the verb twice.

**Remember: Ask *who* or *what* the sentence is about to find the subject.
             Find what happens (happened) or is (was). This is the verb.
             Subject and verb will not be in a prepositional phrase.**

            Example: Two <u>lizards</u> <u>are</u> ~~in the yard~~.

1.   A <u>light</u> <u>hangs</u> ~~above their table~~.

2.   Your <u>mother</u> <u>is</u> ~~in the other room~~.

3.   That <u>frog</u> just <u>jumped</u> ~~into the water~~.

4.   Her <u>brother</u> <u>walked</u> ~~beside us~~.

54

A. Directions: Write a prepositional phrase.

1. <u>between</u>_____

2. <u>under</u>_____

3. <u>for</u>_____

B. Directions: Cross out the prepositional phrase. Then, write <u>O. P.</u> above
                 each object of the preposition.

1. She looked through a telescope.

2. After lunch, they went bowling.

3. Several books are lying on the sofa.

C. Directions: Cross out the prepositional phrase in each sentence.
                  Underline the subject once and the verb twice.

**Remember: Ask *who* or *what* the sentence is about to find the subject.
             Find what happens (happened) or is (was). This is the verb.
             Subject and verb will not be in a prepositional phrase.**

Example: Two <u>lizards</u> <u>are</u> ~~in the yard~~.

1. A light hangs above their table.

2. Your mother is in the other room.

3. That frog just jumped into the water.

4. Her brother walked beside us.

55

WORKBOOK PAGE 28

Date_____

A. **Compound Subject:**

Directions: Cross out the prepositional phrase in each sentence. Then, underline the compound subject once and the verb twice.

Remember: The subject will not be a word in a prepositional phrase.

1. <u>Barbara</u> and <u>I</u> <u>skipped</u> ~~to the store~~.

2. His <u>hat</u> and <u>coat</u> <u>were</u> ~~under some newspapers~~.

3. <u>Toni</u> and her <u>friend</u> <u>sang</u> ~~after dinner~~.

B. **Compound Verb:**

Directions: Cross out the prepositional phrase in each sentence. Then, underline the subject once and the compound verb twice.

Remember: The verb will never be a word in a prepositional phrase.

1. The <u>kite</u> <u>dipped</u> and <u>soared</u> ~~above the trees~~.

2. A <u>policeman</u> <u>whistled</u> and <u>pointed</u> ~~at the driver~~.

3. ~~Before bedtime~~, <u>I</u> <u>wash</u> my face and <u>brush</u> my teeth.

C. **Imperative Sentence:**

Directions: Cross out the prepositional phrase in each sentence. Then, underline the subject once and the verb twice.

Remember: An imperative sentence gives a command.

1. (<u>You</u>) <u>Stand</u> ~~in this line~~.

2. (<u>You</u>) <u>Dust</u> ~~under your bed~~.

3. (<u>You</u>) <u>Put</u> your name ~~on the paper~~, please.

56

A. **Compound Subject:**

Directions: Cross out the prepositional phrase in each sentence. Then, underline the compound subject once and the verb twice.

Remember: **The subject will not be a word in a prepositional phrase.**

1. Barbara and I skipped to the store.

2. His hat and coat were under some newspapers.

3. Toni and her friend sang after dinner.

B. **Compound Verb:**

Directions: Cross out the prepositional phrase in each sentence. Then, underline the subject once and the compound verb twice.

Remember: **The verb will never be a word in a prepositional phrase.**

1. The kite dipped and soared above the trees.

2. A policeman whistled and pointed at the driver.

3. Before bedtime, I wash my face and brush my teeth.

C. **Imperative Sentence:**

Directions: Cross out the prepositional phrase in each sentence. Then, underline the subject once and the verb twice.

Remember: **An imperative sentence gives a command.**

1. Stand in this line.

2. Dust under your bed.

3. Put your name on the paper, please.   57

A.   Directions: Write a prepositional phrase.
ANSWERS WILL VARY.

1.   **across   the   river**_____

2.   **up   the   escalator**_____

3.   **below   a   waterfall**_____

B.   Directions: Cross out the prepositional phrase. Then, write <u>O. P.</u> above
     each object of the preposition.

                                           O. P.
1.   He ordered tiles ~~from Mexico~~.
                                    O. P.
2.   This box ~~of candy~~ is old.
                                                  O. P.
3.   The groom danced ~~with his new bride~~.

C.   Directions: Cross out the prepositional phrase in each sentence.
     Underline the subject once and the verb twice.

Remember: **Ask *who* or *what* the sentence is about to find the subject.**
               Find what happens (happened) or is (was). This is the verb.
               Subject and verb will not be in a prepositional phrase.

               Example: The <u>teenager</u> <u>waved</u> ~~to me~~.

1.   Your <u>coat</u> <u>is</u> ~~inside the closet~~.

2.   The <u>ladies</u> <u>walked</u> ~~around the museum~~.

3.   <u>We</u> <u>fished</u> ~~off the pier~~.

4.   ~~At five o'clock~~, the <u>workers</u> <u>went</u> home.

58

A.   Directions: Write a prepositional phrase.

1.   <u>across</u>_____

2.   <u>up</u>_____

3.   <u>below</u>_____

B.   Directions: Cross out the prepositional phrase. Then, write <u>O. P.</u> above
                   each object of the preposition.

1.   He ordered tiles from Mexico.

2.   This box of candy is old.

3.   The groom danced with his new bride.

C.   Directions: Cross out the prepositional phrase in each sentence.
                   Underline the subject once and the verb twice.

**Remember: Ask *who* or *what* the sentence is about to find the subject.
             Find what happens (happened) or is (was). This is the verb.
             Subject and verb will not be in a prepositional phrase.**

          Example: The <u>teenager waved</u> ~~to me~~.

1.   Your coat is inside the closet.

2.   The ladies walked around the museum.

3.   We fished off the pier.

4.   At five o'clock, the workers went home.   59

WORKBOOK PAGE 30
Date_____

A. Compound Subject:

Directions: Cross out the prepositional phrase in each sentence. Then, underline the compound subject once and the verb twice.

Remember: **The subject will not be a word in a prepositional phrase.**

1. A <u>bear</u> and her <u>cub</u> <u><u>roamed</u></u> ~~through the woods~~.

2. ~~During the rain~~, <u>Mother</u> and <u>Jack</u> <u><u>painted</u></u>.

3. A <u>doctor</u> and <u>nurse</u> <u><u>talked</u></u> ~~beside the water fountain~~.

B. Compound Verb:

Directions: Cross out the prepositional phrase in each sentence. Then, underline the subject once and the compound verb twice.

Remember: **The verb will never be a word in a prepositional phrase.**

1. A first <u>grader</u> <u><u>ran</u></u> ~~into the room~~ and <u><u>shouted</u></u>.

2. Their <u>sister</u> <u><u>washes</u></u> and <u><u>curls</u></u> her hair ~~before school~~.

3. <u>He</u> <u><u>sliced</u></u> tomatoes and <u><u>fried</u></u> them ~~in butter~~.

C. Imperative Sentence:

Directions: Cross out the prepositional phrase in each sentence. Then, underline the subject once and the verb twice.

Remember: **An imperative sentence gives a command.**

1. <u>(You)</u> <u><u>Turn</u></u> ~~to the left~~.

2. <u>(You)</u> <u><u>Hand</u></u> this mug ~~to that waiter~~.

3. <u>(You)</u> Please <u><u>use</u></u> this carton ~~of eggs~~.

60

Name_____

Date_____

A. **Compound Subject:**

Directions: Cross out the prepositional phrase in each sentence. Then, underline the compound subject once and the verb twice.

Remember: **The subject will not be a word in a prepositional phrase.**

1. A bear and her cub roamed through the woods.

2. During the rain, Mother and Jack painted.

3. A doctor and nurse talked beside the water fountain.

B. **Compound Verb:**

Directions: Cross out the prepositional phrase in each sentence. Then, underline the subject once and the compound verb twice.

Remember: **The verb will never be a word in a prepositional phrase.**

1. A first grader ran into the room and shouted.

2. Their sister washes and curls her hair before school.

3. He sliced tomatoes and fried them in butter.

C. **Imperative Sentence:**

Directions: Cross out the prepositional phrase in each sentence. Then, underline the subject once and the verb twice.

Remember: **An imperative sentence gives a command.**

1. Turn to the left.

2. Hand this mug to that waiter.

3. Please use this carton of eggs.

61

Note to Teacher: Sentences 8 and 11 are imperative. Sentence 12 contains a compound verb; sentence 14 contains a compound subject. You may wish to do this page with your students. A similar worksheet has been provided on pages 64-65.

Directions: Cross out any prepositional phrase(s). Underline the subject once and the verb twice.

Example: <u>One</u> ~~of the lambs~~ <u>followed</u> his mother.

1. <u>Jason</u> <u>hid</u> ~~behind a shed~~.

2. The <u>sky</u> <u>grew</u> dark ~~before the storm~~.

3. Deep <u>water</u> <u>rushed</u> ~~over the bridge~~.

4. Several <u>guests</u> <u>lay</u> ~~beside the hotel pool~~.

5. <u>One</u> ~~of her friends~~ <u>works</u> ~~in a hotel~~.

6. The <u>water</u> ~~in the pond~~ <u>dropped</u> ~~below five feet~~.

7. Those <u>girls</u> <u>ride</u> ~~on a bus to the mall~~.

8. (<u>You</u>)   <u>Keep</u> your skates ~~under your bed~~.

9. That <u>man</u> ~~with three small children~~ <u>is</u> my uncle.

10. ~~During the ice storm~~, <u>we</u> <u>played</u> cards ~~by the fire~~.

11. (<u>You</u>)   Please <u>come</u> ~~inside the house~~ ~~with me~~.

12. The <u>runner</u> <u>finished</u> the race and <u>fell</u> ~~on the ground~~.

13. A <u>package</u> ~~from Fred~~ <u>arrived</u> ~~after lunch~~.

14. The <u>lady</u> and her <u>son</u> <u>looked</u> ~~for a book at the library~~.

62

Directions: Cross out any prepositional phrase(s). Underline the subject once and the verb twice.

Example: <u>One</u> ~~of the lambs~~ <u>followed</u> his mother.

1.   Jason hid behind a shed.

2.   The sky grew dark before the storm.

3.   Deep water rushed over the bridge.

4.   Several guests lay beside the hotel pool.

5.   One of her friends works in a hotel.

6.   The water in the pond dropped below five feet.

7.   Those girls ride on a bus to the mall.

8.   Keep your skates under your bed.

9.   That man with three small children is my uncle.

10.   During the ice storm, we played cards by the fire.

11.   Please come inside the house with me.

12.   The runner finished the race and fell on the ground.

13.   A package from Fred arrived after lunch.

14.   The lady and her son looked for a book at the library.

WORKBOOK PAGE 32

Note to Teacher: Sentence 3 contains a compound subject. Sentence 11 contains a compound verb. Sentence 13 is an imperative sentence. Sentence 10 will help you determine if students are thinking about prepositions; some may delete *every day*. *Every*, of course, is not a preposition.

Directions: Cross out any prepositional phrase(s). Underline the subject once and the verb twice.

Example: They ride a merry-go-round on Saturdays.

1. Sheri caught a fish in Mexico.

2. That garden hose wraps around a metal stand.

3. Bo and Carrie ran through the woods.

4. Before church, they eat at a coffee shop.

5. An enormous white cat slipped out the door.

6. During the game, he hopped on one foot.

7. Dad poured food into our dog's bowl.

8. Several cows went up the large, grassy hill.

9. Mrs. Jackson waved a flag above her head.

10. A ferry comes across the lake every day.

11. The actor took off his wig and smiled.

12. They washed their hands with sudsy soap.

13. (You) Wait for me beside the front door.

14. Each of the contestants walked between two white columns.

64

Directions: Cross out any prepositional phrase(s). Underline the subject
             once and the verb twice.

          Example: <u>They</u> <u>ride</u> a merry-go-round ~~on Saturdays~~.

1. Sheri caught a fish in Mexico.

2. That garden hose wraps around a metal stand.

3. Bo and Carrie ran through the woods.

4. Before church, they eat at a coffee shop.

5. An enormous white cat slipped out the door.

6. During the game, he hopped on one foot.

7. Dad poured food into our dog's bowl.

8. Several cows went up the large, grassy hill.

9. Mrs. Jackson waved a flag above her head.

10. A ferry comes across the lake every day.

11. The actor took off his wig and smiled.

12. They washed their hands with sudsy soap.

13. Wait for me beside the front door.

14. Each of the contestants walked between two white columns.

Name_____   **Preposition Test**

Date_____

Note to Teacher: You may want to remind students to look for compound subject, compound verb, and imperative sentence. Score this test as you wish. If you allot one point for the subject, one point for the verb, and one point for each prepositional phrase, the total is 50.

Directions: Cross out any prepositional phrase(s). Underline the subject once and the verb twice.

Example: Your pillow is ~~under your bed~~.

1.   That baby smiles ~~at his mother~~.   3 points

2.   An eagle soared ~~above our house~~.   3 points

3.   Some sheep came ~~down the country road~~.   3 points

4.   A basket ~~of colored eggs~~ is ~~in the kitchen~~.   4 points

5.   The tired hiker walked ~~through a snowstorm~~.   3 points

6.   ~~On Mondays~~, Gail goes ~~to the gym~~.   4 points

7.   Karen plays ~~with her brother~~ ~~after school~~.   4 points

8.   ~~During the play~~, an actor jumped ~~into a box~~.   4 points

9.   Their dad skied ~~between them~~ ~~on the snowy hill~~. 4 points

10. Tina and her husband are ~~from Utah~~.   3 points

11. ~~Before my speech~~, I looked ~~around the room~~.   4 points

12. The toddler giggled and crawled ~~under the table~~.   3 points

13. (You)   Stand ~~beside the Christmas tree~~ ~~for a picture~~. 4 points

14. One ~~of the salesmen~~ hurried ~~across the room~~.   4 points

66

Name_____   **Preposition Test**

Date_____

Directions: Cross out any prepositional phrase(s). Underline the subject
              once and the verb twice.

Example: Your <u>pillow</u> <u>is</u> ~~under your bed~~.

1.   That baby smiles at his mother.

2.   An eagle soared above our house.

3.   Some sheep came down the country road.

4.   A basket of colored eggs is in the kitchen.

5.   The tired hiker walked through a snowstorm.

6.   On Mondays, Gail goes to the gym.

7.   Karen plays with her brother after school.

8.   During the play, an actor jumped into a box.

9.   Their dad skied between them on the snowy hill.

10. Tina and her husband are from Utah.

11. Before my speech, I looked around the room.

12. The toddler giggled and crawled under the table.

13. Stand beside the Christmas tree for a picture.

14. One of the salesmen hurried across the room.

TO THE TEACHER:

<u>**Easy Grammar: Grade 3**</u> does not teach that a word can serve as either a preposition or an adverb.   (Although such words as *in* and *down* will be used when teaching *where* in the adverb unit, no formal explanation will be offered.)   More detail is taught in other **Easy Grammar** texts.

COMPLETE SUBJECT AND VERB:

The next lesson is used to teach students complete subject and complete verb.   This is taught in this text for two reasons.   First, a student may use a different book during an ensuing year.   Because many books use this process, students should, at least, be familiar with it.   In addition, students will be introduced to predicate adjectives in other texts.   Knowing the complete predicate of a sentence will help children to determine where to look for a predicate adjective.

I have not provided students with an introductory (whole page) lesson.   I have simply placed a brief explanation at the top of each practice page.   Therefore, I recommend that you teach the concept using sentences written on a chalkboard or transparency.   Actually seeing the two sentence components makes this an easy task.   (Using colored chalk/pen to draw wavy lines will help students to follow the directions on worksheet pages.)   When teaching this concept, begin with simple sentences and progress to more difficult ones.

      Examples: Your book fell on the floor.

                     His little brother spilled milk at the dinner table.

                     Several bags of groceries are on the counter.

68

Have students do the prepositional process to find subject and verb.

Your <u>book</u>   <u>fell</u> ~~on the floor~~.
~~~~~~~~   ~~~~~~~~~~~~~

Then, teach students that the complete subject is everything **before** the verb; the complete verb includes everything **from the verb to the end of the sentence**. (Most texts instruct students to place double lines under the complete subject and the complete verb. Because we use the double lines for the simple verb, I prefer placing a wavy line under each part.) If you introduce this concept very carefully, students should find the task easy.

Several <u>fish</u>   <u>swam</u> ~~in the pond~~.
~~~~~~~~   ~~~~~~~~~~~~~

His little <u>brother</u>   <u>spilled</u> his milk ~~at the dinner table~~.
~~~~~~~~~~~   ~~~~~~~~~~~~~~~~~~~~~~~~~~~~~~~

Note: I have not included any interrogative (question) sentences for students to determine complete subject and verb. Students have not yet been introduced to verb phrases. However, if the question arises, tell students to change the sentence to a declarative one and proceed in the fashion mentioned above.

Example: Do you like me?

You do like me.

<u>You</u>   <u>do like</u> me.
~~~   ~~~~~~~~~

69

<u>**Note to Teacher: Do this page with the students. If you think that asking students to delete prepositional phrases is confusing (in this process), ask students to merely find subject and verb. Students will need colored pencils or crayons for this worksheet.**</u>

Sometimes, you will be asked to find the complete subject and the complete verb of a sentence. This is very easy. Follow these steps.

1. Cross out any prepositional phrases.

2. Underline the subject with one line.

3. Underline the verb with a double line.

4. With a wavy red line, underline everything **before the verb**.
    This is the complete subject.

5. With a wavy green line, underline the **verb** and everything **after the verb**. This is the complete verb.

        Example: The little girl slid down the slide.

                The little <u>girl</u> <u>slid</u> ~~down the slide~~.
                                The verb is *slid*. Separate the sentence here.
                The little <u>girl</u>   <u>slid</u> ~~down the slide~~.
                        ~~~~~~~~~~~~   ~~~~~~~~~~~~~~~~

Complete subject:_The little girl_   Complete verb:_slid ~~down the slide~~.

🐢 🐢 🐢 🐢 🐢 🐢 🐢 🐢 🐢 🐢 🐢 🐢 🐢 🐢 🐢 🐢 🐢 🐢

Directions: Cross out any prepositional phrase(s). Underline the subject once and the verb twice. Place a wavy red line under the complete subject and a wavy green line under the complete verb.

        Example: A bowl of cherries is on the table.
                    A <u>bowl</u> ~~of cherries~~ <u>is</u> ~~on the table~~.
                      ~~~~~~~~~~~~~~~~ ~~~~~~~~~~~~~~

1. Two <u>girls</u> <u>played</u> ~~in the park~~.
        ~~~~~~~~ ~~~~~~~~~~~~~~~~

2. The <u>boy</u> ~~in the blue sweater~~ <u>is</u> my friend.
        ~~~~~~~~~~~~~~~~~~~~~~ ~~~~~~~~~~~

3. My little <u>brother</u>   <u>cries</u> ~~during his bath~~.
        ~~~~~~~~~~~~~~~~ ~~~~~~~~~~~~~~~~~~~~

70

Sometimes, you will be asked to find the complete subject and the complete verb of a sentence. This is very easy. Follow these steps.

1. Cross out any prepositional phrases.

2. Underline the subject with one line.

3. Underline the verb with a double line.

4. With a wavy red line, underline everything **before the verb**. This is the complete subject.

5. With a wavy green line, underline the **verb** and everything **after the verb**. This is the complete verb.

   Example: The little girl slid down the slide.

   The little girl **slid** down the slide.
   The verb is *slid*. Separate the sentence here.
   The little girl **slid** down the slide.

Complete subject: The little girl   Complete verb: slid down the slide.

🐢 🐢 🐢 🐢 🐢 🐢 🐢 🐢 🐢 🐢 🐢 🐢 🐢 🐢 🐢 🐢 🐢 🐢 🐢

Directions: Cross out any prepositional phrase(s). Underline the subject once and the verb twice. Place a wavy red line under the complete subject and a wavy green line under the complete verb.

   Example: A bowl of cherries is on the table.
   A bowl of cherries is on the table.

1. Two girls played in the park.

2. The boy in the blue sweater is my friend.

3. My little brother cries during his bath.

Name_____

WORKBOOK PAGE 34

Date_____

Complete Subject
and
Complete Verb

Note to Teacher: The steps in finding complete subject and complete verb have been combined to provide more space for student practice.

Follow these steps to find the **complete subject** and the **complete verb**.

1. Cross out any prepositional phrases.

2. Underline the subject with one line and the verb with a double line.

4. With a wavy red line, underline everything **before the verb**. This is the complete subject.

5. With a wavy green line, underline the **verb** and everything **after the verb**. This is the complete verb.

> Example: A <u>bug</u> <u>flew</u> ~~into the house~~.
>
> The verb is *flew*. Separate the sentence here.
>
> A <u>bug</u> **<u>flew</u>** ~~into the house~~.

Directions: Cross out any prepositional phrase(s). Underline the subject once and the verb twice. Place a red wavy line under the complete subject and a green wavy line under the complete verb.

> Example: Her <u>neighbor</u> <u>is</u> ~~in the army~~.

1. <u>We</u>   <u>went</u> ~~to the zoo~~.

2. Their <u>sister</u>   <u>is</u> ~~in college~~.

3. A large <u>tree</u>   <u>grew</u> ~~by the stream~~.

4. This <u>quarter</u>   <u>is</u> ~~for you~~.

5. A <u>lady</u> ~~at the market~~   <u>gave</u> me an apple.

6. Several brown <u>bunnies</u>   <u>sit</u> ~~under our bush~~.

72

Follow these steps to find the **complete subject** and the **complete verb**.

1. Cross out any prepositional phrases.

2. Underline the subject with one line and the verb with a double line.

3. With a wavy red line, underline everything **before the verb**. This is the complete subject.

4. With a wavy green line, underline the **verb** and everything **after the verb**. This is the complete verb.

    Example: A <u>bug</u> <u>flew</u> into the house.

                        The verb is *flew.* Separate the sentence here.

              A <u>bug</u>   **<u>flew</u>** into the house.
                 ~~~~~   ~~~~~~~~~~~~~

🐢 🐢 🐢 🐢 🐢 🐢 🐢 🐢 🐢 🐢 🐢 🐢 🐢 🐢 🐢 🐢 🐢

Directions: Cross out any prepositional phrase(s). Underline the subject once and the verb twice. Place a red wavy line under the complete subject and a green wavy line under the complete verb.

        Example: Her <u>neighbor</u> <u>is</u> in the army.
                       ~~~~~~~~~~ ~~~~~~~~~~~

1. We went to the zoo.

2. Their sister is in college.

3. A large tree grew by the stream.

4. This quarter is for you.

5. A lady at the market gave me an apple.

6. Several brown bunnies sit under our bush.

73

TO THE TEACHER:

As you are well aware, only two worksheets were provided for complete subject and complete verb. These, hopefully, have served to help students who are new to the idea of finding simple subject and verb.

DIRECT OBJECTS:

In teaching direct objects, we continue the process of deleting prepositional phrases. Any word **within** a prepositional phrase will not be a direct object. (At advanced levels, some books teach that an entire prepositional phrase can serve as a direct object. This, of course, is confusing at this level.) In deleting prepositional phrases, students can readily find subject and verb. Also, the process prevents students from determining an inaccurate direct object.

> Example: The boy hid his money from his sister.
>
> > If we do not delete *from his sister,* a student may say that the boy hid his sister.   Of course, *money* is the object he hid.

When **teaching the lesson about direct objects**, I recommend that you involve students.   On the board, write, "I drop my pencil." Have students drop a pencil. What is the object you dropped? Pencil. That's the direct object. Continue with some of the following sentences and proceed in the manner of questioning provided above.

> I raise my hand.
> I clap my hand.
> I untie my shoe. (For students with shoes that don't tie, be creative.)
> I touch my lips.

You will create many more, I'm sure! The objective is for students to have fun while understanding the concept of a direct object.

74

Direct Objects

Name_____   **DIRECT OBJECTS**

WORKBOOK PAGE 35

Date_____

Note to Teacher: Be sure to cover this page carefully.   Reinforce that all sentences do
not contain a prepositional phrase; #4 does not.   I recommend that you do this page
orally with the students.   That should be enough for your lesson.   Do the lesson on
pages 78-79 for the *next* lesson; reteach (reintroduce) the concept again.

A direct object receives an action.

To find a direct object, do the following steps:

1.   Cross out any prepositional phrase(s). Any word in a prepositional
     phrase will **not** be a direct object.

2.   Underline the subject once and the verb twice. Does the verb show an
     action? If the verb shows action, there may be a direct object.

3.   Read your subject and verb. Ask yourself if there is an object that would
     answer *what* .

     Example: <u>Ross made</u> cookies.   Ross made **what**?   cookies

     The object Ross made is cookies. **Cookies** is the direct object.
     Write **D.O.** above a direct object.
                              D.O.
          <u>Ross made</u> cookies.

🐢 🐢 🐢 🐢 🐢 🐢 🐢 🐢 🐢 🐢 🐢 🐢 🐢 🐢 🐢 🐢 🐢

Directions: Cross out any prepositional phrase(s). Underline the subject
              once and the verb twice. Write <u>D.O.</u> above any direct object.

Note to Teacher: You may want to ask students to pretend to do the actions in the
following sentences.   Have them pretend they are eating popcorn, drinking juice,
splashing water, and cutting a cake, too.   This is fun, and it helps to reinforce an action
verb.

                                    D.O.
          Example: <u>Tim empties</u> his trash ~~on Friday~~.

        D.O.
1.   <u>Tyler eats</u> popcorn ~~at the movies~~.

            D.O.
2.   The <u>baby drank</u> juice ~~from a bottle~~.

            D.O.
3.   <u>Lisa splashed</u> water ~~on her face~~.

                      D.O.
4.   Her <u>father cut</u> her birthday cake.

76

Date_____

A direct object receives an action.

To find a direct object, do the following steps:

1. Cross out any prepositional phrase(s). Any word in a prepositional phrase will **not** be a direct object.

2. Underline the subject once and the verb twice. Does the verb show an **action**? If the verb shows action, there may be a direct object.

3. Read your subject and verb. Ask yourself if there is an object that would answer *what* .

    Example: Ross <u>made</u> cookies.   Ross made **what**?   cookies

    The object Ross made is cookies. **Cookies** is the direct object.
    Write **D.O.** above a direct object.
    D.O.
    <u>Ross made</u> cookies.

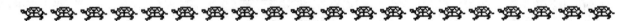

Directions: Cross out any prepositional phrase(s). Underline the subject once and the verb twice. Write <u>D.O.</u> above any direct object.

D.O.
Example: <u>Tim empties</u> his trash ~~on Friday~~.

1. Tyler eats popcorn at the movies.

2. The baby drank juice from a bottle.

3. Lisa splashed water on her face.

4. Her father cut her birthday cake.

WORKBOOK PAGE 36
Date_____

A direct object receives an action.

To find a direct object, do the following steps:

1.   Cross out any prepositional phrase(s). Any word in a prepositional phrase will **not** be a direct object.

2.   Underline the subject once and the verb twice. Does the verb show an **action**? If the verb shows action, there may be a direct object.

3.   Read your subject and verb. Ask yourself if there is an object that would answer *what*.

D.O.
Example: <u>Joan</u> <u>kicked</u> the football <s>to her brother</s>.

Joan kicked what? *football* Football is the direct object.

🐢 🐢 🐢 🐢 🐢 🐢 🐢 🐢 🐢 🐢 🐢 🐢 🐢 🐢 🐢 🐢 🐢 🐢 🐢

Directions: Cross out any prepositional phrase(s). Underline the subject once and the verb twice. Write <u>D.O.</u> above any direct object.

D.O.
Example: <u>They</u> <u>watched</u> television.

           D.O.
1.   <u>She</u> <u>sang</u> a song <s>with her aunt</s>.

           D.O.
2.   The <u>child</u> <u>poured</u> sand <s>into a bucket</s>.

           D.O.
3.   <u>Lance</u> <u>collects</u> baseball cards .

           D.O.
4.   That <u>artist</u> <u>paints</u> pictures <s>of animals</s>.

           D.O.
5.   <u>Mr. Rank</u> <u>bought</u> a gift <s>for his wife</s>.

           D.O.
6.   The <u>plumber</u> <u>fixed</u> a leak <s>in the sink</s>.

Date_____

A direct object receives an action.

To find a direct object, do the following steps:

1. Cross out any prepositional phrase(s).   Any word in a prepositional phrase will **not** be a direct object.

2. Underline the subject once and the verb twice.   Does the verb show an **action**? If the verb shows action, there may be a direct object.

3. Read your subject and verb.   Ask yourself if there is an object that would answer *what*.

D.O.

Example: <u>Joan</u> <u><u>kicked</u></u> the football ~~to her brother~~.

Joan kicked what? *football* Football is the direct object.

🐢 🐢 🐢 🐢 🐢 🐢 🐢 🐢 🐢 🐢 🐢 🐢 🐢 🐢 🐢 🐢 🐢 🐢

Directions: Cross out any prepositional phrase(s). Underline the subject once and the verb twice. Write <u>D.O.</u> above any direct object.

D.O.

Example: <u>They</u> <u><u>watched</u></u> television.

1. She sang a song with her aunt.

2. The child poured sand into a bucket.

3. Lance collects baseball cards.

4. That artist paints pictures of animals.

5. Mr. Rank bought a gift for his wife.

6. The plumber fixed a leak in the sink.

TO THE TEACHER:

1. **Contractions:**

    In addition to the worksheets provided in this text, I recommend that you have students make up contraction study cards. Instruct students to write the contraction on one side of the card and the two words that comprise it on the other. Using these, students can study with a buddy. Be sure that students are saying **and** spelling the word when studying with a buddy. (I recommend that students be given "quizzes" to determine if contractions are being learned.)

2. **They're** versus there and their, **it's** versus its, and **you're** versus your

3. **May and Can**

4. **Helping Verbs:**

    Students need to memorize and learn all twenty-three helping verbs. By learning these, students usually can identify verb phrases easily.

5. **Irregular Verbs:**

    Not all irregular verbs are included. However, be sure that the ones that are included are learned well.

6. **Tenses:**

    Take your time in teaching present and past tenses. Teach future, but don't be discouraged if some students lack understanding at the mastery level.

7. **Subject-Verb Agreement:**

    This concept is very important. Be sure that students understand how to determine usage.

IMPORTANT: No separate cumulative review or cumulative test has been included at the end of this unit. Part H of the review requires deleting prepositional phrases.

PAGE 82 = WORKBOOK PAGE 37
PAGE 83 = WORKBOOK PAGE 38

Verbs

CONTRACTIONS

To contract means to become smaller.

Contractions are formed when two or more words are joined together.

you are = you're

When the words are joined, the new word is smaller because a letter or letters have been dropped.

you are = six letters
you're = five letters
a

Where the letter or letters have been dropped, an apostrophe mark (**'**) is placed.

you**'**re

➜ **a**

Make an apostrophe with a curve in it. Put the apostrophe exactly where the letter or letters have been dropped.

Contractions with **I**:

I am	=	I'm	I will	=	I'll
I have	=	I've			

Contractions with **you**:

you are	=	you're
you will	=	you'll

Contractions with **is**:

he is	=	he's		she is	=	she's
here is	=	here's		what is	=	what's
it is	=	it's		where is	=	where's
that is	=	that's		who is	=	who's
there is	=	there's				

Contractions with **they**:

they are	=	they're
they will	=	they'll
they have	=	they've

Contractions with **we**:

we are	=	we're
we will	=	we'll

Contractions with **not**:

are not	=	aren't
cannot	=	can't
could not	=	couldn't
did not	=	didn't
does not	=	doesn't
do not	=	don't
had not	=	hadn't
has not	=	hasn't
have not	=	haven't
is not	=	isn't
should not	=	shouldn't
was not	=	wasn't
were not	=	weren't
will not	=	won't
would not	=	wouldn't

Directions: Write the contraction.

1.   I am - _____**I'm**_____

2.   I have - _____**I've**_____

3.   I will - _____**I'll**_____

4.   it is - _____**it's**_____

5.   he is - _____**he's**_____

6.   she is - _____**she's**_____

7.   who is - _____**who's**_____

8.   what is - _____**what's**_____

9.   where is - _____**where's**_____

10.   here is - _____**here's**_____

11.   there is - _____**there's**_____

12.   they are - _____**they're**_____

13.   they have - _____**they've**_____

84

Name_____   **VERBS**
                                 Contractions

Date_____

Directions: Write the contraction.

1.   I am - _____

2.   I have - _____

3.   I will - _____

4.   it is - _____

5.   he is - _____

6.   she is - _____

7.   who is - _____

8.   what is - _____

9.   where is - _____

10.   here is - _____

11.   there is - _____

12.   they are - _____

13.   they have - _____

Directions: Write the contraction.

1.   do not - _____**don't**_____

2.   does not - _____**doesn't**_____

3.   did not - _____**didn't**_____

4.   has not - _____**hasn't**_____

5.   have not - _____**haven't**_____

6.   had not - _____**hadn't**_____

7.   is not - _____**isn't**_____

8.   are not - _____**aren't**_____

9.   was not - _____**wasn't**_____

10.   were not - _____**weren't**_____

11.   cannot - _____**can't**_____

12.   will not - _____**won't**_____

13.   would not - _____**wouldn't**_____

Date_____

Directions: Write the contraction.

1.   do not - _____

2.   does not - _____

3.   did not - _____

4.   has not - _____

5.   have not - _____

6.   had not - _____

7.   is not - _____

8.   are not - _____

9.   was not - _____

10.   were not - _____

11.   cannot - _____

12.   will not - _____

13.   would not - _____

Directions: Write the contraction for the words in boldfaced (very black) type.

1. _____I'll_____   **I will** play with you.

2. _____can't_____   Stacey **cannot** come with us.

3. _____He's_____   **He is** my dad's boss.

4. _____shouldn't_____   Tom **should not** play in the street.

5. _____You're_____   **You are** very nice.

6. _____doesn't_____   Janet **does not** like to swing.

7. _____isn't_____   Mrs. Harmon **is not** here yet.

8. _____They're_____   **They are** going to the park today.

9. _____haven't_____   I **have not** done my chores.

10. _____Where's_____   **Where is** your brother?

11. _____You'll_____   **You will** enjoy this game.

12. _____didn't_____   Paul **did not** leave early.

13. _____hasn't_____   One runner **has not** finished.

88

Directions: Write the contraction for the words in boldfaced (very black) type.

1.   _____   **I will** play with you.

2.   _____   Stacey **cannot** come with us.

3.   _____   **He is** my dad's boss.

4.   _____   Tom **should not** play in the street.

5.   _____   **You are** very nice.

6.   _____   Janet **does not** like to swing.

7.   _____   Mrs. Harmon **is not** here yet.

8.   _____   **They are** going to the park today.

9.   _____   I **have not** done my chores.

10.   _____   **Where is** your brother?

11.   _____   **You will** enjoy this game.

12.   _____   Paul **did not** leave early.

13.   _____   One runner **has not** finished.

89

Directions: Write the contraction for the words in boldfaced (very black) type.

1. _____**They're**_____   **They are** having a great time!

2. _____**It's**_____   **It is** raining.

3. _____**wasn't**_____   The hamster **was not** in its cage.

4. _____**wouldn't**_____   The child **would not** answer.

5. _____**I'm**_____   **I am** going to a birthday party.

6. _____**Don't**_____   **Do not** go outside without a coat.

7. _____**won't**_____   Tulips **will not** bloom until spring.

8. _____**They're**_____   **They are** going to the park today.

9. _____**didn't**_____   That player **did not** score any points.

10. _____**What's**_____   **What is** the highest building in the United Sates?

11. _____**That's**_____   **That is** the funniest story I have ever heard.

12. _____**aren't**_____   Those diamonds **are not** real.

Directions: Write the contraction for the words in boldfaced (very black) type.

1. _____   **They are** having a great time!

2. _____   **It is** raining.

3. _____   The hamster **was not** in its cage.

4. _____   The child **would not** answer.

5. _____   **I am** going to a birthday party.

6. _____   **Do not** go outside without a coat.

7. _____   Tulips **will not** bloom until spring.

8. _____   **They are** going to the park today.

9. _____   That player **did not** score any points.

10. _____   **What is** the highest building in the United Sates?

11. _____   **That is** the funniest story I have ever heard.

12. _____   Those diamonds **are not** real.

91

A.   Directions: Write the contractions that begin with **you**:

1.   _____**you'll**_____   2.   _____**you're**_____

B.   Directions: Write the contractions that begin with **they**:

1.   _____**they'll**_____   2.   _____**they're**_____

C.   Directions: Write the contractions that begin with **I**:

1.   _____**I'll**_____   2.   _____**I'm**_____   3.   _____**I've**_____

D.   Directions: Write the contractions that contain **is**:

1.   ___**he's**_____   4.   ___**she's**_____   7.   ___**what's**_____

2.   ___**here's**_____   5.   ___**that's**_____   8.   ___**where's**_____

3.   ___**it's**_____   6.   ___**there's**_____   9.   ___**who's**_____

E.   Directions: Write the contractions that contain **n't (not)**. To help you,
the first letter of each contraction is in parentheses ( ).

1.   ___**aren't**_____   6.   ___**don't**_____   11.   ___**shouldn't**_____

2.   ___**can't**_____   7.   ___**hadn't**_____   12.   ___**wasn't**_____

3.   ___**couldn't**_____   8.   ___**hasn't**_____   13.   ___**weren't**_____

4.   ___**didn't**_____   9.   ___**haven't**_____   14.   ___**won't**_____

5.   ___**doesn't**_____   10.   ___**isn't**_____   15.   ___**wouldn't**_____

A.   Directions: Write the contractions that begin with **you**:

1.   _____   2.   _____

B.   Directions: Write the contractions that begin with **they**:

1.   _____   2.   _____

C.   Directions: Write the contractions that begin with **I**:

1.   _____   2.   _____   3.   _____

D.   Directions: Write the contractions that contain **is**:

1.   _____   4.   _____   7.   _____

2.   _____   5.   _____   8.   _____

3.   _____   6.   _____   9.   _____

E.   Directions: Write the contractions that contain **n't (not)**. To help you,
                   the first letter of each contraction is in parentheses ( ).

1.   _(a)_____   6.   _(d)_____   11.   _(s)_____

2.   _(c)_____   7.   _(h)_____   12.   _(w)_____

3.   _(c)_____   8.   _(h)_____   13.   _(w)_____

4.   _(d)_____   9.   _(h)_____   14.   _(w)_____

5.   _(d)_____   10. _(i)_____   15.   _(w)_____

Name_____   **VERBS**
WORKBOOK PAGE 44   **It's and Its**
Date_____

It's is a contraction meaning **it is**.   An **apostrophe** is used.

The word **its** is a word used to show that something owns or has
something.

> Example: The car lost **its** wheel.

> What does the car have? The car has *its* **wheel.**
> Do **not** use an apostrophe with <u>its</u>.

If you do not remember which word to use, try dividing **it's** into **it is**.

> Example: The car lost **it is** wheel.

> That sounds strange!   Now you know to use <u>its</u>.

🐢🐢🐢🐢🐢🐢🐢🐢🐢🐢🐢🐢🐢🐢🐢🐢🐢🐢🐢🐢🐢🐢🐢

Directions: Circle the correct word.

1. Your hair has lost (it's, **its**) shine.

2. Today, (**it's,** its) very cloudy.

3. (**It's**, Its) your turn.

4. The vase fell over on (it's, **its**) side.

5. The moose raised (it's, **its**) head and looked around.

6. When (**it's**, its) four o'clock, you may go outside and play.

7.   A large kangaroo raised (it's, **its**) tail and hopped away.

8. On Valentine's Day, (**it's**, its) a custom to give cards.

9. Take the cake from the oven if (**it's**, its) baked.

94

It's is a contraction meaning **it is**.   An **apostrophe** is used.

The word **its** is a word used to show that something owns or has something.

> Example: The car lost **its** wheel.
>
> What does the car have? The car has *its* **wheel.**
> Do **not** use an apostrophe with <u>its</u>**.**

If you do not remember which word to use, try dividing **it's** into **it is**.

> Example: The car lost **it is** wheel.
>
> That sounds strange!   Now you know to use **<u>its</u>**.

Directions: Circle the correct word.

1. Your hair has lost (it's, its) shine.

2. Today, (it's, its) very cloudy.

3. (It's, Its) your turn.

4. The vase fell over on (it's, its) side.

5. The moose raised (it's, its) head and looked around.

6.   When (it's, its) four o'clock, you may go outside and play.

7.   A large kangaroo raised (it's, its) tail and hopped away.

8. On Valentine's Day, (it's, its) a custom to give cards.

9. Take the cake from the oven if (it's, its) baked.

TO THE TEACHER:

They're, *their*, and *there* are difficult. Be sure that students understand each word. Again, it is recommended that you do the first worksheet orally with students. Then, make a decision on the second worksheet. (I usually like to introduce a lesson and do the worksheet orally. That is as much as I teach the first day. On the second day, I review the concepts using different examples and then proceed to the second worksheet. If I feel that students comprehend the concept, I do only the first three or four orally and let them finish the page. If I feel that students do not understand the concept, I do the entire page with them.)

PAGE 97 = WORKBOOK PAGE 45

They're/Their/There

They're is a contraction meaning **they are**.   An **apostrophe** is used.

Example: They're finished.

Their is a word used to show that something owns or has something.

Example: The children carried their skis.

What do the children have? The children have *their* **skis.**
Do **not** use an apostrophe with <u>their</u>.

There tells **where**.

Example: I want to go *there*.

Sometimes, **there** is used at the beginning of a sentence.

Example: *There* are thirty pennies in this jar.

<u>If you don't remember which word to use, divide **they're** into **they are**.</u>

Example: The children carried **they're** skis.

The children carried **they are** skis.

That doesn't make sense!   Use ***their***.

97

Name_____
WORKBOOK PAGE 46
Date_____

VERBS
They're, Their, and
There

🐢**They're** is a contraction meaning **they are**.   An **apostrophe** is used.

Example: *They're* in first grade.

🐢**Their** is a word used to show that something owns or has something.

Example: *Their* sister is a golfer.

🐢**There** tells **where**.   Example: I want to go *there*.

Sometimes, **there** is used at the beginning of a sentence.

Example: *There* is a crack in this cup.

🐢🐢🐢🐢🐢🐢🐢🐢🐢🐢🐢🐢🐢🐢🐢🐢🐢🐢🐢🐢🐢

Directions: Circle the correct word in each sentence.

1.   (**Their**, They're, There) scout leader is Mr. Hines.

2.   Josh's family went (their, they're, **there**) last summer.

3.   (Their, **They're**, There) learning about frogs.

4.   After eating lunch, (**their**, they're, there) father took them to the zoo.

5.   (Their, They're, **There**) are no ice cubes in the freezer.

6.   During the storm, (**their**, they're, there) tree blew over.

7.   Did you know (their, they're, **there**) isn't any ice cream left?

8.   I think that (their, **they're**, there) leaving on Friday.

9.   They are taking (**their**, they're, there) cat to a show.

🐢 **They're** is a contraction meaning **they are**.   An **apostrophe** is used.

   Example: *They're* in first grade.

🐢 **Their** is a word used to show that something owns or has something.

   Example: *Their* sister is a golfer.

🐢 **There** tells **where**.   Example: I want to go *there*.

   Sometimes, **there** is used at the beginning of a sentence.

   Example: *There* is a crack in this cup.

🐢🐢🐢🐢🐢🐢🐢🐢🐢🐢🐢🐢🐢🐢🐢🐢🐢🐢🐢🐢🐢🐢🐢🐢

Directions: Circle the correct word in each sentence.

1.   (Their, They're, There) scout leader is Mr. Hines.

2.   Josh's family went (their, they're, there) last summer.

3.   (Their, They're, There) learning about frogs.

4.   After eating lunch, (their, they're, there) father took them to the zoo.

5.   (Their, They're, There) are no ice cubes in the freezer.

6.   During the storm, (their, they're, there) tree blew over.

7.   Did you know (their, they're, there) isn't any ice cream left?

8.   I think that (their, they're, there) leaving on Friday.

9.   They are taking (their, they're, there) cat to a show.

🐢 **They're** is a contraction meaning **they are**.   An **apostrophe** is used.

🐢 **Their** is a word used to show that something owns or has something.

🐢 **There** tells **where**.   Sometimes, **there** is used at the beginning of a sentence.

🐢 🐢

Directions: Circle the correct word in each sentence.

1.   The runners all finished (**their**, they're, there) race.

2.   (Their, They're, **There**) will be no school on Monday.

3.   Do you want (**their**, they're, there) telephone number?

4.   (**Their**, They're, There) plans have changed.

5.   Those birds chirp when (their, **they're**, there) nervous.

6.   We went (their, they're, **there**) last summer.

7.   (**Their**, They're, There) grandma is coming soon.

8.   (Their, **They're**, There) the best two-square players.

9.   Some girls left (**their**, they're, there) papers at home.

10.   I went (their, they're, **there**) during my spring break.

100

🐢 **They're** is a contraction meaning **they are**. An **apostrophe** is used.

🐢 **Their** is a word used to show that something owns or has something.

🐢 **There** tells **where**. Sometimes, **there** is used at the beginning of a sentence.

🐢 🐢

Directions: Circle the correct word in each sentence.

1.   The runners all finished (their, they're, there) race.

2.   (Their, They're, There) will be no school on Monday.

3.   Do you want (their, they're, there) telephone number?

4.   (Their, They're, There) plans have changed.

5.   Those birds chirp when (their, they're, there) nervous.

6.   We went (their, they're, there) last summer.

7.   (Their, They're, There) grandma is coming soon.

8.   (Their, They're, There) the best two-square players.

9.   Some girls left (their, they're, there) papers at home.

10.   I went (their, they're, there) during my spring break.

🐢 **You're** is a contraction for **you are**.   An **apostrophe** is used.

　　　　Example: **You're** funny.
　　　　　　　　　　You are funny.

🐢 **Your** is a word used to show that something owns or has something.

　　　　Example: **Your** pencil is on the floor.

　　　　　　　　　　Your will go over to (modify) another word. It will
　　　　　　　　　　answer <u>what</u>.   *Your what?* Your **pencil**!

🐢 If you are not sure which word to use, try reading the sentence using
　 you are.

　　　　Examples:　　You're right!

　　　　　　　　　　You are right!　　　　　　(This makes sense!)

　　　　　　　　　　You're sister is here.
　　　　　　　　　　You are sister is here.　　(This doesn't make sense!)
　　　　　　　　　　Your sister is here.　　　　　(This is correct!)

🐢🐢🐢🐢🐢🐢🐢🐢🐢🐢🐢🐢🐢🐢🐢🐢🐢🐢🐢🐢🐢🐢🐢

Directions:　　Circle the correct word in each sentence.

1.　Are (you're, **your**) parents here?

2.　(You're, **Your**) friends are waiting for you.

3.　Troy said, "(**You're**, Your) invited to my party."

4.　(You're, **Your**) lunch is in this bag.

5.　(**You're**, Your) the best artist.

🐢 **You're** is a contraction for **you are**.   An **apostrophe** is used.

> Example: **You're** funny.
> You are funny.

🐢 **Your** is a word used to show that something owns or has something.

> Example: **Your** pencil is on the floor.
>
> *Your* will go over to (modify) another word. It will answer <u>what</u>.   *Your what?* Your **pencil**!

🐢 If you are not sure which word to use, try reading the sentence using *you are*.

> Examples: You're right!
> **You are** right!   (This makes sense!)
>
> You're sister is here.
> **You are** sister is here.   (This doesn't make sense!)
> Your sister is here.   (This is correct!)

🐢🐢🐢🐢🐢🐢🐢🐢🐢🐢🐢🐢🐢🐢🐢🐢🐢🐢🐢🐢🐢🐢🐢

Directions: Circle the correct word in each sentence.

1.   Are (you're, your) parents here?

2.   (You're, Your) friends are waiting for you.

3.   Troy said, "(You're, Your) invited to my party."

4.   (You're, Your) lunch is in this bag.

5.   (You're, Your) the best artist.

🐢 **You're** is a contraction for **you are**. An **apostrophe** is used.

🐢 **Your** is a word used to show that something owns or has something.

🐢 If you are not sure which word to use, try reading the sentence using *you are*.

    Examples: You're nice!

               You are nice!   (This makes sense!)

🐢🐢🐢🐢🐢🐢🐢🐢🐢🐢🐢🐢🐢🐢🐢🐢🐢🐢🐢🐢🐢🐢

Directions: Circle the correct word in each sentence.

1.   Does (you're, **your**) name have an <u>o</u> in it?

2.   Don asked if (**you're**, your) going with us.

3.   (You're, **Your**) shoe is under the bed.

4.   (**You're**, Your) lucky.

5.   Has (you're, **your**) uncle written a new song?

6.   Are you sure that (**you're**, your) ready?

7.   (**You're**, Your) a very good actor, Kelly.

8.   Is (you're, **your**) last answer 52?

9.   Jackie has (you're, **your**) bicycle pump.

10. Next week, (**you're**, your) allowed to attend the rodeo.

104

🐢 **You're** is a contraction for **you are**. An **apostrophe** is used.

🐢 **Your** is a word used to show that something owns or has something.

🐢 If you are not sure which word to use, try reading the sentence using *you are.*

   Examples: You're nice!

           You are nice!   (This makes sense!)

🐢🐢🐢🐢🐢🐢🐢🐢🐢🐢🐢🐢🐢🐢🐢🐢🐢🐢🐢🐢🐢🐢🐢

Directions: Circle the correct word in each sentence.

1.   Does (you're, your) name have an <u>o</u> in it?

2.   Don asked if (you're, your) going with us.

3. (You're, Your) shoe is under the bed.

4. (You're, Your) lucky.

5.   Has (you're, your) uncle written a new song?

6.   Are you sure that (you're, your) ready?

7. (You're, Your) a very good actor, Kelly.

8.   Is (you're, your) last answer 52?

9. Jackie has (you're, your) bicycle pump.

10.   Next week, (you're, your) allowed to attend the rodeo.

A. Directions: Write **it's** or **its** in the blank.

1. Jordan said, "_____**It's**_____ time to eat."

2. The book had been damaged; _____**its**_____ pages were torn.

3. _____**It's**_____ cold outside!

4. The worm curled _____**its**_____ tail around a piece of grass.

B. Directions: Write **they're**, **their**, or **there** in the blank.

1. Has _____**their**_____ dog been found?

2. _____**They're**_____ waiting for a phone call.

3. _____**There**_____ is no cereal for breakfast.

4. _____**Their**_____ last house had a fireplace.

5. Gail doesn't know if _____**they're**_____ coming to the party.

C. Directions: Write **you're** or **your** in the blank.

1. _____**You're**_____ standing on my foot!

2. _____**Your**_____ kite is crashing!

3. Yesterday, _____**your**_____ poem won a contest.

4. I think that _____**you're**_____ a good friend.

Name_____

Date_____

A. Directions: Write **it's** or **its** in the blank.

1. Jordan said, "_____ time to eat."

2. The book had been damaged; _____ pages were torn.

3. _____ cold outside!

4. The worm curled _____ tail around a piece of grass.

B. Directions: Write **they're**, **their**, or **there** in the blank.

1. Has _____ dog been found?

2. _____ waiting for a phone call.

3. _____ is no cereal for breakfast.

4. _____ last house had a fireplace.

5. Gail doesn't know if _____ coming to the party.

C. Directions: Write **you're** or **your** in the blank.

1. _____ standing on my foot!

2. _____ kite is crashing!

3. Yesterday, _____ poem won a contest.

4. I think that _____ a good friend.

107

🐢 **Can** means **to be able to**.

      Example: **Can** you fix my bike?

🐢 **May** sometimes **asks permission**.

      Example: **May** I go with you?

May sometimes **gives permission.**

      Example: You **may** eat outside today.

May sometimes suggests a possibility.

      Example: Betty **may** go to the beach soon.

🐢🐢🐢🐢🐢🐢🐢🐢🐢🐢🐢🐢🐢🐢🐢🐢🐢🐢🐢🐢🐢🐢🐢

Directions: Write **can** or **may** in the blank.

1. _____**Can**_____ you hold this for me?

2. You _____**may**_____ begin now.

3. _____**May**_____ Sarah and I make a card?

4. You _____**may**_____ have to wait for a bus.

5. _____**Can**_____ this watch be repaired?

6. _____**May**_____ I say something?

108

🐢 **Can** means **to be able to**.

      Example: **Can** you fix my bike?

🐢 **May** sometimes **asks permission**.

      Example: **May** I go with you?

May sometimes **gives permission.**

      Example: You **may** eat outside today.

May sometimes suggests a possibility.

      Example: Betty **may** go to the beach soon.

🐢🐢🐢🐢🐢🐢🐢🐢🐢🐢🐢🐢🐢🐢🐢🐢🐢🐢🐢🐢🐢🐢

Directions: Write **<u>can</u>** or **<u>may</u>** in the blank.

1. _____ you hold this for me?

2. You _____ begin now.

3. _____ Sarah and I make a card?

4. You _____ have to wait for a bus.

5. _____ this watch be repaired?

6. _____ I say something?

TO THE TEACHER:

Make sure that students understand the conjugation of *to be* and how it is used in our language. Practice of this concept will occur under subject - verb agreement.

Students need to recognize when a verb is showing action. Students are not introduced to linking verbs in this text.

Introduce action verbs carefully in this chapter.

To plus a verb is an infinitive. Introduce students to the term.

Pages 136-137:   **Irregular Verbs**

Students are introduced to a list of irregular verbs. This, of course, is not a complete list. Go over the list with students and explain (again) that an irregular verb will not add <u>ed</u> to the verb in the past tense. In addition, you may wish to point out the following:

1.   Tense means time.   Present is now. For ease, we use *today*.
     The present tense is formed by removing <u>to</u> from the verb (infinitive).

     Example: to run   run or runs

     The reason <u>run</u> or <u>runs</u> is present, is that we must make it agree with the subject.
     Example: Today I <u>run</u>.   They <u>run</u>.
                Mary <u>runs</u>.

2.   Past means time that has already happened. For ease, we use *yesterday*.
     An irregular verb will **not** add <u>ed</u> to the past tense.

     Example: Yesterday they <u>ran</u>.

3.   The present participle* always adds *ing* to the verb; it is not a tense.

4.   The past participle* is not a tense.   It is a form of the verb that usually helps to explain time that has occurred.   Usually, the helping verbs, <u>has</u>, <u>have</u>, or <u>had</u>, are used.
     Example: The joggers <u>had run</u> two miles.

Again, ascertain that students **know** the past and past participle forms of the irregular verbs listed.

PAGE 111 = WORKBOOK PAGE 52
PAGE 123 = WORKBOOK PAGE 58

110   *These form more complex tenses.

VERBS

The verb in a sentence shows an action or says a fact.

A. ACTION VERBS:

Examples: Micah **plays** a guitar.
Devi **laughs** often.
A mouse **darted** across the floor.
Dad **helped** me with the project.

B. STATE OF BEING VERBS:

1. The verb, **to be**, simply states a fact. It is called a state of being verb.
2. The forms of *to be* are: **is**, **am**, **are**, **was**, **were**, **be**, **being**, **been**.

a. For telling present time:

Use **am** with the pronoun, <u>I</u>.
Example: I **am** a good singer.

Use **is** when the subject is only one.
Example: He **is** a great rider.

Use **are** when the subject is <u>you</u>.
Example: You **are** a nice friend.

Use **are** when the subject is more than one.
Examples: The bananas **are** ripe.
Aren and Tito **are** in the kitchen.

b. For telling past time:

Use **was** for only one.
Examples: I **was** scared.
A chair **was** on the patio.

Use **were** when the subject is more than one or with <u>you</u>.
Examples: Her keys **were** lost.
You were not late, Kami.   111

Some verbs show action.

Directions: Write an action verb on the line; then, draw a picture to show
               your sentence.

1.   Dad _____ the floor.
        swept   (sweeps)
        washed   (washes)
        stained   (stains)   **PICTURE WILL VARY.**
        sanded   (sands)
        painted   (paints)

2.   His sister _____ her car.
        washed   (washes)
        drove   (drives)
        wrecked   (wrecks)   **PICTURE WILL VARY.**
        dried   (dries)

3.   A man _____ the trees.
        trimmed   (trims)
        sprayed   (sprays)
        planted   (plants)   **PICTURE WILL VARY.**
        pruned   (prunes)

4.   He _____ in the afternoon.
        ate   (eats)
        slept   (sleeps)
        worked   (works)   **PICTURE WILL VARY.**
        swam   (swims)
        skied   (skis)

112

Name_____

Date_____

Some verbs show action.

Directions: Write an action verb on the line; then, draw a picture to show
your sentence.

1.   Dad _____ the floor.

2.   His sister _____her car.

3.   A man _____the trees.

4.   He _____in the afternoon.

Directions: In the blank, write <u>Yes</u> if the boldfaced word shows action.
Write <u>No</u> if the boldfaced verb does not show action.

Example: _____No_____   Her hair **is** curly.

1. _____**Yes**_____   A golfer **swung** the club.

2. _____**Yes**_____   He **climbs** trees by a small pond.

3. _____**No**_____   Their tricycles **are** in the driveway.

4. _____**Yes**_____   Mother **plants** flowers in her garden.

5. _____**Yes**_____   Several frogs **leaped** into the water.

6. _____**No**_____   All of the workers **were** very hungry.

7. _____**Yes**_____   Janet **draws** cartoons.

8. _____**No**_____   Brian **was** the last one on the stage.

9. _____**Yes**_____   A hummingbird **flaps** his wings fast.

10. _____**Yes**_____   The children **clapped** their hands excitedly.

11. _____**Yes**_____   Joe's brothers and sisters **chop** wood in the winter.

12. _____**No**_____   A special doll **is** on her bed.

114

Directions: In the blank, write <u>Yes</u> if the boldfaced word shows action.
              Write <u>No</u> if the boldfaced verb does not show action.

              Example: ____No____   Her hair **is** curly.

1. _____   A golfer **swung** the club.

2. _____   He **climbs** trees by a small pond.

3. _____   Their tricycles **are** in the driveway.

4. _____   Mother **plants** flowers in her garden.

5. _____   Several frogs **leaped** into the water.

6. _____   All of the workers **were** very hungry.

7. _____   Janet **draws** cartoons.

8. _____   Brian **was** the last one on the stage.

9. _____   A hummingbird **flaps** his wings fast.

10. _____   The children **clapped** their hands excitedly.

11. _____   Joe's brothers and sisters **chop** wood in the winter.

12. _____   A special doll **is** on her bed.

Directions: In the blank, write <u>Yes</u> if the boldfaced word shows action.
Write <u>No</u> if the boldfaced verb does not show action.

Example: ____Yes____   A cow **chews** its cud.

1. ____Yes____   A student **raised** his hand.

2. ____No____   Her uncle **is** a policeman.

3. ____Yes____   Mrs. Kent always **smiles** at us.

4. ____Yes____   Some flour **spilled** on the counter.

5. ____No____   I **am** in the fourth grade.

6. ____Yes____   That jet **lands** at the airport every Friday.

7. ____Yes____   A bowler **rolled** his ball too hard.

8. ____No____   Two bags of candy **were** on the table.

9. ____Yes____   Several girls **jump** rope each afternoon.

10. ____Yes____   Tyler **asked** a question.

11. ____No____   Joan's father **was** sick last week.

12. ____Yes____   A squirrel **gathers** acorns.

116

Directions: In the blank, write <u>Yes</u> if the boldfaced word shows action.
Write <u>No</u> if the boldfaced verb does not show action.

Example: ___<u>Yes</u>___   A cow **chews** its cud.

1. _____   A student **raised** his hand.

2. _____   Her uncle **is** a policeman.

3. _____   Mrs. Kent always **smiles** at us.

4. _____   Some flour **spilled** on the counter.

5. _____   I **am** in the fourth grade.

6. _____   That jet **lands** at the airport every Friday.

7. _____   A bowler **rolled** his ball too hard.

8. _____   Two bags of candy **were** on the table.

9. _____   Several girls **jump** rope each afternoon.

10. _____   Tyler **asked** a question.

11. _____   Joan's father **was** sick last week.

12. _____   A squirrel **gathers** acorns.

Date_____

Past tense means time that has happened.

Examples: Susie **walked** to the store.   (It already happened.)

We **ran** in a race.   (It already happened.)

🐢A regular verb adds **ed** to the verb to form the past tense.

Examples: to hop = hopp**ed**
to stay = stay**ed**
to cry = cri**ed**

🐢An irregular verb does not add **ed** to form the past tense.

Examples: to swim = swam
to fly = flew
to bring = brought

🐢🐢🐢🐢🐢🐢🐢🐢🐢🐢🐢🐢🐢🐢🐢🐢🐢🐢🐢🐢🐢🐢

Directions: Write the past tense of each verb.

1. (to talk)   Steven _____**talked**_____ to his brother about the problem.

2. (to smile)   The baby _____**smiled**_____ at us.

3. (to sing)   We _____**sang**_____ a new song.

4. (to jump)   Five children _____**jumped**_____ into the wading pool at the same time.

5. (to cook)   We _____**cooked**_____ hot dogs on the grill.

6. (to find)   Yesterday, I _____**found**_____ a dime in my pocket.

7. (to laugh)   The crowd _____**laughed**_____ at the seal act.

118

Past tense means time that has happened.

     Examples: Susie **walked** to the store.   (It already happened.)

                We **ran** in a race.   (It already happened.)

🐢 A regular verb adds **ed** to the verb to form the past tense.

      Examples: to hop = hopp**ed**
                 to stay = stay**ed**
                 to cry = cri**ed**

🐢 An irregular verb does not add **ed** to form the past tense.

      Examples: to swim = swam
                 to fly = flew
                 to bring = brought

🐢🐢🐢🐢🐢🐢🐢🐢🐢🐢🐢🐢🐢🐢🐢🐢🐢🐢🐢🐢🐢🐢

Directions: Write the past tense of each verb.

1. (to talk)   Steven _____ to his brother about the problem.

2. (to smile)   The baby _____ at us.

3. (to sing)   We _____ a new song.

4. (to jump)   Five children _____ into the wading pool at the same time.

5. (to cook)   We _____ hot dogs on the grill.

6. (to find)   Yesterday, I _____ a dime in my pocket.

7. (to laugh)   The crowd _____ at the seal act.

Name_____   **VERBS**
WORKBOOK PAGE 57   **Regular or Irregular**
Date_____

Past tense means time that has happened.

     Example: He **sent** a letter.

  🐢A regular verb adds **ed** to the verb to form the past tense.

     Examples: to stop   =   stopp**ed**
                  to whine   =   whin**ed**

  🐢An irregular verb does not add **ed** to form the past tense.

     Examples: to leave   =   left
                to see   =   saw

🐢🐢🐢🐢🐢🐢🐢🐢🐢🐢🐢🐢🐢🐢🐢🐢🐢🐢🐢🐢🐢🐢🐢🐢

Directions: Write the past tense of each verb. Circle any regular verb.
The past tense of regular verbs is in boldfaced print.

   Remember: You will add ed to form the past tense of regular verbs.

1. to dance - ___**danced**___   9. to drink - ___drank___

2. to call - ___**called**___   10. to live - ___**lived**___

3. to go - ___went___   11. to make - ___made___

4. to lock - ___**locked**___   12. to like - ___**liked**___

5. to fall - ___fell___   13. to eat - ___ate___

6. to walk - ___**walked**___   14. to wash - ___**washed**___

7. to yell - ___**yelled**___   15. to ride - ___rode___

8. to clean - ___**cleaned**___   16. to rub - ___**rubbed**___

Name_____

Date_____

Past tense means time that has happened.

    Example: He **sent** a letter.

   A regular verb adds **ed** to the verb to form the past tense.

       Examples: to stop   =   stop**ped**

                   to whine   =   whin**ed**

   An irregular verb does not add **ed** to form the past tense.

       Examples: to leave   =   left

                   to see   =   saw

Directions: Write the past tense of each verb. Circle any regular verb.

Remember: You will add ed to form the past tense of regular verbs.

1.   to dance - _____

2.   to call - _____

3.   to go - _____

4.   to lock - _____

5.   to fall - _____

6.   to walk - _____

7.   to yell - _____

8.   to clean - _____

9.   to drink - _____

10.   to live - _____

11.   to make - _____

12.   to like - _____

13.   to eat - _____

14.   to wash - _____

15.   to ride - _____

16.   to rub - _____

TO THE TEACHER:

Students need to memorize the twenty-three helping verbs. I suggest that you learn them in the groups presented. Practice orally with children; you'll be amazed how quickly they will learn them. If students learn these, finding verb phrases will be very easy.

Teach the concept that a word that can be a helping verb may act as a main verb. Here are other possible examples:

The car **is** in the pit.	(main verb)
Julie **is** sitting by a stream.	(helping verb)
Harriet **had** given her lunch away.	(helping verb)
The clerk **had** money in his hand.	(main verb)

Page 123 will help students to understand the concept of a verb serving either as a main verb or a helping verb. You may want to do that page orally.

Be sure that students comprehend that an interrogative sentence often has the verb phrase separated.

> Example: Does Annie swim on the city's team?

To assist students, you may help them convert an interrogative sentence into a declarative one.

> Example: Does Annie swim on the city's team?
> Changed: Annie does swim on the city's team.

In making the conversion, the helping verb will usually stand beside the main verb.

> Annie <u>does swim</u> on the city's team.

However, you may prefer to guide students to simply look for a helping verb at the beginning of a question. Although not all questions contain a helping verb, many do.

> Example: <u>Are</u> you ready?   (main verb)
>
> <u>Are</u> you <u>going</u> to the grocery store?   (helping verb)

PAGE 136 = WORKBOOK PAGE 65   PAGE 137 = WORKBOOK PAGE 66

122

HELPING VERBS

These verbs help another verb. They are called helping verbs.

do	has	may	can	could	is	was	be
does	have	might	shall	should	am	were	being
did	had	must	will	would	are		been

🐢 Sometimes, a verb on this list can stand **alone** in a sentence. This is called the **main verb**.

Example: Sally is my cousin.   (main verb)

🐢 Sometimes, **one or more** verbs on this list will be **in front of** another verb. This is called a **verb phrase**.

Example: Sharon <u>is **visiting**</u> her grandpa.   (helping verb)

VERB PHRASE	**=**	**HELPING VERB(S)**	**+**	**MAIN VERB**
can go	=	can	+	go
had worked	=	had	+	worked
was broken	=	was	+	broken
should have stayed	=	should have	+	stayed

🐢 The helping verb or verbs may be beside the main verb.

Example: Her sister **has shopped** all day.

🐢 The helping verb or verbs may not be beside the main verb.

Example: Her sister **has** already **shopped** for three hours.

The helping verb or verbs may not be beside the main verb if the sentence asks a question.

Example: **Has** her sister **shopped** all day?   123

Name_____ **VERBS**
WORKBOOK PAGE 59   **Helping Verbs**
Date_____

Note to Teacher: **You may wish to do this page orally with your students.**
Directions: Write <u>H.V.</u> if the boldfaced verb is a helping verb in the
                sentence.   Write <u>M.V.</u> if the boldfaced verb is the main verb.

Example: A.   __M.V.__   **Do** it yourself.

          B.   __H.V.__   **Do** you <u>want</u> to play?

1.   A.   __M.V.__   Keith **does** his chores each day.

     B.   __H.V.__   Mrs. Frame **does** <u>like</u> to sleep late.

2.   A.   __M.V.__   Jeff **has** a cold.

     B.   __H.V.__   She **has** <u>driven</u> her dad's car to work.

3.   A.   __H.V.__   Two boys **were** <u>riding</u> bikes.

     B.   __M.V.__   Their sundaes **were** good.

4.   A.   __M.V.__   Yes, I **can**!

     B.   __H.V.__   She **can** <u>twirl</u> a baton.

5.   A.   __H.V.__   A plumber **is** <u>fixing</u> our sink.

     B.   __M.V.__   She **is** the youngest child in the family.

6.   A.   __H.V.__   **Am** I <u>invited</u> to your party?

     B.   __M.V.__   I **am** nine years old.

124

Name_____

Date_____

Directions: Write <u>H.V.</u> if the boldfaced verb is a helping verb in the
sentence. Write <u>M.V.</u> if the boldfaced verb is the main verb.

Example: A. <u> M.V. </u>   **Do** it yourself.

B. <u> H.V. </u>   **Do** you <u>want</u> to play?

1. A. _____ Keith **does** his chores each day.

   B. _____ Mrs. Frame **does** <u>like</u> to sleep late.

2. A. _____ Jeff **has** a cold.

   B. _____ She **has** <u>driven</u> her dad's car to work.

3. A. _____ Two boys **were** <u>riding</u> bikes.

   B. _____ Their sundaes **were** good.

4. A. _____ Yes, I **can**!

   B. _____ She **can** <u>twirl</u> a baton.

5. A. _____ A plumber **is** <u>fixing</u> our sink.

   B. _____ She **is** the youngest child in the family.

6. A. _____ **Am** I <u>invited</u> to your party?

   B. _____ I **am** nine years old.   125

Note to Teacher: **This is a rather easy page.** **You may want to add more excitement by giving a "prize" to the person (or group) who finishes first.**

Directions: Unscramble the twenty-three helping verbs.

1.   codul - __**could**__

2.   si - __**is**__

3.   ear - __**are**__

4.   sode - __**does**__

5.   sah - __**has**__

6.   stum - __**must**__

7.   nebe - __**been**__

8.   wsa - __**was**__

9.   sdohul - __**should**__

10.   reew - __**were**__

11.   liwl - __**will**__

12.   yam - __**may**__

13.   gitmh - __**might**__

14.   ma - __**am**__

15.   acn - __**can**__

16.   lsahl - __**shall**__

17.   eb - __**be**__

18.   idd - __**did**__

19.   dulow - __**would**__

20.   adh - __**had**__

21.   od - __**do**__

22.   vahe - __**have**__

23.   gneib - __**being**__

Directions: Unscramble the twenty-three helping verbs.

1.   codul - _____

2.   si - _____

3.   ear - _____

4.   sode - _____

5.   sah - _____

6.   stum - _____

7.   nebe - _____

8.   wsa - _____

9.   sdohul - _____

10.   reew - _____

11.   liwl - _____

12.   yam - _____

13.   gitmh - _____

14.   ma - _____

15.   acn - _____

16.   lsahl - _____

17.   eb - _____

18.   idd - _____

19.   dulow - _____

20.   adh - _____

21.   od - _____

22.   vahe - _____

23.   gneib - _____

A. Directions: Write the three helping verbs that begin with <u>d</u>:

1. ___**do**___   2. ___**does**___   3. ___**did**___

B. Directions: Write the three helping verbs that begin with <u>h</u>:

1. ___**have**___   2. ___**has**___   3. ___**had**___

C. Directions: Write the three helping verbs that begin with <u>m</u>:

1. ___**may**___   2. ___**might**___   3. ___**must**___

D. Directions: Write the three helping verbs that end with <u>ould</u>:

1. ___**would**___   2. ___**should**___   3. ___**could**___

E. Directions: Write the forms of the verb, <u>to be</u>:

1. ___**is**___   2. ___**am**___   3. ___**are**___

4. ___**was**___   5. ___**were**___   6. ___**be**___

7. ___**being**___   8. ___**been**___

F. Directions: Write the other three helping verbs on the list:

1. ___**can**___   2. ___**shall**___   3. ___**will**___

Name_____

Date_____

A.   Directions: Write the three helping verbs that begin with <u>d</u>:

1. _____   2. _____   3. _____

B.   Directions: Write the three helping verbs that begin with <u>h</u>:

1. _____   2. _____   3. _____

C.   Directions: Write the three helping verbs that begin with <u>m</u>:

1. _____   2. _____   3. _____

D.   Directions: Write the three helping verbs that end with <u>ould</u>:

1. _____   2. _____   3. _____

E.   Directions: Write the forms of the verb, <u>to be</u>:

1. _____   2. _____   3. _____

4. _____   5. _____   6. _____

7. _____   8. _____

F.   Directions: Write the other three helping verbs on the list:

1. _____   2. _____   3. _____

WORKBOOK PAGE 62
Date_____

Directions: The main verb has been underlined with a double line.
Underline the helping verb with a double line.   Then, write
the verb phrase on the line.

   Example: Your brush **is lying** on the bed. _____is lying_____

1.   A bug **has** crawled up the wall. _____**has crawled**_____

2.   Mother **may buy** a suit. _____**may buy**_____

3.   One of the boys **had** seen a snake. _____**had seen**_____

4.   I **shall** bake bread today. _____**shall bake**_____

5.   Their neighbors **are** camping. _____**are camping**_____

6.   We **should** help you. _____**should help**_____

7.   Dan **was** picking tomatoes. _____**was picking**_____

8.   They **must** clean their bedrooms. _____**must clean**_____

9.   Grandma **might** like this book. _____**might like**_____

10.   She **can** eat three pieces of pizza. _____**can eat**_____

11.   His sisters **have** made breakfast. _____**have made**_____

12.   We **will** leave in a minute. _____**will leave**_____

13.   **Do** you give Valentine cards? _____**Do give**_____

Name_____

Date_____

Directions: The main verb has been underlined with a double line.
Underline the helping verb with a double line. Then, write
the verb phrase on the line.

Example: Your brush **is** lying on the bed. _____is lying_____

1. A bug has crawled up the wall. _____

2. Mother may buy a suit. _____

3. One of the boys had seen a snake. _____

4. I shall bake bread today. _____

5. Their neighbors are camping. _____

6. We should help you. _____

7. Dan was picking tomatoes. _____

8. They must clean their bedrooms. _____

9. Grandma might like this book. _____

10. She can eat three pieces of pizza. _____

11. His sisters have made breakfast. _____

12. We will leave in a minute. _____

13. Do you give Valentine cards? _____

131

Name_____   **VERBS**
WORKBOOK PAGE 63   **Verb Phrases**
Date_____

Note to Teacher: You may want to do this worksheet orally.   Students love to box *not*.   Encourage them to do so.

Not isn't a verb. **Not** is an adverb. **Not** is never part of a verb phrase.

In a contraction, box **n't**.   Example: doesn't

To keep from underlining **not** as part of a verb phrase, *box it*.

Example: The wind was not blowing.

🐢 🐢

Directions: The main verb has been underlined with a double line.
              Underline the helping verb with a double line.   Then, write
              the verb phrase on the line.

Example: Mark **has** not paid his bill.   _____has paid_____

Remember: Be sure to box *not*.
***Not* has been boldfaced rather than boxed.**

1.   I did **not** finish the test.   **did finish**

2.   Bob is**n't** working today.   **is working**

3.   The child would **not** sit still.   **would sit**

4.   You may **not** stand on the bus.   **may stand**

5.   It has**n't** snowed this winter.   **has snowed**

6.   The children had**n't** played long.   **had played**

7.   We are**n't** going until Monday.   **are going**

8.   Fran can**not** find her shoe.   **can find**

9.   Should**n't** we wait for you?   **Should wait**

132

Name_____   **VERBS**
                                              Verb Phrases
Date_____

Not isn't a verb. **Not** is an adverb. **Not** is never part of a verb phrase.

In a contraction, box **n't**.   Example: doesn't

To keep from underlining **not** as part of a verb phrase, *box it*.
      Example: The wind was**not**blowing.

🐢🐢🐢🐢🐢🐢🐢🐢🐢🐢🐢🐢🐢🐢🐢🐢🐢🐢🐢🐢🐢🐢🐢
Directions: The main verb has been underlined with a double line.
               Underline the helping verb with a double line.   Then, write
               the verb phrase on the line.

      Example: Mark **has** not paid his bill.   ____has paid____

Remember: Be sure to box *not*.

1.   I did not <u>finish</u> the test.   _____

2.   Bob isn't <u>working</u> today.   _____

3.   The child would not <u>sit</u> still.   _____

4.   You may not <u>stand</u> on the bus.   _____

5.   It hasn't <u>snowed</u> this winter.   _____

6.   The children hadn't <u>played</u> long.   _____

7.   We aren't <u>going</u> until Monday.   _____

8.   Fran cannot <u>find</u> her shoe.   _____

9.   Shouldn't we <u>wait</u> for you?   _____

133

VERBS
Verb Phrases

Note to Teacher: The bottom part of this worksheet asks students to delete prepositional phrases and to identify verb phrases. You may want to do it orally.

A verb phrase may contain **more than one** helping verb.

     Example: Jeremy **may be** batting next.

🐢🐢🐢🐢🐢🐢🐢🐢🐢🐢🐢🐢🐢🐢🐢🐢🐢🐢🐢🐢🐢🐢🐢🐢

Directions: Underline the subject once and the verb phrase twice.

1.   The driver should have stopped sooner.

2.   Their roof was being repaired.

3.   Her father may have left.

4.   Our dog must have chewed your slippers.

🐢🐢🐢🐢🐢🐢🐢🐢🐢🐢🐢🐢🐢🐢🐢🐢🐢🐢🐢🐢🐢🐢🐢🐢

Review: **To find the subject of the sentence, ask about who or**
              what the sentence is talking.
              To help find subject and verb, cross out any
              prepositional phrase(s).
             Example: ~~During the storm~~, a chair had fallen ~~into the pool~~.

1.   Two raccoons were drinking ~~from a stream~~.

2.   They had blown bubbles ~~with special wands~~.

3.   Mom has been given a present ~~for her birthday~~.

4.   ~~After the blizzard~~, snow was scraped ~~from the roads~~.

5.   The team may be going ~~to Denver~~ ~~for a final game~~.

6.   The toddler would **not** share his toys ~~with his friends~~.

134

A verb phrase may contain **more than one** helping verb.

      Example: Jeremy **may be** batting next.

🐢🐢🐢🐢🐢🐢🐢🐢🐢🐢🐢🐢🐢🐢🐢🐢🐢🐢🐢🐢🐢🐢🐢🐢🐢

Directions: Underline the subject once and the verb phrase twice.

1.   The driver should have stopped sooner.

2.   Their roof was being repaired.

3.   Her father may have left.

4.   Our dog must have chewed your slippers.

🐢🐢🐢🐢🐢🐢🐢🐢🐢🐢🐢🐢🐢🐢🐢🐢🐢🐢🐢🐢🐢🐢🐢🐢🐢

Review: To find the subject of the sentence, ask about who or what the sentence is talking.
To help find subject and verb, cross out any prepositional phrase(s).

      Example: ~~During the storm~~, a chair had fallen ~~into the pool~~.

1.   Two raccoons were drinking from a stream.

2.   They had blown bubbles with special wands.

3.   Mom has been given a present for her birthday.

4.   After the blizzard, snow was scraped from the roads.

5.   The team may be going to Denver for a final game.

6.   The toddler would not share his toys with his friends.   135

IRREGULAR VERBS

Infinitive	Present	Past	Present Participle	Past Participle*
To be	is, am, are	**was, were**	being	**been**
To begin	begin(s)	**began**	beginning	**begun**
To break	break(s)	**broke**	breaking	**broken**
To bring	bring(s)	**brought**	bringing	**brought**
To buy	buy(s)	**bought**	buying	**bought**
To choose	choose(s)	**chose**	choosing	**chosen**
To come	come(s)	**came**	coming	**come**
To dig	dig(s)	**dug**	digging	**dug**
To do	do, does	**did**	doing	**done**
To drink	drink(s)	**drank**	drinking	**drunk**
To drive	drive(s)	**drove**	driving	**driven**
To eat	eat(s)	**ate**	eating	**eaten**
To fall	fall(s)	**fell**	falling	**fallen**
To find	find(s)	**found**	finding	**found**
To fly	fly, flies	**flew**	flying	**flown**
To freeze	freeze(s)	**froze**	freezing	**frozen**
To get	get(s)	**got**	getting	**gotten**
To give	give(s)	**gave**	giving	**given**
To go	go, goes	**went**	going	**gone**
To grow	grow(s)	**grew**	growing	**grown**
To know	know(s)	**knew**	knowing	**known**
To leave	leave(s)	**left**	leaving	**left**

Infinitive	Present	Past	Present Participle	Past Participle*
To ride	ride(s)	**rode**	riding	**ridden**
To ring	ring(s)	**rang**	ringing	**rung**
To rise	rise(s)	**rose**	rising	**risen**
To run	run(s)	**ran**	running	**run**
To see	see(s)	**saw**	seeing	**seen**
To send	send(s)	**sent**	sending	**sent**
To set	set(s)	**set**	setting	**set**
To shake	shake(s)	**shook**	shaking	**shaken**
To sing	sing(s)	**sang**	singing	**sung**
To sink	sink(s)	**sank**	sinking	**sunk**
To sit	sit(s)	**sat**	sitting	**sat**
To speak	speak(s)	**spoke**	speaking	**spoken**
To stand	stand(s)	**stood**	standing	**stood**
To steal	steal(s)	**stole**	stealing	**stolen**
To swim	swim(s)	**swam**	swimming	**swum**
To swing	swing(s)	**swung**	swinging	**swung**
To swear	swear(s)	**swore**	swearing	**sworn**
To take	take(s)	**took**	taking	**taken**
To teach	teach(es)	**taught**	teaching	**taught**
To throw	throw(s)	**threw**	throwing	**thrown**
To wear	wear(s)	**wore**	wearing	**worn**
To write	write(s)	**wrote**	writing	**written**

*Uses a helping verb such as <u>has</u>, <u>have</u>, <u>had</u>. Other helping verbs such as *was* or *were* may also be used.

Note to Teacher: **You may wish to do this worksheet orally.**

Directions: Write the past participle form of the following verb infinitives:
              (Use *has*, *have*, or *had* with the word.)

Example: to set -   _had set_____

1. to do - _____had **done**_____   13. to fall - _____had **fallen**_____

2. to leave - _____had **left**_____   14. to sit - _____had **sat**_____

3. to teach - _____had **taught**_____   15. to eat - _____had **eaten**_____

4. to know - _____had **known**_____   16. to see - _____had **seen**_____

5. to drink - _____had **drunk**_____   17. to go - _____had **gone**_____

6. to bring - _____had **brought**_____   18. to sing - _____had **sung**_____

7. to swear - _____had **sworn**_____   19. to ride - _____had **ridden**_____

8. to choose - _____had **chosen**_____   20. to swim - _____had **swum**_____

9. to throw - _____had **thrown**_____   21. to grow - _____had **grown**_____

10. to steal - _____had **stolen**_____   22. to dig - _____had **dug**_____

11. to shake - _____had **shaken**_____   23. to fly - _____had **flown**_____

12. to write - _____had **written**_____   24. to rise - _____had **risen**_____

Name_____

Date_____

Directions: Write the past participle form of the following verb infinitives:
(Use *has*, *have*, or *had* with the word.)

Example: to set -   __had set__

1. to do - _____

2. to leave - _____

3. to teach - _____

4. to know - _____

5. to drink - _____

6. to bring - _____

7. to swear - _____

8. to choose - _____

9. to throw - _____

10. to steal - _____

11. to shake - _____

12. to write - _____

13. to fall - _____

14. to sit - _____

15. to eat - _____

16. to see - _____

17. to go - _____

18. to sing - _____

19. to ride - _____

20. to swim - _____

21. to grow - _____

22. to dig - _____

23. to fly - _____

24. to rise - _____

Note to Teacher: You may wish to do this worksheet orally.
Directions: Write the past participle form of the following verb infinitives:
(Use *has*, *have*, or *had* with the word.)

Example: to ride - ___had ridden___

1. to stand - ___**had stood**___   13. to run - ___**had run**___

2. to begin - ___**had begun**___   14. to set - ___**had set**___

3. to swing - ___**had swung**___   15. to dig - ___**had dug**___

4. to freeze - ___**had frozen**___   16. to take - ___**had taken**___

5. to drive - ___**had driven**___   17. to be - ___**had been**___

6. to break - ___**had broken**___   18. to find - ___**had found**___

7. to sink - ___**had sunk**___   19. to wear - ___**had worn**___

8. to come - ___**had come**___   20. to buy - ___**had bought**___

9. to give - ___**had given**___   21. to get - ___**had gotten**___

10. to swim - ___**had swum**___   22. to write - ___**had written**___

11. to speak - ___**had spoken**___   23. to see - ___**had seen**___

12. to send - ___**had sent**___   24. to ring - ___**had rung**___

Name_____

VERBS
Irregular Verbs

Date_____

Directions: Write the past participle form of the following verb infinitives:
(Use *has*, *have*, or *had* with the word.)

Example: to ride -   _had ridden_

1. to stand - _____

2. to begin - _____

3. to swing - _____

4. to freeze - _____

5. to drive - _____

6. to break - _____

7. to sink - _____

8. to come - _____

9. to give - _____

10. to swim - _____

11. to speak - _____

12. to send - _____

13. to run - _____

14. to set - _____

15. to dig - _____

16. to take - _____

17. to be - _____

18. to find - _____

19. to wear - _____

20. to buy - _____

21. to get - _____

22. to write - _____

23. to see - _____

24. to ring - _____

Name_____   **VERBS**

WORKBOOK PAGE 69   **Irregular Verbs**

Date_____

Note to Teacher: **You may wish to do this worksheet orally.**

Directions: Underline the correct verb with double lines.

Example: A <u>boy</u> **had** (brang, <u>brought</u>) a snake.

1. <u>Ellen</u> **has** (broke, **<u>broken</u>**) her finger.

2. <u>I</u> **have** (**<u>bought</u>**, boughten) a ruler.

3. <u>Ice</u> **had** (froze, **<u>frozen</u>**) on the pond.

4. <u>We</u> **have** (**<u>written</u>**, wrote) letters.

5. During breakfast, <u>he</u> **had** (ate, **<u>eaten</u>**) all of the cereal.

6. <u>Jake</u> **has** (**<u>given</u>**, gave) his basketball to a friend.

7. Several <u>kittens</u> **have** (drank, **<u>drunk</u>**) milk.

8. <u>Snow</u> **had** (fell, **<u>fallen</u>**) during the night.

9. <u>Jan</u> and <u>David</u> **have** (**<u>flown</u>**, flew) to Idaho.

10. <u>One</u> of the dogs **has** (**<u>run</u>**, ran) into the street.

11. His <u>sister</u> **had** (spoke, **<u>spoken</u>**) to him harshly.

12. Bob's <u>brothers</u> **have** (**<u>taken</u>**, took) a taxi.

13. Our <u>bus</u> **had** (came, **<u>come</u>**) early.

142

Name_____   **VERBS**
                                              Irregular Verbs
Date_____

Directions: Underline the correct verb with double lines.

Example: A boy **had** (brang, brought) a snake.

1. Ellen **has** (broke, broken) her finger.

2. I **have** (bought, boughten) a ruler.

3. Ice **had** (froze, frozen) on the pond.

4. We **have** (written, wrote) letters.

5. During breakfast, he **had** (ate, eaten) all of the cereal.

6. Jake **has** (given, gave) his basketball to a friend.

7. Several kittens **have** (drank, drunk) milk.

8. Snow **had** (fell, fallen) during the night.

9. Jan and David **have** (flown, flew) to Idaho.

10. One of the dogs **has** (run, ran) into the street.

11. His sister **had** (spoke, spoken) to him harshly.

12. Bob's brothers **have** (taken, took) a taxi.

13. Our bus **had** (came, come) early.

Directions: Underline the correct verb with double lines.

Example: He **has** (sang, **sung**) a solo.

1.   Marcie **had** (swang, **swung**) for an hour.

2.   I **have** never (**ridden**, rode) on a subway.

3.   The pitcher **should have** (**thrown**, threw) the ball to first base.

4.   Her watch **may have been** (stole, **stolen**).

5.   Five robins **have** (flew, **flown**) to that branch.

6.   He **has** (rang, **rung**) the buzzer three times.

7.   Sally **had** (gave, **given**) the cashier three dimes.

8.   They **must have** (went, **gone**) somewhere.

9.   Both Joan and Brian **had** (**run**, ran) a mile.

10.   One bear **must have** (ate, **eaten**) too much honey.

11.   **Have** you (**seen**, saw) that video about snakes?

12.   The injured person **had been** (took, **taken**) to the hospital.

13.   Mr. Kent **should have** (**bought**, boughten) another car.

Name_____

Date_____

Directions: Underline the correct verb with double lines.

Example: <u>He **has**</u> (sang, **<u>sung</u>**) a solo.

1.   <u>Marcie **had**</u> (swang, swung) for an hour.

2.   <u>I **have**</u> never (ridden, rode) on a subway.

3.   The <u>pitcher</u> **<u>should have</u>** (thrown, threw) the ball to first base.

4.   Her <u>watch</u> **<u>may have been</u>** (stole, stolen).

5.   Five <u>robins</u> **<u>have</u>** (flew, flown) to that branch.

6.   <u>He **has**</u> (rang, rung) the buzzer three times.

7.   <u>Sally</u> **<u>had</u>** (gave, given) the cashier three dimes.

8.   <u>They</u> **<u>must have</u>** (went, gone) somewhere.

9.   Both <u>Joan</u> and <u>Brian</u> **<u>had</u>** (run, ran) a mile.

10.   One <u>bear</u> **<u>must have</u>** (ate, eaten) too much honey.

11.   **<u>Have</u>** <u>you</u> (seen, saw) that video about snakes?

12.   The injured <u>person</u> **<u>had been</u>** (took, taken) to the hospital.

13.   <u>Mr. Kent</u> **<u>should have</u>** (bought, boughten) another car.

Note to Teacher: You may want to do this page orally.
Directions: Underline the subject once and the verb phrase twice.

Example: They had (rode, ridden) two miles.

1.   Their choir had (sang, **sung**) two songs.

2.   The taxi has (came, **come**).

3.   He had (**stolen**, stole) third base.

4.   A witness has (swore, **sworn**) an oath.

5.   The ladies have (spoke, **spoken**).

6.   Ken has (ate, **eaten**) two hot dogs.

7.   Her sister had (drank, **drunk**) several milkshakes.

8.   Many birds have (flew, **flown**) by here.

9.   These steaks were (froze, **frozen**) last week.

10.   Mindy had (fell, **fallen**) down.

11.   The coach must have (went, **gone**) early.

12.   I should have (knew, **known**) the answer.

13.   Some gloves had been (**left**, leaved) behind.

146

Name_____   **VERBS**
                                Irregular Verbs
Date_____

Directions: Underline the subject once and the verb phrase twice.

        Example: <u>They</u> <u>had</u> (rode, <u>ridden</u>) two miles.

1.   Their choir had (sang, sung) two songs.

2.   The taxi has (came, come).

3.   He had (stolen, stole) third base.

4.   A witness has (swore, sworn) an oath.

5.   The ladies have (spoke, spoken).

6.   Ken has (ate, eaten) two hot dogs.

7.   Her sister had (drank, drunk) several milkshakes.

8.   Many birds have (flew, flown) by here.

9.   These steaks were (froze, frozen) last week.

10. Mindy had (fell, fallen) down.

11. The coach must have (went, gone) early.

12. I should have (knew, known) the answer.

13. Some gloves had been (left, leaved) behind.   147

TO THE TEACHER: Read this page carefully. A student page appears on 149. Past tense was introduced on pages 118-121; therefore, tenses should be easy.

VERB TENSES:

A. Present Tense:

Be sure that students understand that **tense means time. Present tense signifies present time.** Although present can mean at this moment, it is easier to use "today" as a point of reference for present tense. It's helpful for students to know that present tense **never** has a helping verb.*

To form the present tense, remove *to* from the infinitive:

1. **If the subject is singular (one), add <u>s</u> to the verb.** (<u>es</u> to some)

   Examples: to eat: A <u>horse eats</u> hay.

   to do: That <u>child does</u> funny tricks.

2. **If the subject is <u>you</u>, <u>I</u>, or is plural (more than one), simply remove the *to* from the infinitive.**

   Examples: to live: <u>You live</u> near a fire station.

   <u>I live</u> in an apartment.

   Their <u>grandparents live</u> in Maine.

B. Past Tense:

Past tense indicates that which **has happened.** Although past can mean a second ago, it is easier to use the term, "yesterday." Teach students that past tense **never** has a helping verb.**

1. **To form the past tense of a regular verb, add <u>ed</u> to the verb.**

   to dance: danc**ed**   to yell: yell**ed**

2. **To form the past tense of an irregular verb, change the verb to its appropriate form.**

   to do: did   to dig: dug

C. Future Tense:

Future tense indicates time yet to happen. There are two helping verbs that indicate future tense: *shall* and *will*. Although future may be any time yet to occur, using *"tomorrow"* helps students comprehend it. Be sure that students understand that *shall* or *will* must be used with the future tense.

   to send: **shall** send or **will** send
   to stay: **shall** stay or **will** stay

*am running = progressive tense   **had written = perfect tense.

PAGE 149 = WORKBOOK PAGE 72

148   Students will learn more complex tenses in <u>Easy Grammar</u> or <u>Easy Grammar Plus</u>.

VERB TENSES

➪ **Present Tense:**
    Tense means time. Present tense means present time.
Although present can mean now, it is easier to use "today" to help you
remember. Present tense **never** has a helping verb. To form the present
tense, remove *to* from the infinitive:

1. **If the subject is singular (one), add <u>s</u> to the verb. (<u>es</u> to some)**
        to wave: The <u>baby waves</u> to everybody. (one child)
                       He <u>does</u> exercises.   (one boy)

2. **If the subject is <u>you</u>, remove the *to* from the infinitive.**
        to need: **You <u>need</u>** a bath.

3. **If the subject is <u>I</u>, remove the *to* from the infinitive.**
        to need: **I <u>need</u>** a bath.

4. **If the subject is <u>PLURAL</u> (more than one), remove the *to* from
the infinitive.**
        to need: Those **<u>children</u> <u>need</u>** baths.

➪ **Past Tense:**
    Past tense indicates that which has happened. Although past
can mean a second ago, it is easier to use the term, "yesterday." Past tense
never has a helping verb.

1. **To form the past tense of a regular verb, add <u>ed</u> to the verb.**
        to fix: fix**ed**   <u>Mom fix**ed**</u> the stereo.

2. **To form the past tense of an irregular verb, change the verb
to its correct form.**
        to bring: **brought**   <u>Kent **brought**</u> his dog along.

➪ **Future Tense:**
    Future tense indicates time yet to happen. There are two
helping verbs that indicate future tense: *shall* and *will*. Future may be
any time yet to occur. To make it easier, we shall use "tomorrow" as a guide.
        to go: I **<u>shall go</u>** to a movie.

                       His <u>sister</u> **<u>will go</u>** to the mall tomorrow   149

A.   Directions: Write a complete sentence to answer each question.
ANSWERS WILL VARY.

1.   Write a sentence telling something you did yesterday.

    Yesterday, I walked my dog._____

    This is the **past tense**.

2.   Write a complete sentence telling something you will do tonight.

    Tonight, I shall (will) watch television._____

    This is the **future tense**.

3.   Write a complete sentence telling something that you do every day.

    Every day, I brush my teeth._____

    This is the **present tense**.

B.   Directions: Write a complete sentence to answer each question.

1.   What will a friend and you do next week? (**future tense**)

    _____**Next week, Chad and I will build a fort.**_____

2.   What did a friend and you do last week? (**past tense**)

    _____**Last week, Brianna and I played dolls.**

Name_____   **VERBS**
                                        Tenses
Date_____

A.   Directions: Write a complete sentence to answer each question.

1.   Write a sentence telling something you did yesterday.

     <u>Yesterday,</u>_____

     This is the **past tense**.

2.   Write a complete sentence telling something you will do tonight.

     <u>Tonight,</u>_____

     This is the **future tense**.

3.   Write a complete sentence telling something that you do every day.

     <u>Every day,</u>_____

     This is the **present tense**.

B.   Directions: Write a complete sentence to answer each question.

1.   What will a friend and you do next week?   (**future tense**)

     _____

2.   What did a friend and you do last week?   (**past tense**)

     _____

Directions: Read each sentence.   The verb or verb phrase has been
              underlined for you. Write the tense of the verb on each line.

Remember: The verb tenses are *present*, *past*, and *future*.

Example: _____past_____   A clown <u>juggled</u> three balls.

1. _____**past**_____   Their car <u>broke</u> down.

2. _____**present**_____   Sarah <u>rides</u> her bike every day.

3. _____**future**_____   They <u>will go</u> grocery shopping.

4. _____**past**_____   She <u>frosted</u> a cake for her friend.

5. _____**future**_____   I <u>shall try</u> to help you.

6. _____**present**_____   Mary's cousin <u>races</u> cars.

7. _____**past**_____   Jack <u>sewed</u> a button on his jacket.

8. _____**present**_____   They <u>paint</u> mailboxes for extra
                              money.

9. _____**future**_____   The bus <u>will arrive</u> soon.

10. _____**past**_____   The umpire <u>yelled</u>, "Strike!"

11. _____**present**_____   Jody and I <u>buy</u> lunch at a deli.

Directions: Read each sentence.   The verb or verb phrase has been
                    underlined for you. Write the tense of the verb on each line.

Remember: The verb tenses are *present*, *past*, and *future*.

Example: ____past____   A clown <u>juggled</u> three balls.

1. _____   Their car <u>broke</u> down.

2. _____   Sarah <u>rides</u> her bike every day.

3. _____   They <u>will go</u> grocery shopping.

4. _____   She <u>frosted</u> a cake for her friend.

5. _____   I <u>shall try</u> to help you.

6. _____   Mary's cousin <u>races</u> cars.

7. _____   Jack <u>sewed</u> a button on his jacket.

8. _____   They <u>paint</u> mailboxes for extra
                                         money.

9. _____   The bus <u>will arrive</u> soon.

10. _____   The umpire <u>yelled</u>, "Strike!"

11. _____   Jody and I <u>buy</u> lunch at a deli.

Directions: Read each sentence. The subject and verb/verb phrase have been underlined for you. Write the tense of the verb on each line.

Remember: The verb tenses are *present*, *past*, and *future*.

Example: _____future_____ I shall give you some candy.

1. _____**present**_____ Lanzo loves his dog.

2. _____**past**_____ Lanzo loved going to Happyland.

3. _____**future**_____ Lanzo will love his new house.

1. _____**present**_____ His sisters skate on the sidewalk.

2. _____**past**_____ His sisters skated yesterday.

3. _____**future**_____ His sisters will skate with me tomorrow.

1. _____**future**_____ Loni will bake cookies tonight.

2. _____**past**_____ Loni baked a cake yesterday.

3. _____**present**_____ Loni bakes nearly every week.

154

Name_____   **VERBS**
                                            Tenses
Date_____

Directions: Read each sentence. The subject and verb/verb phrase have
              been underlined for you. Write the tense of the verb on each
              line.

Remember: The verb tenses are *present*, *past*, and *future*.

        Example: _____future_____   I shall give you some candy.

1. _____   Lanzo loves his dog.

2. _____   Lanzo loved going to Happyland.

3. _____   Lanzo will love his new house.

1. _____   His sisters skate on the sidewalk.

2. _____   His sisters skated yesterday.

3. _____   His sisters will skate with me
                                   tomorrow.

1. _____   Loni will bake cookies tonight.

2. _____   Loni baked a cake yesterday.

3. _____   Loni bakes nearly every week.

155

Directions: Cross out any prepositional phrases. Underline the subject once and the verb/verb phrase twice. On the line provided, write the tense: *present*, *past*, or *future*.

to look:

1. ___**past**_____ They <u>looked</u> ~~at the sunset~~.

2. ___**present**_____ He <u>looks</u> sad.

3. ___**future**_____ <u>Dad</u> <u>will look</u> ~~for another car~~.

to sit:

1. ___**present**_____ <u>Grandpa</u> <u>sits</u> ~~on the porch~~.

2. ___**future**_____ <u>Tom</u> <u>will sit</u> ~~beside me~~.

3. ___**past**_____ Baseball <u>players</u> <u>sat</u> ~~by the dugout~~.

to speak:

1. ___**future**_____ <u>Mrs. Martin</u> <u>will speak</u> ~~at a meeting~~.

2. ___**past**_____ <u>He</u> <u>spoke</u> ~~to me~~.

3. ___**present**_____ <u>Scott</u> <u>speaks</u> slowly.

to sing:

1. ___**present**_____ <u>They</u> <u>sing</u> ~~in the car~~.

2. ___**future**_____ <u>She</u> <u>will sing</u> ~~by herself~~.

3. ___**past**_____ The <u>group</u> <u>sang</u> ~~for ten minutes~~.

156

Name_____

Date_____

Directions: Cross out any prepositional phrases. Underline the subject once and the verb/verb phrase twice. On the line provided, write the tense: *present*, *past*, or *future*.

to look:

1. _____   They looked at the sunset.

2. _____   He looks sad.

3. _____   Dad will look for another car.

to sit:

1. _____   Grandpa sits on the porch.

2. _____   Tom will sit beside me.

3. _____   Baseball players sat by the dugout.

to speak:

1. _____   Mrs. Martin will speak at a meeting.

2. _____   He spoke to me.

3. _____   Scott speaks slowly.

to sing:

1. _____   They sing in the car.

2. _____   She will sing by herself.

3. _____   The group sang for ten minutes.

TO THE TEACHER: Concepts are presented for students on the next page.

PAGE 159 = WORKBOOK PAGE 77

SUBJECT-VERB AGREEMENT (Present Tense):
1. Review present tense.
2. Be sure that students understand that **singular** means one and **plural** means more than one.
3. Continue to teach students to delete prepositional phrases to help find the subject. This is important in making subject and verb agree.

Rules:

A. If the **subject is singular** (one), add <u>s</u> to the verb.

> Example: A <u>dog</u> <u>bark**s**</u>.

> However:
> 1. Some **irregular** verbs completely change form for the present tense.
>   Examples: to have: One <u>student</u> **has** a cold.
>
>   to be: Janell <u>is</u> ~~in third grade~~.
> 2. The pronoun, **I**, is singular; however, the verb does not add <u>s</u>.
>   Example: <u>I</u> <u>like</u> mushrooms.
>
> 3. The pronoun, <u>**you**</u>, is singular; however, the verb does not add <u>s</u>.
>   Example: <u>You</u> <u>talk</u> too much.

B. If the **subject is plural** (more than one), do **NOT** add <u>s</u> to the verb.

> Examples: His <u>cousins</u> <u>play</u> together.
>
> Two <u>birds</u> <u>drink</u> ~~from our fountain~~.

Sometimes, the subject is compound; do not add <u>s</u> if the subjects are joined by **and.**

> Example: His <u>mom</u> and <u>dad</u> <u>leave</u> early.

However: Some irregular verbs completely change form for the present tense.

> Example: His <u>marbles</u> <u>are</u> lost.

This concept is very difficult and is introduced formally in <u>Easy Grammar: Level 1</u>.
If a compound subject (two or more) is joined by *or*, follow these rules:
>   **A. If the subject closer to the verb is singular, add <u>s</u> to the verb.**

> Example: His brothers or <u>**sister**</u> <u>plays</u> the piano.

>   **B. If the subject closer to the verb is plural, don't add <u>s</u> to the verb.**

158   Example: His sister or <u>**brothers**</u> <u>play</u> the piano.

SUBJECT-VERB AGREEMENT

Rules:
A. If the subject is singular (one), add _s_ to the verb.

>   Example: A <u>fish</u> <u>swim**s**</u>.

We will continue to **cross out prepositional phrases** to help find the subject. Then, it will be easier to make the verb agree.

>   One of the girls (race, races) every day.

The prepositional phrase is ~~of the girls~~. Therefore, **_girls_** cannot be the subject.

>   <u>One</u> ~~of the girls~~ (race, <u>races</u>) every day.   (**_One_** is the subject!)

1. Some **_irregular_** verbs completely change form for the present tense.
>   Examples: to have: My <u>friend</u> **has** a hamster.
>   to be: Her <u>brother</u> **is** funny.

2. Do **not** add _s_ to a verb after **_I_**.
>   Example: <u>I want</u> a sandwich.

3. Do **not** add _s_ to a verb after **_you._**
>   Example: <u>You drink</u> your milk fast.

B. If the subject is plural (more than one), do NOT add _s_ to the verb.

>   Examples: Some <u>babies nap</u> every afternoon.

>   Several <u>children eat</u> their snacks outside.

Sometimes, the subject is compound; do not add _s_ if the subjects are joined by **_and._**
>   Example: My <u>friend</u> and <u>I walk</u> home together.

However: Some irregular verbs completely change form for the present tense.
>   Example: <u>Sundaes are</u> good.   159

Important note: After students complete part A, ask them if their verbs ended with s.
Students need to comprehend this concept.
If the subject is singular (one), add s to the verb.

Example: A <u>snake</u> <u>live**s**</u> in a hole.

ANSWERS WILL VARY.

A. Directions: Write a sentence that tells what each animal does.

1. A cat **likes to drink milk.**_____

2. A bear **lives in the woods.**_____

3. A cow **chews its cud.**_____

4. A turtle **eats leaves.**_____

5. A dog **sleeps under a tree.**_____

B. Directions: Complete each sentence.
     After *I*, do not add s to the verb in the present tense.

1. Often, I **play basketball with my friends.**_____

2. Every summer, I **go to Oklahoma to visit my grandma.**_____

C. Directions: Complete each sentence.
     After *you*, do not add s to the verb in the present tense.

1. Every day, you **eat breakfast in a hurry.**_____

2. Every week, you **wash the family car.**_____
160

Name_____

Date_____

If the subject is singular (one), add s to the verb.

Example: A <u>snake</u> <u>lives</u> in a hole.

A. Directions: Write a sentence that tells what each animal does.

1. A cat _____.

2. A bear _____.

3. A cow _____.

4. A turtle _____.

5. A dog _____.

B. Directions: Complete each sentence.
    After I, do not add s to the verb in the present tense.

1. Often, I_____.

2. Every summer, I_____.

C. Directions: Complete each sentence.
    After you, do not add s to the verb in the present tense.

1. Every day, you_____.

2. Every week, you_____.

161

Name_____

WORKBOOK PAGE 79

Date_____

VERBS
Subject/Verb
Agreement

A. **If the subject is singular (one), add s to the verb.**

Do **not** add s to a verb after *I* or *you.*
Some verbs like *to have* and *to be* totally change forms.

B. **If the subject is plural (more than one), do NOT add s to the verb.**

Some irregular verbs like *to be* completely change form.

Directions: Cross out any prepositional phrases. Underline the subject once and the verb twice.

1.   <u>Mom</u> (tape, <u>tapes</u>) some programs.

2.   Our <u>dogs</u> (<u>dig</u>, digs) ~~in the yard~~.

3.   <u>She</u> always (lie, <u>lies</u>) ~~on her tummy~~.

4.   <u>I</u> (<u>swing</u>, swings) ~~during recess~~.

5.   <u>Katie</u> (tell, <u>tells</u>) funny stories.

6.   <u>Mike</u> (do, <u>does</u>) his chores carefully.

7.   Those <u>children</u> (<u>play</u>, plays) ~~after lunch~~.

8.   <u>Bob</u> and <u>Tammy</u> (<u>wash</u>, washes) their van.

9.   <u>One</u> ~~of the boys~~ (walk, <u>walks</u>) home ~~with his brother~~.

162

A. **If the subject is singular (one), add s to the verb.**

Do **not** add s to a verb after *I* or *you.*
Some verbs like *to have* and *to be* totally change forms.

B. **If the subject is plural (more than one), do NOT add s to the verb.**

Some irregular verbs like *to be* completely change form.

🐢 🐢 🐢 🐢 🐢 🐢 🐢 🐢 🐢 🐢 🐢 🐢 🐢 🐢 🐢 🐢 🐢 🐢 🐢

Directions: Cross out any prepositional phrases. Underline the subject once and the verb twice.

1. Mom (tape, tapes) some programs.

2. Our dogs (dig, digs) in the yard.

3. She always (lie, lies) on her tummy.

4. I (swing, swings) during recess.

5. Katie (tell, tells) funny stories.

6. Mike (do, does) his chores carefully.

7. Those children (play, plays) after lunch.

8. Bob and Tammy (wash, washes) their van.

9. One of the boys (walk, walks) home with his brother.

A.   If the subject is singular (one), add s to the verb.

Do **not** add s to a verb after *I* or **you.**
Some verbs like **to have** and **to be** totally change forms.

B.   If the subject is plural (more than one), do NOT add s to the verb.

Some irregular verbs like **to be** completely change form.

Directions: Cross out any prepositional phrases. Underline the subject once and the verb twice.

1.   I (like, likes) juice.

2.   Dad (buy, buys) ice cream cones ~~for us~~.

3.   You (clean, cleans) your room well.

4.   Skunks (smell, smells) bad.

5.   A tent (cover, covers) their picnic area.

6.   She (write, writes) her name ~~in cursive~~.

7.   Fred and Bonnie (shop, shops) every week.

8.   One ~~of the teddy bears~~ (is, are) mine.

164

A. If the subject is singular (one), add s to the verb.

Do **not** add s to a verb after *I* or *you.*
Some verbs like *to have* and *to be* totally change forms.

B. If the subject is plural (more than one), do NOT add s to the verb.

Some irregular verbs like *to be* completely change form.

🐢 🐢 🐢 🐢 🐢 🐢 🐢 🐢 🐢 🐢 🐢 🐢 🐢 🐢 🐢 🐢 🐢 🐢 🐢

Directions: Cross out any prepositional phrases. Underline the subject once and the verb twice.

1. I (like, likes) juice.

2. Dad (buy, buys) ice cream cones for us.

3. You (clean, cleans) your room well.

4. Skunks (smell, smells) bad.

5. A tent (cover, covers) their picnic area.

6. She (write, writes) her name in cursive.

7. Fred and Bonnie (shop, shops) every week.

8. One of the teddy bears (is, are) mine.

Name_____ **VERBS**
WORKBOOK PAGE 81 **Review**
Date_____

A. Contractions:

   Directions: Write the contraction in the space provided.

1. I have - ____**I've**____   5. is not - ____**isn't**____

2. I am - ____**I'm**____   6. have not - ____**haven't**____

3. cannot - ____**can't**____   7. she is - ____**she's**____

4. they are - ____**they're**____   8. will not - ____**won't**____

B.   It's/Its   They're/There/Their   You're/Your:

   Directions: Circle the correct word.

1. (**You're**, Your) not supposed to leave.

2. Has (they're, there, **their**) cat come home?

3. (**It's**, Its) time to eat.

4.   (**They're**, There, Their) toasting marshmallows.

5. (You're, **Your**) bike has been moved.

6.   (They're, **There**, Their) are ten dimes in a dollar.

7. Did you know that (**they're**, there, their) in a play?

8.   A gerbil was running around in (it's, **its**) cage.
166

Name_____   **VERBS**
                                         Review
Date_____

A.   Contractions:

Directions: Write the contraction in the space provided.

1.   I have - _____   5.   is not - _____

2.   I am - _____   6.   have not - _____

3.   cannot - _____   7.   she is - _____

4.   they are - _____   8.   will not - _____

B.   It's/Its   They're/There/Their   You're/Your:

Directions: Circle the correct word.

1.   (You're, Your) not supposed to leave.

2.   Has (they're, there, their) cat come home?

3.   (It's, Its) time to eat.

4.   (They're, There, Their) toasting marshmallows.

5.   (You're, Your) bike has been moved.

6.   (They're, There, Their) are ten dimes in a dollar.

7.   Did you know that (they're, there, their) in a play?

8.   A gerbil was running around in (it's, its) cage.

C. Can/May:

Directions: Circle the correct word.

1. (Can, **May**) I play with you?

2. Bob (**can**, may) jump nearly six feet.

3. (Can, **May**) John and I go there?

4. I (**can**, may) finish this later.

D. State of Being:

Directions: Use *is, am, are, was,* or *were* to fill in the blanks.

Present: 1.   I ____**am**____ nice.

2.   Honey ____**is**____ sweet.

3.   We ____**are**____ good students.

Past: 1.   Pat ____**was**____ the winner.

2.   The judges ____**were**____ from Kansas.

168

C. Can/May:

   Directions: Circle the correct word.

1.   (Can, May) I play with you?

2.   Bob (can, may) jump nearly six feet.

3.   (Can, May) John and I go there?

4.   I (can, may) finish this later.

D. State of Being:

   Directions: Use *is, am, are, was,* or *were* to fill in the blanks.

Present: 1.   I _____ nice.

   2.   Honey _____ sweet.

   3.   We _____ good students.

Past: 1.   Pat _____ the winner.

   2.   The judges _____ from Kansas.

E.   Helping (Auxiliary) Verbs:

Directions: List the twenty-three helping verbs.

1. d**o**	7. m**ay**	13. c**an**	19. w**as**
2. d**oes**	8. m**ight**	14. s**hall**	20. w**ere**
3. d**id**	9. m**ust**	15. w**ill**	21. b**e**
4. h**as**	10. c**ould**	16. i**s**	22. b**eing**
5. h**ave**	11. s**hould**	17. a**m**	23. b**een**
6. h**ad**	12. w**ould**	18. a**re**	

F.   Helping or Main Verb?:

Directions: Write the helping verb(s) on the first line; write the main verb on the second line.

1.   <u>Ben</u> is running a race.   _____**is**_____   _____**running**_____

2.   One <u>boy</u> had eaten three hot dogs.   _____**had**_____   _____**eaten**_____

3.   A <u>note</u> was written quickly.   _____**was**_____   _____**written**_____

4.   The <u>rain</u> must have stopped.   _____**must have**_____   _____**stopped**_____

170

E.   Helping (Auxiliary) Verbs:

Directions: List the twenty-three helping verbs.

1. d _	7. m _ _	13. c _ _	19. w _ _
2. d _ _ _	8. m _ _ _ _	14. s _ _ _ _	20. w _ _ _
3. d _ _	9. m _ _ _	15. w _ _ _	21. b _
4. h _ _	10. c _ _ _ _	16. i _	22. b _ _ _ _
5. h _ _ _	11. s _ _ _ _ _	17. a _	23. b _ _ _
6. h _ _	12. w _ _ _ _	18. a _ _	

F.   Helping or Main Verb?:

Directions: Write the helping verb(s) on the first line; write the main
verb on the second line.

1. Ben is running a race.   _____   _____

2. One boy had eaten.
    three hot dogs.   _____   _____

3. A note was written
    quickly.   _____   _____

4. The rain must have
    stopped.   _____   _____

Name_____   **VERBS**
WORKBOOK PAGE 84   **Review**
Date_____

G. Action?:

Directions: Write <u>Yes</u> if the boldfaced verb shows action; write <u>No</u> if the boldfaced verb does not show action.

1. __**Yes**__   The elephant **lifted** his trunk.

2. __**Yes**__   Several bees **buzzed** around her head.

3. __**No**__   I **am** a good swimmer.

4. __**Yes**__   Mike **gave** his friend some cookies.

5. __**No**__   Sheena **is** in fifth grade.

H. Regular or Irregular:

Directions: Write the past and past participle in the blank. Then, answer the question.

1. (to brush) Yesterday, I ___**brushed**___ my dog.

      I had ___**brushed**___ my teeth before bedtime.

      To brush is a regular verb if you added *ed.* Is *to brush* a regular or an irregular verb? ___**regular**___

2. (to throw) Yesterday, she ___**threw**___ away her sneakers.

      Trina has ___**thrown**___ the ball to her little sister.

      To throw is a regular verb if you added *ed.* Is *to throw* a regular or an irregular verb? ___**irregular**___

172

G. Action?:

Directions: Write <u>Yes</u> if the boldfaced verb shows action; write <u>No</u> if the boldfaced verb does not show action.

1. _____ The elephant **lifted** his trunk.

2. _____ Several bees **buzzed** around her head.

3. _____ I **am** a good swimmer.

4. _____ Mike **gave** his friend some cookies.

5. _____ Sheena **is** in fifth grade.

H. Regular or Irregular:

Directions: Write the past and past participle in the blank. Then, answer the question.

1. (to brush) Yesterday, I _____ my dog.

   I had _____ my teeth before bedtime.

   To brush is a regular verb if you added *ed.* Is *to brush* a regular or an irregular verb? _____

2. (to throw) Yesterday, she _____ away her sneakers.

   Trina has _____ the ball to her little sister.

   To throw is a regular verb if you added *ed.* Is *to throw* a regular or an irregular verb? _____

I.   Subject/Verb:

   Directions: Cross out any prepositional phrase(s). Underline the
                 subject once and the verb/verb phrase twice.

1.   **They** **live** ~~by a farm~~.

2.   **Larry** **bit** his tongue.

3.   Her **dad** **drives** a bus ~~in the city~~.

4.   Some **girls** **are sitting** ~~under a tree~~.

5.   **Betty** **stayed** ~~with her aunt for a week~~.

6.   **Will** **you** **help** me?

J. Irregular Verbs:

   Directions: Cross out any prepositional phrase(s). Underline the
                 subject once and the verb or verb phrase twice.

1.   Their **mom** **has** (flew, **flown**) ~~to Texas~~.

2.   **Mary** **had** (brung, **brought**) a sack lunch.

3.   **You** **should have** (**come**, came) earlier.

4.   **Mrs. Cann** **was** (chose, **chosen**) the winner.

5.   **I** **have** (**drunk**, drank) too much ginger ale.

6.   **They** **have** (<u>eaten</u>, ate) pancakes ~~for breakfast~~.

174

I. Subject/Verb:

Directions: Cross out any prepositional phrase(s). Underline the
subject once and the verb/verb phrase twice.

1. They live by a farm.

2. Larry bit his tongue.

3. Her dad drives a bus in the city.

4. Some girls are sitting under a tree.

5. Betty stayed with her aunt for a week.

6. Will you help me?

J. Irregular Verbs:

Directions: Cross out any prepositional phrase(s). Underline the
subject once and the verb or verb phrase twice.

1. Their mom has (flew, flown) to Texas.

2. Mary had (brung, brought) a sack lunch.

3. You should have (come, came) earlier.

4. Mrs. Cann was (chose, chosen) the winner.

5. I have (drunk, drank) too much ginger ale.

6. They have (eaten, ate) pancakes for breakfast.

K. Tenses:

Directions: Write the tense of the boldfaced verb.

Remember: The tenses are *present*, *past*, and *future*.

1. _____**present**_____   Kay **likes** ice cream.

2. _____**past**_____   He **hopped** on one foot.

3. _____**future**_____   I **shall sit** here.

4. _____**present**_____   Jo's brothers **go** to bed at 8:00.

5. _____**future**_____   The clerk **will give** you change.

6. _____**past**_____   The bell **rang**.

L.   Subject/Verb Agreement:

Directions: Circle the correct verb.

1.   The baby (sleep, **sleeps**) in a crib.

2.   Those cooks (**give**, gives) lessons.

3.   He (**lifts**, lift) weights.

4.   Our dog (play, **plays**) with our cat.

5.   Many singers (**perform**, performs) at the fair.

6.   Debra and Lori (is, **are**) friends.

176

K. Tenses:

Directions: Write the tense of the boldfaced verb.

Remember: The tenses are *present*, *past*, and *future*.

1. _____   Kay **likes** ice cream.

2. _____   He **hopped** on one foot.

3. _____   I **shall sit** here.

4. _____   Jo's brothers **go** to bed at 8:00.

5. _____   The clerk **will give** you change.

6. _____   The bell **rang**.

L.   Subject/Verb Agreement:

Directions: Circle the correct verb.

1. The baby (sleep, sleeps) in a crib.

2. Those cooks (give, gives) lessons.

3. He (lifts, lift) weights.

4. Our dog (play, plays) with our cat.

5. Many singers (perform, performs) at the fair.

6. Debra and Lori (is, are) friends.

Name_____   **Verb Test**

Date_____

A. Directions: Write the contraction.

1. we are - _____**we're**_____   9. I have - _____**I've**_____

2. should not - ___**shouldn't**___   10. cannot - _____**can't**_____

3. I am - _____**I'm**_____   11. they are - _____**they're**_____

4. will not - _____**won't**_____   12. she is - _____**she's**_____

5. have not - ___**haven't**___   13. has not - _____**hasn't**_____

6. they have - ___**they've**___   14. what is - _____**what's**_____

7. is not- _____**isn't**_____   15. you will - _____**you'll**_____

8. you are - _____**you're**_____   16. here is - _____**here's**_____

B. Directions: Write <u>Yes</u> if the boldfaced verb shows action; write <u>No</u> if the
boldfaced verb does not show action.

1. ___**Yes**___   A cow **chews** its cud.
2. ___**No**___   Denny **is** a singer.
3. ___**Yes**___   I **stuck** out my tongue.
4. ___**Yes**___   Jenny **sewed** a shirt.
5. ___**No**___   Mr. Moss **became** their friend.

C. Directions: Write <u>RV</u> if the verb is a regular verb; write <u>IV</u> if the verb is
irregular.

1. ___**RV**___ to bark 2. ___**RV**___ to roll 3. ___**IV**___ to see

178

Date_____

A. Directions: Write the contraction.

1. we are - _____   9. I have - _____

2. should not - _____   10. cannot - _____

3. I am - _____   11. they are - _____

4. will not - _____   12. she is - _____

5. have not - _____   13. has not - _____

6. they have - _____   14. what is - _____

7. is not- _____   15. you will - _____

8. you are - _____   16. here is - _____

B. Directions: Write <u>Yes</u> if the boldfaced verb shows action; write <u>No</u> if the
boldfaced verb does not show action.

1. _____   A cow **chews** its cud.
2. _____   Denny **is** a singer.
3. _____   I **stuck** out my tongue.
4. _____   Jenny **sewed** a shirt.
5. _____   Mr. Moss **became** their friend.

C. Directions: Write <u>RV</u> if the verb is a regular verb; write <u>IV</u> if the verb is
irregular.

1. _____ to bark 2. _____ to roll 3. _____ to see

D. Directions: Circle the correct verb.

1. He has (**swum**, swam) in an ocean.

2. Jack must have (drank, **drunk**) the lemonade.

3. Chimes have (**rung**, rang) several times.

4. You should have (saw, **seen**) the parade.

5. Has Dad (went, **gone**) to work yet?

6. I could have (ate, **eaten**) more.

7. Tyler had (rode, **ridden**) his bike.

8. Joy had (**flown**, flew) to Mexico.

9. The bus has (**come**, came).

10. His friend must have (brung, **brought**) chips.

E. Directions: Write <u>can</u> or <u>may</u> on the line.

1. _____**May**_____ I go to the bathroom?

2. _____**Can**_____ you fasten this for me?

F. Directions: Write the tense of the boldfaced verb or verb phrase.

1. _____**future**_____ They **will help** you.

2. _____**past**_____ Ken **found** a dollar.

3. _____**present**_____ He **answers** the phone on the first ring.

4. _____**present**_____ Brandy and I **need** a haircut.

180

D. Directions: Circle the correct verb.

1. He has (swum, swam) in an ocean.

2. Jack must have (drank, drunk) the lemonade.

3. Chimes have (rung, rang) several times.

4. You should have (saw, seen) the parade.

5. Has Dad (went, gone) to work yet?

6. I could have (ate, eaten) more.

7. Tyler had (rode, ridden) his bike.

8. Joy had (flown, flew) to Mexico.

9. The bus has (come, came).

10. His friend must have (brung, brought) chips.

E. Directions: Write can or may on the line.

1. _____ I go to the bathroom?

2. _____ you fasten this for me?

F. Directions: Write the tense of the boldfaced verb or verb phrase.

1. _____ They **will help** you.

2. _____ Ken **found** a dollar.

3. _____ He **answers** the phone on the first ring.

4. _____ Brandy and I **need** a haircut.

G.   Directions: Circle the correct word.

1.   (You're, **Your**) cat is in a tree.

2.   (**They're**, Their, There) making a playhouse.

3.   (They're, **Their**, There) mom goes to college.

4.   That car is missing (it's, **its**) bumper.

5.   I think that (**you're**, your) wrong.

H.   Directions: Circle the verb that agrees with the subject.

1.   Three hamsters (**live**, lives) in that cage.

2.   I (**add**, adds) in my head.

3.   Those brothers (**do**, does) their own washing.

4.   One of the babies (cry, **cries**) after every bath.

5.   Jana and Layla (**go**, goes) to a lake with Aunt Mona.

I.   Directions: Cross out any prepositional phrases. Underline the subject
                once and the verb/verb phrase twice.

1.   A <u>woman</u> <u>waded</u> ~~in the lake~~.

2.   The <u>family</u> <u>will eat</u> ~~at a cafe~~.

3.   This <u>road</u> <u>leads</u> ~~to an old barn~~.

4.   <u>She</u> <u>rinsed</u> her hair ~~with lemon juice~~.

5.   ~~Before the meeting,~~ <u>they</u> <u>must have talked</u> ~~for several minutes~~.

182

G. Directions: Circle the correct word.

1. (You're, Your) cat is in a tree.

2. (They're, Their, There) making a playhouse.

3. (They're, Their, There) mom goes to college.

4. That car is missing (it's, its) bumper.

5. I think that (you're, your) wrong.

H. Directions: Circle the verb that agrees with the subject.

1. Three hamsters (live, lives) in that cage.

2. I (add, adds) in my head.

3. Those brothers (do, does) their own washing.

4. One of the babies (cry, cries) after every bath.

5. Jana and Layla (go, goes) to a lake with Aunt Mona.

I. Directions: Cross out any prepositional phrases. Underline the subject once and the verb/verb phrase twice.

1. A woman waded in the lake.

2. The family will eat at a cafe.

3. This road leads to an old barn.

4. She rinsed her hair with lemon juice.

5. Before the meeting, they must have talked for several minutes.   183

TO THE TEACHER:

The emphasis of this unit is for students to comprehend that nouns name people, places, and things. Ideas have not been included at this level. Also, students are **not** introduced to the concept that a word can serve as a noun in some sentences and as another part of speech in other sentences.

Many worksheets feature singular and plural nouns. Seek complete understanding.

NOUNS

Note to Teacher: You may wish for students to label their drawings.

A **noun** names a person, a place, or a thing.

🐢 🐢 🐢 🐢 🐢 🐢 🐢 🐢 🐢 🐢 🐢 🐢 🐢 🐢 🐢 🐢 🐢 🐢 🐢

PICTURES WILL VARY.

Directions: Read each sentence and draw a picture.

1.   A person is a **noun**. Draw a picture of someone in your family.

2.   A place is a **noun**. Draw a picture of where you live.

3.   A thing is a **noun**. Draw a picture of something that you really like.

186

Name_____

Date_____

A **noun** names a person, a place, or a thing.

🐢 🐢 🐢 🐢 🐢 🐢 🐢 🐢 🐢 🐢 🐢 🐢 🐢 🐢 🐢 🐢 🐢 🐢

Directions: Read each sentence and draw a picture.

1.   A person is a **noun**. Draw a picture of someone in your family.

2.   A place is a **noun**. Draw a picture of where you live.

3.   A thing is a **noun**. Draw a picture of something that you really like.

Note to Teacher: Because *a* and *an* have been written before several blanks, this would be a good place to discuss using *an* before a word beginning with a vowel. Also, when students give answers, it's always fun to take a quick poll to see how many have the same answer. This maintains students' interest.

A **noun** names a person, a place, or a thing.

🐢 🐢 🐢 🐢 🐢 🐢 🐢 🐢 🐢 🐢 🐢 🐢 🐢 🐢 🐢 🐢 🐢 🐢

Directions: Write a noun that fits in the meaning of each sentence.
ANSWERS WILL VARY.

1. An object in this room is a (an) ___**picture, chair, table**, etc.___.
        (noun)

2. A part of my head is my ___**nose, ear, eye**, etc.___.
        (noun)

3. In the summer, I like to go to a (an) ___**park, lake, pond**, etc.___.
        (noun)

4. My ___**dad, dog, friend**, etc.___ is very funny.
        (noun)

5. My family lives in a (an) ___**house, apartment**, etc.___.
        (noun)

6. I really like my ___**bunny, cat, bike**, etc.___.
        (noun)

7. Something I hold in my hand is a (an) ___**coin, bird, apple**, etc.___.
        (noun)

8. I might see a (an) ___**monkey, zebra, giraffe**, etc.___ at the zoo.
        (noun)

Name_____

Date_____

A **noun** names a person, a place, or a thing.

🐢 🐢 🐢 🐢 🐢 🐢 🐢 🐢 🐢 🐢 🐢 🐢 🐢 🐢 🐢 🐢 🐢

Directions: Write a noun that fits in the meaning of each sentence.

1. An object in this room is a (an) _____.
                                              (noun)

2. A part of my head is my _____.
                                     (noun)

3. In the summer, I like to go to a (an) _____.
                                                    (noun)

4. My _____ is very funny.
              (noun)

5. My family lives in a (an) _____.
                                      (noun)

6. I really like my _____.
                            (noun)

7. Something I hold in my hand is a (an) _____.
                                                     (noun)

8. I might see a (an) _____ at the zoo.
                              (noun)

A **noun** names a person, a place, or a thing.

🐢🐢🐢🐢🐢🐢🐢🐢🐢🐢🐢🐢🐢🐢🐢🐢🐢🐢

ANSWERS WILL VARY.
Directions: Write the answers.

1. Objects are nouns.   Name two objects that are round.

   ____**ball**_____   ____**orange**_____

2. People are nouns. Name three people you know.

   ____**Joe**_____   (my) **grandma**   (my) **sister**

3. Places are nouns.   Name two places you like to go.

   ____**circus**_____   ____**fair**_____

4. Things that you can see are nouns. Name ten things you can see now.

   ____**paper**_____   ____**ceiling**_____

   ____**book**_____   ____**flag**_____

   ____**pencil**_____   ____**friend**_____

   ____**hand**_____   ____**picture**_____

   ____**wall**_____   ____**clock**_____

190

A **noun** names a person, a place, or a thing.

🐢 🐢 🐢 🐢 🐢 🐢 🐢 🐢 🐢 🐢 🐢 🐢 🐢 🐢 🐢 🐢 🐢 🐢

Directions: Write the answers.

1.   Objects are nouns.   Name two objects that are round.

    _____   _____

2.   People are nouns. Name three people you know.

    _____   _____   _____

3.   Places are nouns.   Name two places you like to go.

    _____   _____

4.   Things that you can see are nouns. Name ten things you can see now.

    _____   _____

    _____   _____

    _____   _____

    _____   _____

    _____   _____

Note to Teacher: You may want to do this worksheet orally.

A **common noun** does not name a specific person, place, or thing.

Most nouns are common.   *Example:* football   thumb

Do not capitalize a common noun.

If a type of noun is given, it is still common.   *Example:* dog   collie

A **proper noun** names a **specific** person, place, or thing. **Capitalize** a proper noun.

Example: lake   **L**inx **L**ake

A.   Directions: Fill in the blank.

1.   My *friend* is a common noun.   There are many ____**friends**____ in the world. My friend's name is ____**Kimo***____. I am naming a specific friend; this is a proper noun.   ***ANSWERS WILL VARY.***

2.   A store is a common noun. There are many ____**stores**____ in the world.   The name of a specific store is a proper noun. The name of a store that I know is ____**Yassie's Market***_____.
                                              ANSWERS WILL VARY.

B.   Directions: Circle the proper noun.

1. boy   **Franco**   5. leader   **Abraham Lincoln**

2. river   **Hudson River**   6. **Miami**   city

3. country   **Mexico**   7. dam   **Hoover Dam**

4. **Bambi**   deer   8. **Judson School** school

192

A **common noun** does not name a specific person, place, or thing.

Most nouns are common.   *Example:* football   thumb

Do not capitalize a common noun.

If a type of noun is given, it is still common.   *Example:* dog   collie

A **proper noun** names a **specific** person, place, or thing. **Capitalize** a proper noun.

Example: lake   **Linx Lake**

🐢 🐢 🐢 🐢 🐢 🐢 🐢 🐢 🐢 🐢 🐢 🐢 🐢 🐢 🐢 🐢 🐢 🐢 🐢

A. Directions: Fill in the blank.

1. My *friend* is a common noun. There are many _____ in the world. My friend's name is _____. I am naming a specific friend; this is a proper noun.

2.   A store is a common noun. There are many _____ in the world. The name of a specific store is a proper noun. The name of a store that I know is _____.

🐢 🐢 🐢 🐢 🐢 🐢 🐢 🐢 🐢 🐢 🐢 🐢 🐢 🐢 🐢 🐢 🐢 🐢 🐢

B. Directions: Circle the proper noun.

1.	boy	Franco	5.	leader	Abraham Lincoln
2.	river	Hudson River	6.	Miami	city
3.	country	Mexico	7.	dam	Hoover Dam
4.	Bambi	deer	8.	Judson School	school

ANSWERS WILL VARY.

A **common noun** does not name a specific person, place, or thing.

Most nouns are common and are not capitalized.

Examples: doll   glass

If a type of noun is given, it is still common.   *Example:* horse   pinto

A **proper noun** names a **specific** person, place, or thing. **Capitalize** a proper noun.

Example: <u>town</u> - <u>**Crossville**</u>
              common   proper
               noun   noun

🐢🐢🐢🐢🐢🐢🐢🐢🐢🐢🐢🐢🐢🐢🐢🐢🐢🐢

Directions: Write a **proper noun** on the line.

  Example: The name of a bridge near my town is   <u>**White Run Bridge**</u> .

1.   A person I like is <u>**Sarah**</u> .

2.   The name of my town (city) is <u>**Cashtown**</u> .

3.   The name of a street or road in my town is <u>**Low Dutch Road**</u> .

4.   The name of a store in my town is <u>**Jack's Hardware Store**</u> .

5.   The name of a restaurant I like is <u>**Casual Cafe**</u> .

6.   I live in the state of <u>**North Dakota**</u> .

7.   The name of my country is <u>**United States**</u> .

Name_____

Date_____

A **common noun** does not name a specific person, place, or thing.

Most nouns are common and are not capitalized.

     Examples: doll   glass

If a type of noun is given, it is still common.   *Example:* horse   pinto

A **proper noun** names a **specific** person, place, or thing. **Capitalize** a proper noun.

     Example: <u> town </u> - <u>Crossville</u>
                      common   proper
                      noun   noun

🐢 🐢 🐢 🐢 🐢 🐢 🐢 🐢 🐢 🐢 🐢 🐢 🐢 🐢 🐢 🐢 🐢 🐢

Directions: Write a **proper noun** on the line.

  Example: The name of a bridge near my town is<u> **White Run Bridge** </u>.

1.   A person I like is _____.

2.   The name of my town (city) is _____.

3.   The name of a street or road in my town is _____.

4.   The name of a store in my town is _____.

5.   The name of a restaurant I like is _____.

6.   I live in the state of _____.

7.   The name of my country is _____.   195

Note to Teacher: A discussion of abstract nouns is included in *Easy Grammar: Grades 4 and 5.*

Most nouns are <u>concrete</u> nouns. That means you can see them.

Read this sentence. How many things can be seen?

The boy drives a car down the road.

Can you see a boy? Yes, <u>boy</u> is a noun.

Can you see a car? Yes, <u>car</u> is a noun.

Can you see a road? Yes, <u>road</u> is a noun.

🐢🐢🐢🐢🐢🐢🐢🐢🐢🐢🐢🐢🐢🐢🐢🐢🐢🐢

Directions: Circle any nouns.

1.   **Dad** likes **cereal** and **milk**.

2.   My **sister** drives a **truck**.

3.   **Mrs. Jones** walks to the **store**.

4.   A **ladder** is leaning against the **house**.

5.   The **fork** and **knife** just fell on the **floor**.

6.   A **turtle** and an **owl** live in our **backyard**.

7.   **Mom** put **sheets** and a **blanket** on that **bed**.

8.   A **football** and **baseball** are in the **closet**.

196

Most nouns are <u>concrete</u> nouns. That means you can see them.

Read this sentence. How many things can be seen?

The boy drives a car down the road.
Can you see a boy? Yes, <u>boy</u> is a noun.
Can you see a car? Yes, <u>car</u> is a noun.
Can you see a road? Yes, <u>road</u> is a noun.

🐢 🐢 🐢 🐢 🐢 🐢 🐢 🐢 🐢 🐢 🐢 🐢 🐢 🐢 🐢 🐢 🐢 🐢

Directions: Circle any nouns.

1.   Dad likes cereal and milk.

2.   My sister drives a truck.

3.   Mrs. Jones walks to the store.

4.   A ladder is leaning against the house.

5.   The fork and knife just fell on the floor.

6.   A turtle and an owl live in our backyard.

7.   Mom put sheets and a blanket on that bed.

8.   A football and baseball are in the closet.   197

Most nouns are <u>concrete</u> nouns. That means you can see them.

Read this sentence. How many things can be seen?

Mary put icing on the cake.

Can you see Mary? Yes, <u>Mary</u> is a noun.

Can you see icing? Yes, <u>icing</u> is a noun.

Can you see a cake? Yes, <u>cake</u> is a noun.

Directions: Circle any nouns.

1. That **flower** has lost its **petals**.

2. My **grandfather** buys many **books**.

3. Your new **shirt** is in this **bag**.

4. A **bowl** of **cherries** is on the **table**.

5. **Jan** and her **brother** washed their **car**.

6. The **gift** with a red **bow** is for my **mother**.

7. Several **nails** are lying on the **floor** by the **television**.

8. **Mr. Jacobs** likes to eat **chips** with his **sandwiches**.

Name_____

Date_____

Most nouns are <u>concrete</u> nouns. That means you can see them.

Read this sentence. How many things can be seen?

Mary put icing on the cake.

Can you see Mary? Yes, <u>Mary</u> is a noun.

Can you see icing? Yes, <u>icing</u> is a noun.

Can you see a cake? Yes, <u>cake</u> is a noun.

Directions: Circle any nouns.

1.   That flower has lost its petals.

2.   My grandfather buys many books.

3.   Your new shirt is in this bag.

4.   A bowl of cherries is on the table.

5.   Jan and her brother washed their car.

6.   The gift with a red bow is for my mother.

7.   Several nails are lying on the floor by the television.

8.   Mr. Jacobs likes to eat chips with his sandwiches.

Singular means one.
Plural means more than one.

<u>Singular</u>	<u>Plural</u>
skunk	skunks
grape	grapes
dish	dishes
child	children

🐢🐢🐢🐢🐢🐢🐢🐢🐢🐢🐢🐢🐢🐢🐢🐢🐢🐢🐢🐢

Directions: Write **S** if the noun is singular (one) and **P** if the noun is plural (more than one).

1. __S__ comb

2. __P__ songs

3. __S__ bottle

4. __S__ powder

5. __P__ ears

6. __S__ lion

7. __S__ tooth

8. __P__ apples

9. __S__ rug

10. __P__ watches

11. __P__ pennies

12. __S__ lamp

13. __S__ goose

14. __P__ geese

15. __P__ stamps

16. __P__ calves

17. __S__ pear

18. __P__ men

200

Singular means one.
Plural means more than one.

<u>Singular</u>	<u>Plural</u>
skunk	skunks
grape	grapes
dish	dishes
child	children

🐢 🐢 🐢 🐢 🐢 🐢 🐢 🐢 🐢 🐢 🐢 🐢 🐢 🐢 🐢 🐢 🐢 🐢

Directions:　Write **<u>S</u>** if the noun is singular (one) and **<u>P</u>** if the noun is plural (more than one).

1. _____ comb

2. _____ songs

3. _____ bottle

4. _____ powder

5. _____ ears

6. _____ lion

7. _____ tooth

8. _____ apples

9. _____ rug

10. _____ watches

11. _____ pennies

12. _____ lamp

13. _____ goose

14. _____ geese

15. _____ stamps

16. _____ calves

17. _____ pear

18. _____ men

WORKBOOK PAGE 95

Date_____

Singular means one.
Plural means more than one.

🐢 To form the plural of most nouns, add <u>s</u>.

🐢 If a word ends in <u>ch</u>, <u>sh</u>, <u>s</u>, <u>z</u>, or <u>x</u>, add <u>es</u> to form the plural.

Use a dictionary to check the plural form. If <u>es</u> should be added to a noun, it will say, **pl. es.** <u>If no plural (pl.) is given, you know to simply add</u> **s**.

🐢 🐢 🐢 🐢 🐢 🐢 🐢 🐢 🐢 🐢 🐢 🐢 🐢 🐢 🐢 🐢 🐢 🐢

Directions: Write the plural.

1. star - _____**stars**_____

2. wish - _____**wishes**_____

3. dime - _____**dimes**_____

4. rock - _____**rocks**_____

5. box - _____**boxes**_____

6. car - _____**cars**_____

7. bush - _____**bushes**_____

8. fizz - _____**fizzes**_____

9. juice - _____**juices**_____

10. lunch - _____**lunches**_____

11. club - _____**clubs**_____

12. mix - _____**mixes**_____

13. light - _____**lights**_____

14. bus - _____**buses**_____

15. spoon - _____**spoons**_____

16. catch - _____**catches**_____

17. bone - _____**bones**_____

18. loss - _____**losses**_____

202

Name_____

Date_____

Singular means one.
Plural means more than one.

🐢 To form the plural of most nouns, add <u>s</u>.

🐢 If a word ends in <u>**ch**</u>, <u>**sh**</u>, <u>**s**</u>, <u>**z**</u>, or <u>**x**</u>, add <u>es</u> to form the plural.

Use a dictionary to check the plural form. If <u>es</u> should be added to a noun, it will say, **pl. es.** <u>If no plural (pl.) is given, you know to simply add</u> ***s***.

🐢 🐢 🐢 🐢 🐢 🐢 🐢 🐢 🐢 🐢 🐢 🐢 🐢 🐢 🐢 🐢 🐢 🐢

Directions: Write the plural.

1.   star - _____

2.   wish - _____

3.   dime - _____

4.   rock - _____

5.   box - _____

6.   car - _____

7.   bush - _____

8.   fizz - _____

9.   juice - _____

10.   lunch - _____

11.   club - _____

12.   mix - _____

13.   light - _____

14.   bus - _____

15.   spoon - _____

16.   catch - _____

17.   bone - _____

18.   loss - _____

Name_____   **NOUNS**
WORKBOOK PAGE 96   **Singular and Plural**
Date_____
**Note to Teacher: Be sure students understand vowels and consonants.
Begin the lesson with this discussion.   Although i + y combination has
been included in the lesson, no English words presently end in *iy*.**
Singular means one.
Plural means more than one.

🐢 To form the plural of a noun ending in <u>ay</u>, <u>ey</u>, <u>oy</u>, or <u>uy</u>, add **s**. As you know, <u>a</u>, <u>e</u>, <u>i</u>, <u>o</u>, and <u>u</u> are vowels. If a word ends in <u>a</u>, <u>e</u>, <u>i</u>, <u>o</u>, or <u>u</u> **+ y**, add **s**.

	<u>singular</u>	<u>plural</u>
Examples:	bay	bays
	key	keys
	boy	boys
	buy	buys

🐢 To form the plural of a noun ending in a **consonant + y**, change the **y** to <u>i</u> and add **es**.

	penny	pennies
Examples:	lily	lilies

Use a dictionary to check the plural form. If the <u>y</u> should be changed to <u>i</u> and **es** added to a noun, it will say, **pl. *ies*.** <u>If no plural (pl.) is given, you know to simply add **s**.</u>

🐢 🐢 🐢 🐢 🐢 🐢 🐢 🐢 🐢 🐢 🐢 🐢 🐢 🐢 🐢 🐢 🐢 🐢

Directions: Write the plural.

1. baby - _____ **babies** _____   5. buggy - _____ **buggies** _____

2. monkey - _____ **monkeys** _____   6. toy - _____ **toys** _____

3. lady - _____ **ladies** _____   7. bunny - _____ **bunnies** _____

4. guy - _____ **guys** _____   8. ray - _____ **rays** _____

204

Singular means one.
Plural means more than one.

🐢 To form the plural of a noun ending in <u>ay</u>, <u>ey</u>, <u>oy</u>, or <u>uy</u>, add <u>**s**</u>. As you know, <u>a</u>, <u>e</u>, <u>i</u>, <u>o</u>, and <u>u</u> are vowels. If a word ends in <u>a</u>, <u>e</u>, <u>i</u>, <u>o</u>, or <u>u</u> **+ y**, add <u>**s**</u>.

	Examples:	<u>singular</u>	<u>plural</u>
		bay	bays
		key	keys
		boy	boys
		buy	buys

🐢 To form the plural of a noun ending in a **consonant + y**, change the <u>y</u> to <u>i</u> and add <u>**es**</u>.

	Examples:	penny	pennies
		lily	lilies

Use a dictionary to check the plural form. If the <u>y</u> should be changed to <u>i</u> and <u>**es**</u> added to a noun, it will say, **pl.** *ies.* <u>If no plural (pl.) is given, you know to simply add</u> <u>**s**</u>.

🐢 🐢 🐢 🐢 🐢 🐢 🐢 🐢 🐢 🐢 🐢 🐢 🐢 🐢 🐢 🐢 🐢 🐢

Directions: Write the plural.

1. baby - _____

2. monkey - _____

3. lady - _____

4. guy - _____

5. buggy - _____

6. toy - _____

7. bunny - _____

8. ray - _____

Note to Teacher: <u>Explain to students that even if they don't recognize a word such as *filly*, they can still form the plural following these rules.</u>

Singular means one.

Plural means more than one.

🐢 To form the plural of a noun ending in <u>ay</u>, <u>ey</u>, <u>oy</u>, or <u>uy</u>, add <u>s</u>. As you know, <u>a</u>, <u>e</u>, <u>i</u>, <u>o</u>, and <u>u</u> are vowels. If a word ends in <u>a</u>, <u>e</u>, <u>i</u>, <u>o</u>, or <u>u</u> **+ y**, add <u>s</u>.

Example: monk**ey**   monk**eys**

🐢 To form the plural of a noun ending in a **consonant + y**, change the **y** to <u>i</u> and add <u>es</u>.

Example: strawber**ry**   strawberr**ies**

Use a dictionary to check the plural form. If the <u>y</u> should be changed to <u>i</u> and <u>es</u> added to a noun, it will say, **pl. *ies*.** <u>If no plural (pl.) is given, you know to simply add s.</u>

🐢 🐢 🐢 🐢 🐢 🐢 🐢 🐢 🐢 🐢 🐢 🐢 🐢 🐢 🐢 🐢 🐢 🐢

Directions: Write the plural.

1. pony - _____**ponies**_____   7. dummy - _____**dummies**_____

2. day - _____**days**_____   8. buy - _____**buys**_____

3. filly - _____**fillies**_____   9. pansy - _____**pansies**_____

4. donkey - _____**donkeys**_____   10. ruby - _____**rubies**_____

5. joy - _____**joys**_____   11. stray - _____**strays**_____

6. berry - _____**berries**_____   12. mommy - _____**mommies**_____

206

Name_____

Date_____

Singular means one.
Plural means more than one.

🐢 To form the plural of a noun ending in <u>ay, ey, oy,</u> or <u>uy,</u> add <u>**s**</u>. As you know, <u>a, e, i, o,</u> and <u>u</u> are vowels. If a word ends in <u>a, e, i, o,</u> or <u>u</u> + <u>**y**</u>, add <u>**s**</u>.

Example: monk**ey**   monk**eys**

🐢 To form the plural of a noun ending in a **consonant** + <u>**y**</u>, change the <u>**y**</u> to <u>**i**</u> and add <u>**es**</u>.

Example: strawbe**rry**   strawber**ries**

Use a dictionary to check the plural form. If the <u>y</u> should be changed to <u>i</u> and <u>es</u> added to a noun, it will say, **pl.** *ies.* <u>If no plural (pl.) is given, you know to simply add</u> *s*.

🐢 🐢 🐢 🐢 🐢 🐢 🐢 🐢 🐢 🐢 🐢 🐢 🐢 🐢 🐢 🐢 🐢 🐢

Directions: Write the plural.

1. pony - _____

2. day - _____

3. filly - _____

4. donkey - _____

5. joy - _____

6. berry - _____

7. dummy - _____

8. buy - _____

9. pansy - _____

10. ruby - _____

11. stray - _____

12. mommy - _____

207

Name_____   **NOUNS**
WORKBOOK PAGE 98   **Singular and Plural**
Date_____
<u>**Note to Teacher:** Be sure that students know the plural spelling of the following words: *calf, half, leaf, loaf,* and *dwarf.* Usually, if a word ends in the same double consonant *(puff),* s is added to form the plural *(puffs).*</u>
Singular means one.
Plural means more than one.

🐢 To form the plural of some nouns ending in <u>f</u>, change the <u>f</u> to <u>v</u> and add **es**.

Examples: **calf - cal<u>ves</u>**
             leaf - lea<u>ves</u>
             loaf - loa<u>ves</u>
             dwarf - dwar<u>ves</u>

🐢 To form the plural of some nouns ending in <u>f</u>, simply add **s**.

Examples: puff - puff**s**
             roof - roof**s**
             belief - belief**s**

Use a dictionary to check the plural form. If the <u>f</u> should be changed to <u>v</u> and **es** added to a noun such as *calf,* it will say, **pl. ves** or **pl., calves.** <u>If no plural (pl.) is given, you know to simply add **s**.</u>

🐢 🐢 🐢 🐢 🐢 🐢 🐢 🐢 🐢 🐢 🐢 🐢 🐢 🐢 🐢 🐢 🐢

Directions: Write the plural.

1. loaf - _____**loaves**_____   5. cuff - _____**cuffs**_____

2. whiff - _____**whiffs**_____   6. half - _____**halves**_____

3. leaf - _____**leaves**_____   7. staff - _____**staffs**_____

4. proof - _____**proofs**_____   8. leaf - _____**leaves**_____

208

Singular means one.
Plural means more than one.

🐢 To form the plural of some nouns ending in f, change the f to v and add
es.

	Examples:	**calf - calves**
		leaf - leaves
		loaf - loaves
		dwarf - dwarves

🐢 To form the plural of some nouns ending in f, simply add **s**.

	Examples:	puff - puffs
		roof - roofs
		belief - beliefs

Use a dictionary to check the plural form. If the f should be changed to v
and **es** added to a noun such as *calf,* it will say, **pl. ves** or *pl., calves.* If
no plural (pl.) is given, you know to simply add *s.*

🐢 🐢 🐢 🐢 🐢 🐢 🐢 🐢 🐢 🐢 🐢 🐢 🐢 🐢 🐢 🐢 🐢

Directions: Write the plural.

1. loaf - _____

2. whiff - _____

3. leaf - _____

4. proof - _____

5. cuff - _____

6. half - _____

7. staff - _____

8. leaf - _____

NOUNS
Singular and Plural

<u>**Note to Teacher:**</u> <u>Forming the plural with nouns ending in *o* is tricky. Be</u> <u>sure to allow students to use a dictionary. A small problem also arises in</u> <u>that dictionary spellings vary. I accept a variant spelling if a student can</u> <u>show me the spelling in the dictionary used.</u>

Singular means one.
Plural means more than one.

🐢 To form the plural of some nouns ending in <u>o</u>, add **s**.

Examples: zoo   -   zoo**s**
silo   -   silo**s**

🐢 To form the plural of some nouns ending in <u>o</u>, add **es**.

Example: tomato   -   tomato**es**

🐢 Some nouns ending in <u>o</u> will add **s** or **es**. When two spellings are given, the first one is preferred. Use the first spelling.

Example: **lasso**....pl., *sos, soes...*

This means that more than one lasso can be spelled *lassos* or *lassoes*. Do you see that *sos* is listed first? Therefore, the best spelling of more than one lasso is *lassos*.

Use a dictionary to check the plural form. <u>If no plural (pl.) is given, you</u> <u>know to simply add *s*.</u>

🐢 🐢 🐢 🐢 🐢 🐢 🐢 🐢 🐢 🐢 🐢 🐢 🐢 🐢 🐢 🐢 🐢

Directions: Write the plural.

1. potato - ____**potatoes**____   4. pogo - ____**pogos**____

2. yoyo - ____**yoyos**____   5. stereo - ____**stereos**____

3. rodeo - ____**rodeos**____   6. domino - ____**dominoes**____

210

Singular means one.
Plural means more than one.

🐢 To form the plural of some nouns ending in <u>o</u>, add **s**.

          Examples: zoo   -   zoo**s**
                        silo   -   silo**s**

🐢 To form the plural of some nouns ending in <u>o</u>, add **es**.

          Example: tomato   -   tomato**es**

🐢 Some nouns ending in <u>o</u> will add **s** or **es**. When two spellings are given, the first one is preferred. Use the first spelling.

          Example: **lasso**....pl., *sos, soes*...

This means that more than one lasso can be spelled *lassos* or *lassoes*. Do you see that *sos* is listed first? Therefore, the best spelling of more than one lasso is *lassos*.

Use a dictionary to check the plural form. <u>If no plural (pl.) is given, you know to simply add **s**.</u>

🐢 🐢 🐢 🐢 🐢 🐢 🐢 🐢 🐢 🐢 🐢 🐢 🐢 🐢 🐢 🐢 🐢 🐢 🐢

Directions: Write the plural.

1. potato - _____

2. yoyo - _____

3. rodeo - _____

4. pogo - _____

5. stereo - _____

6. domino - _____

Singular means one.
Plural means more than one.

🐢Some nouns do not change to form the plural.

Example: deer   -   deer

Use a dictionary to check the plural form. If the word does not change, the dictionary will say (pl. deer).

deer...*pl.* deer

🐢Some nouns totally change to form the plural.

Example: child   -   child**ren**

Use a dictionary to check the plural form. If the word does change, the dictionary will say the plural.

child...*pl.* children

🐢🐢🐢🐢🐢🐢🐢🐢🐢🐢🐢🐢🐢🐢🐢🐢🐢🐢

Directions: Write the plural.

1.   tooth - _____**teeth**_____

2.   sheep - _____**sheep**_____

3.   mouse - _____**mice**_____

4.   goose - _____**geese**_____

5.   elk - _____**elk**_____

6.   moose - _____**moose**_____

7.   foot - _____**feet**_____

8.   woman - _____**women**_____

9.   trout - _____**trout**_____

10.   child - _____**children**_____

212

Name_____

Date_____

Singular means one.
Plural means more than one.

🐢 Some nouns do not change to form the plural.

Example: deer   -   deer

Use a dictionary to check the plural form. If the word does not change, the dictionary will say (pl. deer).

deer...*pl.* deer

🐢 Some nouns totally change to form the plural.

Example: child   -   child**ren**

Use a dictionary to check the plural form. If the word does change, the dictionary will say the plural.

child...*pl.* children

🐢 🐢 🐢 🐢 🐢 🐢 🐢 🐢 🐢 🐢 🐢 🐢 🐢 🐢 🐢 🐢 🐢 🐢

Directions: Write the plural.

1. tooth - _____

2. sheep - _____

3. mouse - _____

4. goose - _____

5. elk - _____

6. moose - _____

7. foot - _____

8. woman - _____

9. trout - _____

10. child - _____

213

Name_____   **NOUNS**
WORKBOOK PAGE 101   **Possessives**
Date_____

<u>**Note to Teacher:**</u>   **<u>In teaching this concept, create your own examples</u>**
<u>using your students and things they own or items in your classroom and</u>
<u>things that may belong to them. (Example: flag's stars)</u>
Possessive nouns show ownership or that something is part of
something else.

Examples: Manny's shoes

a pencil's eraser

🐢 To a singular (one) noun, add **'s** to the noun.

Example: horse   -   horse's stall

It does not matter how many items are owned; **'s** is added to the noun.

Examples: Chan**'s** sister
Chan**'s** sisters

🐢🐢🐢🐢🐢🐢🐢🐢🐢🐢🐢🐢🐢🐢🐢🐢🐢🐢🐢

Directions: Write the possessive for each noun.

Example: a purse belonging to my mom - __my mom's purse__

1. a quarter belonging to Yancy - _____**Yancy's quarter**_____

2. dogs belonging to Jina - _____**Jina's dogs**_____

3. a notebook belonging to her brother - _____**her brother's notebook**_____

4. a birthday party for Chessa - _____**Chessa's birthday party**_____

5. a van belonging to Grandma - _____**Grandma's van**_____

214

Possessive nouns show ownership or that something is part of something else.

Examples: Manny's shoes

a pencil's eraser

🐢 To a singular (one) noun, add **'s** to the noun.

Example: horse   -   horse's stall

It does not matter how many items are owned; **'s** is added to the noun.

Examples: Chan**'s** sister
Chan**'s** sisters

🐢 🐢 🐢 🐢 🐢 🐢 🐢 🐢 🐢 🐢 🐢 🐢 🐢 🐢 🐢 🐢 🐢 🐢

Directions: Write the possessive for each noun.

Example: a purse belonging to my mom - __my mom's purse__

1.   a quarter belonging to Yancy - _____

2.   dogs belonging to Jina - _____

3.   a notebook belonging to her brother - _____

4.   a birthday party for Chessa - _____

5.   a van belonging to Grandma - _____

Possessive nouns show ownership or that something is part of something else.

Examples: Mr. Benson's job

sisters' playhouse

🐢 To a plural (more than one) noun that ends in s, add **'** after the **s**.

Example: more than one bird   =   bird**s**   -   bird**s'** nest

It does not matter how many items are owned; **s'** is added to the noun.

Examples: boys' baseball

boys' baseballs

🐢🐢🐢🐢🐢🐢🐢🐢🐢🐢🐢🐢🐢🐢🐢🐢🐢🐢🐢

Directions: Write the possessive for each noun.

Example: a ball belonging to two girls - ___girls' ball___

1.   an apartment shared by three ladies - __**ladies' apartment**__

2.   a room shared by two sisters - _____**sisters' room**_____

3.   a report done by two boys - _____**boys' report**_____

4.   the balloons belonging to three clowns - __**clowns' balloons**__

5.   a store belonging to his aunts - _____**aunts' store**_____

6.   cake eaten by all the guests - _____**guests' cake**_____

216

Name_____

NOUNS
Possessives

Date_____

Possessive nouns show ownership or that something is part of something else.

Examples: Mr. Benson's job

sisters' playhouse

🐢 To a plural (more than one) noun that ends in s, add ' after the **s**.

Example: more than one bird = bird**s**   -   bird**s'** nest

It does not matter how many items are owned; **s'** is added to the noun.

Examples: boys' baseball

boys' baseballs

🐢 🐢 🐢 🐢 🐢 🐢 🐢 🐢 🐢 🐢 🐢 🐢 🐢 🐢 🐢 🐢 🐢 🐢

Directions: Write the possessive for each noun.

Example: a ball belonging to two girls - __girls' ball__

1. an apartment shared by three ladies - _____

2. a room shared by two sisters - _____

3. a report done by two boys - _____

4. the balloons belonging to three clowns - _____

5. a store belonging to his aunts - _____

6. cake eaten by all the guests - _____

217

Name_____   **NOUNS**
WORKBOOK PAGE 103   **Possessives**
Date_____

<u>**Note to Teacher: Be sure to review the concept that it does not matter how many items are owned.**</u>

TO REVIEW:

🐢 To a singular (one) noun, add **'s** to the noun.

        Example: pig   -   pig's tail

🐢 To a plural (more than one) noun that ends in s, add **'** after the **s**.

    Example: more than one boy = boy**s** - boy**s'** coach

NEW RULE:

🐢 If a noun is **plural** (more than one) and **does not end in s**, place an apostrophe(**'**) **+ s** at the end of the word.

    Example: more than one child = **children** - children**'s** sand box

🐢🐢🐢🐢🐢🐢🐢🐢🐢🐢🐢🐢🐢🐢🐢🐢🐢🐢

Directions: Write the possessive for each noun.

1.   (review) cheese belonging to a mouse - _____ **mouse's cheese** _____

2.   (review) tickets belonging to a woman - _____ **woman's tickets** _____

3.   (review) a dog owned by two friends - _____ **friends' dog** _____

4.   a box belonging to more than one mouse - _____ **mice's box** _____

5.   an office shared by more than one woman - _____ **women's office** _____

6.   a restroom belonging to more than one man - _____ **men's restroom** _____

218

TO REVIEW:

🐢 To a singular (one) noun, add **'s** to the noun.

        Example: pig   -   pig's tail

🐢 To a plural (more than one) noun that ends in s, add **'** after the **s**.

   Example: more than one boy = boy**s** - boy**s'** coach

NEW RULE:

🐢 If a noun is **plural** (more than one) and **does not end in s**, place an apostrophe(') **+ s** at the end of the word.

   Example: more than one child = **children** - children**'s** sand box

🐢🐢🐢🐢🐢🐢🐢🐢🐢🐢🐢🐢🐢🐢🐢🐢🐢🐢🐢

Directions: Write the possessive for each noun.

1.   (review)   cheese belonging to a mouse - _____

2.   (review)   tickets belonging to a woman - _____

3.   (review)   a dog owned by two friends - _____

4.   a box belonging to more than one mouse - _____

5.   an office shared by more than one woman - _____

6.   a restroom belonging to more than one man - _____

Name_____   **NOUNS**
WORKBOOK PAGE 104   **Review**
Date_____

A.   Common and Proper Nouns:

   Directions: Circle the proper noun.

1. girl   **Ellen**   3. town   **Littlestown**

2. **Pacific Ocean**   ocean   4. creek   **Potts Creek**

B.   Identifying Nouns:

   Directions: Circle any nouns.

1. Two **horses** pulled a **wagon**.

2. **Jan** likes **chicken** with **noodles**.

3. Several **friends** met in the **cafeteria**.

C.   Singular and Plural Nouns:

   Directions: Write <u>S</u> if the noun is singular; write <u>P</u> if the noun is plural.

             Remember: Singular means only one.
             Plural means more than one.

1. __**S**__ pan

2. __**P**__ crackers

3. __**S**__ potato

4. __**P**__ blisters
220

A. Common and Proper Nouns:

Directions: Circle the proper noun.

1. girl   Ellen   3. town   Littlestown

2. Pacific Ocean   ocean   4. creek   Potts Creek

B.   Identifying Nouns:

Directions: Circle any nouns.

1. Two horses pulled a wagon.

2. Jan likes chicken with noodles.

3. Several friends met in the cafeteria.

C.   Singular and Plural Nouns:

Directions: Write <u>S</u> if the noun is singular; write <u>P</u> if the noun is plural.

Remember: Singular means only one.
Plural means more than one.

1. _____ pan

2. _____ crackers

3. _____ potato

4. _____ blisters

D. Plural Nouns:

Directions: Write the plural of each noun.

1. floor - _____**floors**_____   7. city - _____**cities**_____

2. tomato - _____**tomatoes**_____   8. watch - _____**watches**_____

3. calf - _____**calves**_____   9. boy - _____**boys**_____

4. dairy - _____**dairies**_____   10. box - _____**boxes**_____

5. deer - _____**deer**_____   11. child - _____**children**_____

6. flash - _____**flashes**_____   12. roof - _____**roofs**_____

E. Possessive Nouns:

Directions: Write the possessive.

1. a coat belonging to Jim - _____**Jim's coat**_____

2. socks belonging to her brother - _____**(her) brother's socks**_____

3. a ball shared by two friends - _____**(two) friends' ball**_____

4. the workroom for teachers - _____**teachers' workroom**_____

5. a theater for more than one child - _____**(a) children's theater**_____

Name_____   **NOUNS**
                                         Review
Date_____

D. Plural Nouns:

Directions: Write the plural of each noun.

1. floor - _____   7. city -_____

2. tomato - _____   8. watch - _____

3. calf -_____   9. boy - _____

4. dairy - _____   10. box - _____

5. deer - _____   11. child - _____

6. flash -_____   12. roof - _____

E.   Possessive Nouns:

Directions: Write the possessive.

1. a coat belonging to Jim - _____

2. socks belonging to her brother - _____

3. a ball shared by two friends - _____

4. the workroom for teachers - _____

5. a theater for more than one child - _____

Name_____   **Noun Test**

Date_____

A. Directions: Circle the proper noun.

1. country   **Canada**   2.   **Mammoth Cave**   cave

B. Directions: Circle any nouns.

1. **Kelly** colored a **picture** for her **grandpa**.

2. His **shoes** and **socks** are under the **bed**.

C. Directions: Write the plural.

1. doughnut - __**doughnuts**__   5.   story - _____**stories**_____

2. half - _____**halves**_____   6.   tomato - _____**tomatoes**____

3. key - _____**keys**_____   7.   foot - _____**feet**_____

4. deer - _____**deer**_____   8.   latch - _____**latches**_____

D. Directions: Write the possessive.

1. balloons belonging to one girl - _____**(one) girl's balloons**____

2. balloons belonging to more than one girl - ____**girls' balloons**_____

3. a book owned by one child - _____**child's book**_____

4. a book shared by more than one child - _____**children's book**_____
224

Name_____   **Noun Test**

Date_____

A.   Directions: Circle the proper noun.

1.   country   (Canada)   2.   (Mammoth Cave)   cave

B.   Directions: Circle any nouns.

1.   (Kelly) colored a (picture) for her (grandpa).

2.   His (shoes) and (socks) are under the (bed).

C.   Directions: Write the plural.

1.   doughnut - _doughnuts_   5.   story - _stories_

2.   half - _halves_   6.   tomato - _tomatoes_

3.   key - _keys_   7.   foot - _feet_

4.   deer - _deer_   8.   latch - _latches_

D.   Directions: Write the possessive.

1.   balloons belonging to one girl - _girl's ballons_

2.   balloons belonging to more than one girl - _girls' ballons_

3.   a book owned by one child - _child's book_

4.   a book shared by more than one child - _childrens' book_

225

Name_____   **Cumulative Review**
WORKBOOK PAGE 106   **Nouns**
Date_____

A.   List of Prepositions:
     Directions: List the twenty-eight prepositions that you have learned.

1. **above**	15. **from**
2. **across**	16. **in**
3. **after**	17. **inside**
4. **around**	18. **into**
5. **at**	19. **of**
6. **before**	20. **off**
7. **behind**	21. **on**
8. **below**	22. **out**
9. **beside**	23. **over**
10. **between**	24. **through**
11. **by**	25. **to**
12. **down**	26. **under**
13. **during**	27. **up**
14. **for**	28. **with**

226

Name_____ **Cumulative Review**
Nouns

Date_____

A. **List of Prepositions:**
Directions: List the twenty-eight prepositions that you have learned.

1. _____   15. _____

2. _____   16. _____

3. _____   17. _____

4. _____   18. _____

5. _____   19. _____

6. _____   20. _____

7. _____   21. _____

8. _____   22. _____

9. _____   23. _____

10. _____   24. _____

11. _____   25. _____

12. _____   26. _____

13. _____   27. _____

14. _____   28. _____   227

B. Compound Subject:

Directions: Cross out the prepositional phrase in each sentence. Then, underline the compound subject once and the verb twice.

Remember: The subject will not be a word in a prepositional phrase.

1.   <u>Judy</u> and her <u>brother</u> <u><u>go</u></u> ~~to a cabin~~.

2.   Their <u>bikes</u> and <u>skates</u> <u><u>are</u></u> ~~in the garage~~.

C. Compound Verb:

Directions: Cross out the prepositional phrase in each sentence. Then, underline the subject once and the compound verb twice.

Remember: The verb will never be a word in a prepositional phrase.

1.   <u>Mom</u> <u><u>sang</u></u> and <u><u>danced</u></u> ~~around the kitchen~~.

2.   His <u>sister</u> <u><u>looked</u></u> ~~into the bag~~ and <u><u>laughed</u></u>.

D. Imperative Sentence:

Directions: Cross out the prepositional phrase in each sentence. Then, underline the subject once and the verb twice.

Remember: An imperative sentence gives a command.

1.   <u>(You)</u> <u><u>Keep</u></u> this ~~in your room~~.

2.   <u>(You)</u> <u><u>Wait</u></u> ~~for a few minutes~~.

B. Compound Subject:

Directions: Cross out the prepositional phrase in each sentence.
               Then, underline the compound subject once and the
               verb twice.

Remember: The subject will not be a word in a prepositional phrase.

1.   Judy and her brother go to a cabin.

2.   Their bikes and skates are in the garage.

C. Compound Verb:

Directions: Cross out the prepositional phrase in each sentence.
               Then, underline the subject once and the compound
               verb twice.

Remember: The verb will never be a word in a prepositional phrase.

1.   Mom sang and danced around the kitchen.

2.   His sister looked into the bag and laughed.

D. Imperative Sentence:

Directions: Cross out the prepositional phrase in each sentence.
               Then, underline the subject once and the verb twice.

Remember: An imperative sentence gives a command.

1.   Keep this in your room.

2.   Wait for a few minutes.   229

E.   Contractions:

Directions: Write the contraction in the space provided.

1.   we are - ___**we're**___   4.   they are - ___**they're**___

2.   I have - ___**I've**___   5.   you will - ___**you'll**___

3.   will not - ___**won't**___   6.   had not - ___**hadn't**___

F.   It's/Its   They're/There/Their   You're/Your:

Directions: Circle the correct word.

1.   (**It's**, Its) snowing.

2.   (**You're**, Your) supposed to be polite.

3.   (They're, There, **Their**) brother is fishing today.

4.   (**They're**, There, Their) helping to build a tree house.

G.   Can/May:

Directions: Circle the correct word.

1.   (**Can**, May) you hold this?

2.   (Can, **May**) we sit with you?

3.   Harry (**can**, may) hop on one foot.

230

E. Contractions:

Directions: Write the contraction in the space provided.

1. we are - _____   4. they are - _____

2. I have - _____   5. you will - _____

3. will not - _____   6. had not - _____

F. It's/Its   They're/There/Their   You're/Your:

Directions: Circle the correct word.

1. (It's, Its) snowing.

2. (You're, Your) supposed to be polite.

3. (They're, There, Their) brother is fishing today.

4. (They're, There, Their) helping to build a tree house.

G. Can/May:

Directions: Circle the correct word.

1. (Can, May) you hold this?

2. (Can, May) we sit with you?

3. Harry (can, may) hop on one foot.   231

H.   State of Being:

Directions: Use *is, am, are, was,* or *were* to fill in the blanks.

Present: 1.   I ____**am**____ tired.

2.   Today ____**is**____ cloudy.

3.   Those children ____**are**____ funny.

Past: 1.   Gail ____**was**____ afraid of the snake.

2.   Both boys ____**were**____ in the pool.

I.   Helping (Auxiliary) Verbs:

Directions: List the twenty-three helping verbs.

d<u>o</u>___	h<u>as</u>___	m<u>ay</u>___	c<u>ould</u>___	c<u>an</u>___	<u>is</u>___	w<u>ere</u>___
d<u>oes</u>___	h<u>ave</u>___	m<u>ight</u>___	sh<u>ould</u>___	sh<u>all</u>___	<u>am</u>___	b<u>e</u>___
d<u>id</u>___	h<u>ad</u>___	m<u>ust</u>___	w<u>ould</u>___	will___	<u>are</u>___	be<u>ing</u>___
					w<u>as</u>___	b<u>een</u>___

J. Action?:

Directions: Write <u>Yes</u> if the boldfaced verb shows action. Write <u>No</u> if the boldfaced verb does not show action.

1. __**Yes**__   Kenny **pitched** a ball.

2. __**Yes**__   She **tasted** the stew.

3. __**No**__   The stew **tastes** good.

232

H.   State of Being:

Directions: Use *is, am, are, was,* or *were* to fill in the blanks.

Present: 1.   I _____ tired.

2.   Today _____ cloudy.

3.   Those children _____ funny.

Past: 1.   Gail _____ afraid of the snake.

2.   Both boys _____ in the pool.

I.   Helping (Auxiliary) Verbs:

Directions: List the twenty-three helping verbs.

d_____   h_____   m_____   c_____   c_____   i____   w_____

d_____   h_____   m_____   sh____   sh____   a____   b_____

d_____   h_____   m_____   w_____   w_____   a____   b_____

w____   b_____

J. Action?:

Directions: Write <u>Yes</u> if the boldfaced verb shows action. Write <u>No</u> if the boldfaced verb does not show action.

1.   _____   Kenny **pitched** a ball.

2.   _____   She **tasted** the stew.

3.   _____   The stew **tastes** good.   233

K. Regular or Irregular:

Directions: Write the past and past participle in the blank. Then, answer the question.

1. (to paint) Yesterday, they ____**painted**____ a house.

   They have ____**painted**____ two houses on this street.

   To paint is a regular verb if you added *ed.* Is *to paint* a regular or an irregular verb? ____**regular**____

2. (to write) Yesterday, I ____**wrote**____ a letter.

   Glen has ____**written**____ his name on his baseball.

   To write is a regular verb if you added *ed.* Is *to write* a regular or an irregular verb? ____**irregular**____

L. Irregular Verbs:

Directions: Cross out any prepositional phrase(s). Underline the subject once and the verb or verb phrase twice.

1. <u>Larry</u> <u>had</u> (ate, **eaten**) earlier.

2. <u>Sharon</u> <u>may have</u> (went, **gone**) ~~with her family~~.

3. <u>Water</u> <u>was</u> (froze, **frozen**) ~~in the bucket~~.

4. The <u>king</u> <u>has</u> (**fallen**, fell) ~~off his horse~~.

5. <u>Have</u> <u>you</u> ever (rode, **ridden**) ~~on a city bus~~?

234

K.   Regular or Irregular:

   Directions: Write the past and past participle in the blank. Then,
                  answer the question.

1.   (to paint)   Yesterday, they _____ a house.

        They have _____ two houses on this street.

     To paint is a regular verb if you added *ed.* Is *to paint* a regular or
     an irregular verb? _____

2.   (to write)   Yesterday, I _____ a letter.

        Glen has _____ his name on his baseball.

     To write is a regular verb if you added *ed.* Is *to write* a regular or
     an irregular verb? _____

L. Irregular Verbs:

   Directions: Cross out any prepositional phrase(s). Underline the
                  subject once and the verb or verb phrase twice.

1.   Larry had (ate, eaten) earlier.

2.   Sharon may have (went, gone) with her family.

3.   Water was (froze, frozen) in the bucket.

4.   The king has (fallen, fell) off his horse.

5.   Have you ever (rode, ridden) on a city bus?

M. Tenses:

Directions: Write the tense of the boldfaced verb.

Remember: The tenses are *present*, *past*, and *future*.

1. ____**past**_____   Janet **walked** past me.

2. ____**future**_____   I **shall leave** soon.

3. ____**present**_____   Scott **loves** to eat.

4. ____**past**_____   That baby **smiled** at us.

5. ____**future**_____   Tara and Kent **will stay** home.

N. Subject/Verb Agreement:

Directions: Circle the correct verb.

1. Her aunt (make, **makes**) dolls.

2. That lamp (shine, **shines**) too brightly.

3. Misty and her dad (rides, **ride**) bikes together.

4. Several men (**meet**, meets) for breakfast.

5. Everyone (**is**, are) very friendly.

6. One ~~of their friends~~ (collect, **collects**) stamps.

M. Tenses:

Directions: Write the tense of the boldfaced verb.

Remember: The tenses are *present*, *past*, and *future*.

1. _____   Janet **walked** past me.

2. _____   I **shall leave** soon.

3. _____   Scott **loves** to eat.

4. _____   That baby **smiled** at us.

5. _____   Tara and Kent **will stay** home.

N. Subject/Verb Agreement:

Directions: Circle the correct verb.

1. Her aunt (make, makes) dolls.

2. That lamp (shine, shines) too brightly.

3. Misty and her dad (rides, ride) bikes together.

4. Several men (meet, meets) for breakfast.

5. Everyone (is, are) very friendly.

6. One of their friends (collect, collects) stamps.

A. Directions: Cross out the prepositional phrase in each sentence.
                     Then, underline the subject once and the verb twice.

1.   I ate two bowls ~~of cereal~~.

2.   A paper and crayons are ~~on the floor~~.

3.   Mrs. Jones washed two spoons and dried them.

4.   Do you want an ice cream cone?

5.   (You) Hold this ~~for me~~.

B. Directions: Write the contraction in the space provided.

1.   we have - ____**we've**____   4.   they will - _____**they'll**_____

2.   I am - _____**I'm**_____   5.   she is - _____**she's**_____

3.   has not - ____**hasn't**____   6.   should not - ____**shouldn't**____

C. Directions: Circle the correct word.

1.   (**It's**, Its) a very sad story.

2.   (You're, **Your**) dad is here for you.

3.   (**They're**, There, Their) planning a camping trip.

4.   (Can, **May**) I help you?

5.   I know (they're, there, **their**) grandmother.

238

A. Directions: Cross out the prepositional phrase in each sentence.
Then, underline the subject once and the verb twice.

1. I ate two bowls of cereal.

2. A paper and crayons are on the floor.

3. Mrs. Jones washed two spoons and dried them.

4. Do you want an ice cream cone?

5. Hold this for me.

B. Directions: Write the contraction in the space provided.

1. we have - _____

2. I am - _____

3. has not - _____

4. they will - _____

5. she is - _____

6. should not - _____

C. Directions: Circle the correct word.

1. (It's, Its) a very sad story.

2. (You're, Your) dad is here for you.

3. (They're, There, Their) planning a camping trip.

4. (Can, May) I help you?

5. I know (they're, there, their) grandmother.

D. Directions: Write <u>Yes</u> if the boldfaced verb shows action. Write <u>No</u> if the boldfaced verb does not show action.

1. __**Yes**__   Rob **paddles** a canoe.

2. __**No**__   An ostrich **is** a fast bird.

E. Directions: Write <u>RV</u> if the verb is regular and <u>IV</u> if the verb is irregular.

1. __**IV**__   to do   2. __**RV**__   to walk

F. Directions: Circle the correct verb.

1. Dad must have (ate, **eaten**) all of the chips.

2. Lenny has (went, **gone**) to a horse show.

3. The child should have (gave, **given**) me the note.

4. A fork had (**fallen**, fell) into the trash.

G. Directions: Write the tense (*present*, *past*, or *future*) of the boldfaced verb.

1. __**future**__   He **will** not **stop**.

2. __**present**__   Jana and Jody **are** twins.

3. __**past**__   The car **stopped** suddenly.

H. Directions: Circle the correct verb.

1. My sister and I (wants, **want**) dessert.

2. A rose (**opens**, open) slowly.

3. They always (**drink**, drinks) milk for lunch.

240

D. Directions: Write <u>Yes</u> if the boldfaced verb shows action. Write <u>No</u> if the boldfaced verb does not show action.

1. _____ Rob **paddles** a canoe.

2. _____ An ostrich **is** a fast bird.

E. Directions: Write <u>RV</u> if the verb is regular and <u>IV</u> if the verb is irregular.

1. _____ to do 2. _____ to walk

F. Directions: Circle the correct verb.

1. Dad must have (ate, eaten) all of the chips.

2. Lenny has (went, gone) to a horse show.

3. The child should have (gave, given) me the note.

4. A fork had (fallen, fell) into the trash.

G. Directions: Write the tense (*present*, *past*, or *future*) of the boldfaced verb.

1. _____ He **will** not **stop**.

2. _____ Jana and Jody **are** twins.

3. _____ The car **stopped** suddenly.

H. Directions: Circle the correct verb.

1. My sister and I (wants, want) dessert.

2. A rose (opens, open) slowly.

3. They always (drink, drinks) milk for lunch. 241

TO THE TEACHER:

This adjective unit is limited to descriptive adjectives, the limiting adjectives, *a*, *an*, and *the*, and those that tell *how many*, plus a brief discussion of degrees. A more complete unit is included in the ensuing text, *Easy Grammar: Grade 4*.

Adjectives

Most adjectives are describing words.

A red ball is on the long table.

First, find the things you can see in the sentence. These are nouns.

You can see a ball and a table.

Is there a word that describes ball?   **RED** ball

Is there a word that describes table?   **LONG** table

Red and **long** are adjectives.

🐢 🐢 🐢 🐢 🐢 🐢 🐢 🐢 🐢 🐢 🐢 🐢 🐢 🐢 🐢 🐢 🐢 🐢

Directions: Write an adjective that can describe each noun.
ANSWERS WILL VARY.

Example: _____**smart**_____ girl

1. _____**white**_____ bread   7. _____**chicken**_____ soup

2. _____**breakable**_____ toy   8. _____**cardboard**_____ box

3. _____**sour**_____ milk   9. _____**willow**_____ tree

4. _____**big**_____ house   10. _____**sports**_____ car

5. _____**shy**_____ boy   11. _____**colorful**_____ rock

6. _____**good**_____ friend   12. _____**sharpened**_____ pencil

Name_____

Date_____

Most adjectives are describing words.

A red ball is on the long table.

First, find the things you can see in the sentence. These are nouns.

You can see a ball and a table.

Is there a word that describes ball?   **RED** ball

Is there a word that describes table?   **LONG** table

Red and *long* are adjectives.

🐢 🐢 🐢 🐢 🐢 🐢 🐢 🐢 🐢 🐢 🐢 🐢 🐢 🐢 🐢 🐢 🐢 🐢

Directions: Write an adjective that can describe each noun.

Example: _____**smart**_____ girl

1. _____ bread   7. _____ soup

2. _____ toy   8. _____ box

3. _____ milk   9. _____ tree

4. _____ house   10. _____ car

5. _____ boy   11. _____ rock

6. _____ friend   12. _____ pencil

245

Name_____   **ADJECTIVES**

WORKBOOK PAGE 113

Date_____

<u>Note to Teacher:</u>   <u>Lines for placing adjectives have been spaced. However, this may</u>
<u>be an excellent place to teach the rule for commas between more than one adjective.</u>

Rule: If two describing adjectives precede a noun, place a comma between the
          adjectives.   However, if one adjective is a color, a number, or is a closely-related
          word, do not place a comma.)   Examples: **funny, happy child**
                                                      tiny red ball   (no comma)
                                                      one hot day   (no comma)
                                                      large oak tree   (no comma)

Most adjectives are describing words.

A large, furry bear lives in that dark cave.

First, find the things you can see in the sentence. These are **nouns**.

You can see a **bear** and a **cave**.

Sometimes, **more than one word** will describe a noun.

Two words describe bear: **large** bear   **furry** bear

Only one word describes cave: **dark** cave

Large, *furry*, and *dark* are **adjectives**.

🐢🐢🐢🐢🐢🐢🐢🐢🐢🐢🐢🐢🐢🐢🐢🐢🐢🐢

Directions: Write two adjectives that can describe each noun.

ANSWERS WILL VARY.

Example: ___**little**___   ___**green**___   bug

1.   ___**white**___   ___**fluffy**___   rabbit

2.   ___**pretty**___   ___**pink**___   flower

3.   ___**tall**___   ___**smiling**___   lady

4.   ___**brick**___   ___**school**___   building

5.   ___**cute**___   ___**cuddly**___   baby

6.   ___**tiny**___   ___**funny**___   monkey

7.   ___**huge**___   ___**whaling**___   boat

246

Name_____

Date_____

Most adjectives are describing words.

A large, furry bear lives in that dark cave.

First, find the things you can see in the sentence. These are **nouns**.
You can see a **bear** and a **cave**.

Sometimes, **more than one word** will describe a noun.
Two words describe bear: **large** bear   **furry** bear

Only one word describes cave: **dark** cave

Large, *furry*, and *dark* are **adjectives**.

🐢🐢🐢🐢🐢🐢🐢🐢🐢🐢🐢🐢🐢🐢🐢🐢🐢🐢

Directions: Write two adjectives that can describe each noun.

Example: __**little**__ __**green**__ bug

1. _____ _____ rabbit

2. _____ _____ flower

3. _____ _____ lady

4. _____ _____ building

5. _____ _____ baby

6. _____ _____ monkey

7. _____ _____ boat

Name_____   **ADJECTIVES**

WORKBOOK PAGE 114

Date_____

Note to Teacher: I recommend that prior to doing this page, you model using an animal such as a raccoon. Lead students to understand that a word such as *playful* is an adjective, but *playing in the bushes* tells what the animal is doing. Also, explain that if they were to write *black eyes, black* describes eyes, not the entire animal. (However, for this exercise, I would certainly accept the answer. Our purpose is to create describing words.)

Give ample time for students to draw and color pictures. Point out what to write on the lines and double lines. Due to lack of space, no example has been provided.

Most adjectives are describing words.

Directions: Draw a picture of a forest with at least two animals in it.
Color your picture.

DRAWINGS WILL VARY.

🐢🐢🐢🐢🐢🐢🐢🐢🐢🐢🐢🐢🐢🐢🐢🐢🐢🐢🐢🐢

ANSWERS WILL VARY.

Directions: On the top lines, write two animals you drew in your forest.
On the double lines, write adjectives that describe each animal.

deer	squirrel
small	gray
quiet	playful
brown	noisy

248

Name_____   **ADJECTIVES**

Date_____

Most adjectives are describing words.

Directions: Draw a picture of a forest with at least two animals in it.
Color your picture.

🐢 🐢 🐢 🐢 🐢 🐢 🐢 🐢 🐢 🐢 🐢 🐢 🐢 🐢 🐢 🐢 🐢 🐢

Directions: On the top lines, write two animals you drew in your forest.
On the double lines, write adjectives that describe each animal.

_____   _____

\=\=\=\=\=\=\=\=\=\=\=\=\=\=   \=\=\=\=\=\=\=\=\=\=\=\=\=\=

\=\=\=\=\=\=\=\=\=\=\=\=\=\=   \=\=\=\=\=\=\=\=\=\=\=\=\=\=

\=\=\=\=\=\=\=\=\=\=\=\=\=\=   \=\=\=\=\=\=\=\=\=\=\=\=\=\=

\=\=\=\=\=\=\=\=\=\=\=\=\=\=   \=\=\=\=\=\=\=\=\=\=\=\=\=\=

249

<u>**Note to teacher:**</u> **Before teaching this lesson, ascertain that students truly comprehend *vowels* and *consonants*.**

Articles are special adjectives. A, *an*, and *the* are articles.

They do not describe. They are called limiting adjectives.

Rules for using *a*, *an*, and *the*.

> A.   **Use <u>the</u> before words beginning with both vowels and consonants.**
>
> B.   **Use <u>an</u> before words beginning with a vowel.**
>
>> an **a**pple
>> an **e**gg
>> an **i**ce cream cone
>> an **o**strich
>> an **u**mbrella
>
> C.   **Use <u>a</u> before words beginning with a consonant.**
>
>> a dollar   a flag   a zebra

🐢🐢🐢🐢🐢🐢🐢🐢🐢🐢🐢🐢🐢🐢🐢🐢🐢🐢

A.   Directions: Write <u>a</u> or <u>an</u> before each word.

1.	<u>**an**</u> arm	5.	<u>**a**</u> storm	9.	<u>**a**</u> bridge
2.	<u>**a**</u> chance	6.	<u>**an**</u> elephant	10.	<u>**an**</u> inn
3.	<u>**an**</u> elk	7.	<u>**an**</u> afternoon	11.	<u>**an**</u> urn
4.	<u>**an**</u> icicle	8.	<u>**an**</u> open door	12.	<u>**a**</u> shower

B.   Directions: Read each sentence. Circle each article. Then, reread the sentence and circle any describing adjectives.

1.   **The** doll has **glass** eyes.

2.   **An** otter is **a fast** swimmer.

Articles are special adjectives. *A*, *an*, and *the* **are articles.**
They do not describe. They are called limiting adjectives.

Rules for using *a*, *an*, and *the*.

A. **Use the before words beginning with both vowels and
     consonants.**

B. **Use an before words beginning with a vowel.**

> an **a**pple
> an **e**gg
> an **i**ce cream cone
> an **o**strich
> an **u**mbrella

C. **Use a before words beginning with a consonant.**

> a dollar   a flag   a zebra

🐢🐢🐢🐢🐢🐢🐢🐢🐢🐢🐢🐢🐢🐢🐢🐢🐢🐢🐢

A. Directions: Write a or an before each word.

1. _____ arm   5. _____ storm   9. _____ bridge

2. _____ chance   6. _____ elephant   10. _____ inn

3. _____ elk   7. _____ afternoon   11. _____ urn

4. _____ icicle   8. _____ open door   12. _____ shower

B. Directions: Read each sentence. Circle each article. Then, reread the
                  sentence and circle any describing adjectives.

1. The doll has glass eyes.

2. An otter is a fast swimmer.   251

WORKBOOK PAGE 116

Date_____

Most adjectives describe. Often, descriptive adjectives tell *what kind*.

> Examples: cherry pie
>
> What kind of pie?   cherry

A, *an*, and *the* are called limiting adjectives.

Some limiting adjectives tell *how many*.

> one icy road   How many?   one
>
> several cereal boxes   How many?   several

NUMBERS can be limiting adjectives that tell *how many*.

***Several*, *some*, *many*, *few*, *no*, and *any* can be limiting adjectives that tell *how many*.**

🐢 🐢 🐢 🐢 🐢 🐢 🐢 🐢 🐢 🐢 🐢 🐢 🐢 🐢 🐢 🐢 🐢 🐢

A.   Directions: Write a number that tells *how many*. The number is an adjective.

ANSWERS WILL VARY.

> Example: _____**one**_____ bird

1. _____**two**_____ socks   3. _____**three**_____ dimes

2. _____**seventeen**_____ days   4. _____**fifty**_____ hours

B.   Directions: Write *several*, *some*, *many*, *few*, *no*, or *any* on each line. These words that tell *how many* serve as adjectives.

ANSWERS WILL VARY.

1. ____**several**____ dollars   3. _____**no**_____ money

2. _____**many**_____ boys   4. _____**few**_____ people

252

Most adjectives describe. Often, descriptive adjectives tell *what kind*.

        Examples: cherry pie

                What kind of pie?   cherry

***A*, *an*, and *the* are called limiting adjectives.**
Some limiting adjectives tell *how many*.

    one icy road   How many?   one
    several cereal boxes   How many?   several

NUMBERS can be limiting adjectives that tell *how many*.

***Several*, *some*, *many*, *few*, *no*, and *any* can be limiting adjectives that tell *how many*.**

A.   Directions: Write a number that tells *how many*. The number is an adjective.

      Example: _____**one**_____ bird

1. _____ socks   3. _____ dimes

2. _____ days   4. _____ hours

B.   Directions: Write *several*, *some*, *many*, *few*, *no*, or *any* on each line. These words that tell *how many* serve as adjectives.

1. _____ dollars   3. _____ money

2. _____ boys   4. _____ people

Name_____

Date_____

Most adjectives describe. Often, descriptive adjectives tell *what kind*.

       Examples: race car

                 What kind of car?   race

A, *an*, and *the* are called limiting adjectives.
Some limiting adjectives tell *how many*.

    two shoes   How many?   two

    many men   How many?   many

NUMBERS can be limiting adjectives that tell *how many*.

Several*, *some*, *many*, *few*, *no*,** and ***any can be limiting adjectives that tell *how many*.

Directions: Read each sentence. First, circle *a, an,* or *the*. Next, look
               for words that tell *how many*. Then, circle any describing
               adjectives.

1.   **A strong** wind blew **the palm** trees.

2.   **The short** man sat on **an old park** bench.

3.   **Three big** goats crossed **a troll** bridge.

4.   **Several tall** candles are on **the birthday** cake.

5.   **Four orange striped** balls bounced by me.

6.   **Many red** roses are growing in **a flower** garden.

254

Most adjectives describe. Often, descriptive adjectives tell *what kind.*

Examples: race car

What kind of car?   race

***A*, *an*, and *the* are called limiting adjectives.**
Some limiting adjectives tell *how many*.

two shoes   How many?   two
many men   How many?   many

NUMBERS can be limiting adjectives that tell *how many*.

Several*, *some*, *many*, *few*, *no*, and *any can be limiting adjectives that tell *how many*.

🐢 🐢 🐢 🐢 🐢 🐢 🐢 🐢 🐢 🐢 🐢 🐢 🐢 🐢 🐢 🐢 🐢 🐢 🐢

Directions: Read each sentence. First, circle *a, an,* or *the.* Next, look for words that tell *how many.* Then, circle any describing adjectives.

1.   A strong wind blew the palm trees.

2.   The short man sat on an old park bench.

3.   Three big goats crossed a troll bridge.

4.   Several tall candles are on the birthday cake.

5.   Four orange striped balls bounced by me.

6.   Many red roses are growing in a flower garden.   255

TO THE TEACHER:

PAGE 257 = WORKBOOK PAGE 118

Review syllables before teaching the comparative adjective lesson. I always recommend having students clap out syllables. Below is a list of adjectives that you may want to "clap out" to determine number of syllables.

fast	pretty
funny	sensible
beautiful	talkative
gentle	cute
dumb	cuddly
fantastic	different
happy	dangerous
remarkable	reversible

Review the rule that a one-syllable word ending in CVC (consonant-vowel-consonant) will double the final consonant **if** the suffix (ending) begins with a **vowel**.

big - bigger   (biggest)

happy - happier   (happiest)

Review the rule that a one-syllable word ending in **e** will drop the *e* when adding a suffix (ending) that begins with a **vowel**.

cute - cuter   (cutest)

tame - tamer   (tamest)

Be sure to teach students to use a dictionary to help determine if a two-syllable word should add er(est).

Note: If the adjective should add er and est, they will appear in the entry.

shiny (shīn) - *adj.* **shinier, shiniest**

256

Adjectives can make comparisons.

The comparative form compares two items.

Example: big   -   bigger

The pan is big, but the kettle is bigger.

Here, a *pan* and a *kettle* (2 items) are being compared in size.

THERE ARE SEVERAL WAYS TO FORM THE COMPARATIVE:

Add er to most one-syllable adjectives.
small - smaller
This bee is smaller than that bug.

Add er to some two-syllable adjectives.
happy - happier
After the game, Adam was happier than his sister.

Place more (or less) before some two-syllable adjectives.
trusting - more trusting
Our beagle is more trusting than our poodle.

Place more (or less) before adjectives of three or more syllables.
beautiful - more beautiful
Of the two gowns, the satin one is more beautiful.

Some adjectives totally change forms when comparing two items.
good - better   bad - worse
She is a better painter than her brother.

257

Adjectives can make comparisons.

The comparative form compares two items.

🐢 **Add er to most one-syllable adjectives.**
dumb - dumber

🐢 **Add er to some two-syllable adjectives.**
funny - funnier

🐢 **Place more (or less) before some two-syllable adjectives.**
loving - more loving

🐢 **Place more (or less) before adjectives of three or more syllables.**
fantastic - more fantastic

🐢 **Some adjectives totally change forms when comparing two items.**
good - better   *bad - worse*

🐢🐢🐢🐢🐢🐢🐢🐢🐢🐢🐢🐢🐢🐢🐢🐢🐢🐢🐢

A.   Directions: Write the comparative form (for comparing two items).
     Remember: Use a dictionary if necessary.

1.   fast - _____**faster**_____   3.   patient - _____**more patient**_____

2.   tiny - _____**tinier**_____   4.   bad - _____**worse**_____

B.   Directions: Circle the comparative form.

1.   Jill's left foot is (**smaller**, more small) than her right one.

2.   The gray kitten is (energeticer, **more energetic**) than the white one.

3.   She's (upseter, **more upset**) about losing her ring than her keys.

258

Adjectives can make comparisons.

The comparative form compares two items.

🐢 **Add er to most one-syllable adjectives.**
     dumb - dumber

🐢 **Add er to some two-syllable adjectives.**
     funny - funnier

🐢 **Place more (or less) before some two-syllable adjectives.**
     loving - more loving

🐢 **Place more (or less) before adjectives of three or more syllables.**
     fantastic - more fantastic

🐢 **Some adjectives totally change forms when comparing two items.**
     good - better   bad - worse

🐢 🐢 🐢 🐢 🐢 🐢 🐢 🐢 🐢 🐢 🐢 🐢 🐢 🐢 🐢 🐢 🐢 🐢

A.   Directions: Write the comparative form (for comparing two items).
     Remember: Use a dictionary if necessary.

1.   fast - _____   3.   patient - _____

2.   tiny - _____   4.   bad - _____

B.   Directions: Circle the comparative form.

1.   Jill's left foot is (smaller, more small) than her right one.

2.   The gray kitten is (energeticer, more energetic) than the white one.

3.   She's (upseter, more upset) about losing her ring than her keys.

259

PAGE 261 = WORKBOOK PAGE 120

Adjectives can make comparisons.

The superlative form compares three or more items.

Example: tall - tallest

Of the three girls, Molly is tallest.

Molly and two other girls are being compared.

THERE ARE SEVERAL WAYS TO FORM THE SUPERLATIVE:

🐢 **Add <u>est</u> to most one-syllable adjectives.**

long - longest

Of the four tables, the wooden one is longest.

🐢 **Add <u>est</u> to some two-syllable adjectives.**

pretty - prettiest

This is the prettiest dress in the store.

🐢 **Place most (or least) before some two-syllable adjectives.**

patient - most patient

Mrs. Kent is the most patient person I know.

🐢 **Place most (or least) before adjectives of three or more syllables.**

delicious - most delicious

All of the pies are delicious, but your apple pie is most delicious.

🐢 **Some adjectives totally change forms when comparing three or more items.**

good - best   bad - worst

"I am the worst speller in our family," said Anne.   261

Adjectives can make comparisons.
The superlative form compares three or more items.

- **Add <u>est</u> to most one-syllable adjectives.**
  dumb - dumbest

- **Add <u>est</u> to some two-syllable adjectives.**
  funny - funniest

- **Place most (or least) before some two-syllable adjectives.**
  loving - most loving

- **Place most (or least) before adjectives of three or more syllables.**
  fantastic - most fantastic

- **Some adjectives totally change forms when comparing two items.**
  good - best   *bad - worst*

A.   Directions: Write the superlative form (for comparing three or more items). **Remember: Use a dictionary if necessary.**

1.   kind - _____***kindest***_____   3.   timid - _____***most timid***_____

2.   quiet - _____***quietest***_____   4.   brilliant - _____***most brilliant***_____

B.   Directions: Circle the superlative form.

1.   Of the triplets, Jana is the (**hardest**, most hard) worker.

2.   When Scott told four jokes, his last one was (**funniest**, most funny).

3.   The runner's fifth jump was (perfectest, **most perfect**).

4.   Of the three teachers, Miss Henry is (understandingest, **most understanding**).

262

Adjectives can make comparisons.

The superlative form compares three or more items.

- Add <u>est</u> to most one-syllable adjectives.
    dumb - dumbest

- Add <u>est</u> to some two-syllable adjectives.
    funny - funniest

- Place most (or least) before some two-syllable adjectives.
    loving - most loving

- Place most (or least) before adjectives of three or more syllables.

    fantastic - most fantastic

- Some adjectives totally change forms when comparing two items.
    good - best   bad - worst

A. Directions: Write the superlative form (for comparing three or more items). **Remember: Use a dictionary if necessary.**

1. kind - _____   3. timid - _____

2. quiet - _____   4. brilliant - _____

B. Directions: Circle the superlative form.

1. Of the triplets, Jana is the (hardest, most hard) worker.

2. When Scott told four jokes, his last one was (funniest, most funny).

3. The runner's fifth jump was (perfectest, most perfect).

4. Of the three teachers, Miss Henry is (understandingest, most understanding).

The comparative form compares two items.

🐢 Add <u>er</u> to most one-syllable adjectives.   (tough - tougher)

🐢 Add <u>er</u> to some two-syllable adjectives. (icy - icier)

🐢 Place more (or less) before some two-syllable adjectives.
(unkind - more unkind)

🐢 Place more (or less) before adjectives of three or more syllables.   (different - more different)

🐢 Some adjectives totally change forms when comparing two items.   (good - better   bad - worse)

The superlative form compares three or more items.

🐢 Add <u>est</u> to most one-syllable adjectives.   (tough - toughest)

🐢 Add <u>est</u> to some two-syllable adjectives.   (icy - iciest)

🐢 Place most (or least) before some two-syllable adjectives.
(unkind - most unkind)

🐢 Place most (or least) before adjectives of three or more syllables.   (different - most different)

🐢 Some adjectives totally change forms when comparing two items.   (good - best   bad - worst)

🐢🐢🐢🐢🐢🐢🐢🐢🐢🐢🐢🐢🐢🐢🐢🐢🐢🐢

Directions: Circle the correct adjective form.

1.   Our first roller coaster ride was (**shorter**, shortest) than our second one.

2.   Clint is the (quieter, **quietest**) member of his family.

3.   Her serve is (**more powerful**, most powerful) than her backhand.

4.   Of all the dogs in the show, Troubles was the (noisier, **noisiest**).

264

Name_____

Date_____

The comparative form compares two items.

- Add **er** to most one-syllable adjectives.   (tough - tougher)

- Add **er** to some two-syllable adjectives.   (icy - icier)

- Place **more** (or **less**) before some two-syllable **adjectives.**
  (unkind - more unkind)

- Place **more** (or **less**) before adjectives of three or more
  syllables.   (different - more different)

- Some adjectives totally change forms when comparing
  two items.   (good - better   bad - worse)

The superlative form compares three or more items.

- Add **est** to most one-syllable adjectives.   (tough - toughest)

- Add **est** to some two-syllable adjectives.   (icy - iciest)

- Place **most** (or **least**) before some two-syllable **adjectives.**
  (unkind - most unkind)

- Place **most** (or **least**) before adjectives of three or more
  syllables.   (different - most different)

- Some adjectives totally change forms when comparing
  two items.   (good - best   bad - worst)

Directions: Circle the correct adjective form.

1. Our first roller coaster ride was (shorter, shortest) than our second one.

2. Clint is the (quieter, quietest) member of his family.

3. Her serve is (more powerful, most powerful) than her backhand.

4. Of all the dogs in the show, Troubles was the (noisier, noisiest).

265

A. Describing Words:
ANSWERS WILL VARY.

    Directions: Write two describing words for each noun.

1. ____**white**____   ____**frisky**____   mouse

2. ____**huge**____   ____**dented**____   van

3. ____**yellow**____   ____**ripe**____   banana

B. A, An, and The:

    Directions: Write *a* or *an* before each word or group of words.

1. __**a**__ bottle   4. __**an**__ end

2. __**an**__ ant   5. __**an**__ organ

3. __**a**__ grocery store   6. __**an**__ ice cream sundae

C. Limiting Adjectives:

    Directions: Fill in the blank.

1.   The articles that are always adjectives are __**a**__ , __**an**__ , and __**the**__ .
ANSWERS WILL VARY.

2.   Write an example of a number used as an adjective: __**five**__ pennies.

3.   Write adjectives that tell how many:

       s e v e r a l   **s o m e**   **m a n y**   **f e w**   **a n y**   **n o**

A.   Describing Words:

Directions: Write two describing words for each noun.

1.   _____   _____ mouse

2.   _____   _____ van

3.   _____   _____ banana

B.   A, An, and The:

Directions: Write *a* or *an* before each word or group of words.

1.   _____ bottle   4.   _____ end

2.   _____ ant   5.   _____ organ

3.   _____ grocery store   6.   _____ ice cream sundae

C.   Limiting Adjectives:

Directions: Fill in the blank.

1.   The articles that are always adjectives are _____, _____, and _____.

2.   Write an example of a number used as an adjective: _____ pennies.

3.   Write adjectives that tell how many:

   s e _ _ _ _ _   s o _ _   m _ _ _   f _ _   a _ _   n _

D.   Identifying Adjectives:

Directions: Circle each adjective.

Remember: *A*, *an*, and *the* are adjectives.

Numbers and words like **some**, **several**, **few**, **many**, **no**, and **any** can be limiting adjectives.

Most adjectives are describing words.

1.   Rex looked at **a gold** watch.

2.   **The old** car has **two flat** tires.

3.   She likes **peach** pie with **whipped** cream.

4.   **Several little** puppies slept in **an orange** basket.

5.   **Some** kittens have **blue** eyes and **soft** whiskers.

E.   Degrees of Adjectives:

Directions: Circle the correct form.

1.   Mike's new bike is (**bigger**, biggest) than his old one.

2.   This pink mattress is (**firmer**, more firm) that the blue one.

3.   My aunt is (**more athletic**, most athletic) than my mother.

4.   Janell chose the (more colorful, **most colorful**) blouse on the rack.

5.   Of the two coats, the short one has the (**better**, best) price.

268

D. Identifying Adjectives:

Directions: Circle each adjective.
Remember: *A*, *an*, and *the* are adjectives.

Numbers and words like *some*, *several*, *few*, *many*, *no*, and *any* can be limiting adjectives.

Most adjectives are describing words.

1. Rex looked at a gold watch.

2. The old car has two flat tires.

3. She likes peach pie with whipped cream.

4. Several little puppies slept in an orange basket.

5. Some kittens have blue eyes and soft whiskers.

E.   Degrees of Adjectives:

Directions: Circle the correct form.

1. Mike's new bike is (bigger, biggest) than his old one.

2. This pink mattress is (firmer, more firm) that the blue one.

3. My aunt is (more athletic, most athletic) than my mother.

4. Janell chose the (more colorful, most colorful) blouse on the rack.

5. Of the two coats, the short one has the (better, best) price.

Name_____   **Adjective Test**

Date_____

A. Directions: Write <u>a</u> or <u>an</u> before each word.

1. __**an**__ orange   3. __**an**__ apple   5. __**an**__ eye

2. __**a**__ pancake   4. __**a**__ tent   6. __**an**__ umbrella

B. Directions: Circle each adjective.

1. **A few wild** geese flew over **the** lake.

2. **The old** house needs **a new** roof.

3. Brent likes **mystery** books and **animal** stories.

4. **Three young** girls rode **small** ponies.

5. **The young** woman ordered **an egg** sandwich.

C. Directions: Circle the correct form.

1. The green jello is (more firm, **firmer**) than the red jello.

2. Joyann is the (**shorter**, shortest) twin.

3. His red car was the (cleaner, **cleanest**) one in the parking lot.

4. The second test was (badder, **worse**) than the first one.

5. Of all the pictures in the album, Grandma's wedding picture is (lovelier, **loveliest**).

270

Name_____ **Adjective Test**

Date_____

A. Directions: Write <u>a</u> or <u>an</u> before each word.

1. _____ orange   3. _____ apple   5. _____ eye

2. _____ pancake   4. _____ tent   6. _____ umbrella

B. Directions: Circle each adjective.

1. A few wild geese flew over the lake.

2. The old house needs a new roof.

3. Brent likes mystery books and animal stories.

4. Three young girls rode small ponies.

5. The young woman ordered an egg sandwich.

C. Directions: Circle the correct form.

1. The green jello is (more firm, firmer) than the red jello.

2. Joyann is the (shorter, shortest) twin.

3. His red car was the (cleaner, cleanest) one in the parking lot.

4. The second test was (badder, worse) than the first one.

5. Of all the pictures in the album, Grandma's wedding picture is (lovelier, loveliest.)
271

A.   List of Prepositions:
    Directions: List the twenty-eight prepositions that you have learned.

1. ab **o v e**

2. ac **r o s s**

3. af **t e r**

4. ar **o u n d**

5. a **t**

6. be **f o r e**

7. be **h i n d**

8. be **l o w**

9. be **s i d e**

10. be **t w e e n**

11. b **y**

12. d **o w n**

13. du **r i n g**

14. f **o r**

15. fr **o m**

16. i **n**

17. in **s i d e**

18. in **t o**

19. **o f**

20. **o f f**

21. **o n**

22. **o u t**

23. **o v e r**

24. th **r o u g h**

25. t **o**

26. **u n d e r**

27. u **p**

28. w **i t h**

A.   List of Prepositions:

Directions: List the twenty-eight prepositions that you have learned.

1. <u>ab</u> _ _ _   15. <u>f</u>_ _ _

2. <u>ac</u> _ _ _ _   16. <u>i</u>_

3. <u>af</u> _ _ _   17. <u>in</u> _ _ _ _

4. <u>ar</u> _ _ _ _   18. <u>in</u> _ _

5. <u>a</u>_   19. <u>o</u>_

6. <u>be</u> _ _ _ _   20. <u>o</u>_ _

7. <u>be</u> _ _ _ _   21. <u>o</u>_

8. <u>be</u> _ _ _   22. <u>o</u>_ _

9. <u>be</u> _ _ _ _   23. <u>o</u> _ _ _

10. <u>be</u> _ _ _ _ _   24. <u>th</u> _ _ _ _ _

11. <u>b</u>_   25. <u>t</u>_

12. <u>d</u>_ _ _   26. <u>u</u>_ _ _ _

13. <u>du</u> _ _ _ _   27. <u>u</u>_

14. <u>f</u>_ _   28. <u>w</u>_ _ _   273

B. Compound Subject and Compound Verb:

Directions: Cross out the prepositional phrase in each sentence.
Then, underline the subject once and the verb twice.

Remember: The subject or verb will not be a word in a prepositional phrase.

1. <u>Craig</u> and his <u>mother</u> <u>went</u> ~~to the beach~~.

2. <u>Hannah</u> <u>lay</u> ~~in a chair~~ and <u>read</u> a magazine.

C. Imperative Sentence:

Directions: Cross out the prepositional phrase in each sentence.
Then, underline the subject once and the verb twice.

Remember: An imperative sentence gives a command.

1. (<u>You</u>) <u>Hang</u> this ~~on the wall~~.

2. (<u>You</u>) ~~After lunch~~, <u>meet</u> me ~~by that tree~~.

D. It's/Its They're/There/Their You're/Your:

Directions: Circle the correct word.

1. (**It's**, Its) two o'clock.

2. (They're, **There**, Their) are five fish in this bowl.

3. Do you know if (**you're**, your) in the next race?

4. (**They're**, There, Their) writing a letter to a pen pal.

274

B. Compound Subject and Compound Verb:

Directions: Cross out the prepositional phrase in each sentence.
Then, underline the subject once and the verb twice.

Remember: **The subject or verb will not be a word in a prepositional phrase.**

1.   Craig and his mother went to the beach.

2.   Hannah lay in a chair and read a magazine.

C. Imperative Sentence:

Directions: Cross out the prepositional phrase in each sentence.
Then, underline the subject once and the verb twice.

Remember: **An imperative sentence gives a command.**

1.   Hang this on the wall.

2.   After lunch, meet me by that tree.

D.   It's/Its   They're/There/Their   You're/Your:

Directions: Circle the correct word.

1.   (It's, Its) two o'clock.

2.   (They're, There, Their) are five fish in this bowl.

3.   Do you know if (you're, your) in the next race?

4.   (They're, There, Their) writing a letter to a pen pal.

E.   Can/May:

   Directions: Circle the correct word.

1.   (Can, **May**) I be excused?

2.   (**Can**, May) you untie this for me?

3.   She (can, **may**) be arriving soon.

F.   Contractions:

   Directions: Write the contraction in the space provided.

1.   I will - _____**I'll**_____   10.   is not - _____**isn't**_____

2.   who is - _____**who's**_____   11.   they are - _____**they're**_____

3.   cannot - _____**can't**_____   12.   are not - _____**aren't**_____

4.   here is - _____**here's**_____   13.   will not - _____**won't**_____

5.   you are - _____**you're**_____   14.   what is - _____**what's**_____

6.   there is - _____**there's**_____   15.   they will - _____**they'll**_____

7.   it is- _____**it's**_____   16.   do not - _____**don't**_____

8.   they will - _____**they'll**_____   17.   what is - _____**what's**_____

9.   I am - _____**I'm**_____   18.   we are - _____**we're**_____

276

E.   Can/May:

Directions: Circle the correct word.

1.   (Can, May) I be excused?

2.   (Can, May) you untie this for me?

3.   She (can, may) be arriving soon.

F.   Contractions:

Directions: Write the contraction in the space provided.

1. I will - _____	10. is not - _____
2. who is - _____	11. they are - _____
3. cannot - _____	12. are not - _____
4. here is - _____	13. will not - _____
5. you are - _____	14. what is - _____
6. there is - _____	15. they will - _____
7. it is- _____	16. do not - _____
8. they will - _____	17. what is - _____
9. I am - _____	18. we are - _____

WORKBOOK PAGE 128   **Adjectives**
Date_____

G.   State of Being:

Directions: Underline the subject once and the verb twice. Label the
direct object - D.O.

Remember: The direct object receives the action of the verb.

D.O.
Example: Her <u>mom</u> <u>paints</u> cars.   The **object** her mom paints is *cars*.

D.O.
1.   <u>She</u> <u>packs</u> her lunch.

D.O.
2.   <u>Gary</u> <u>blew</u> bubbles.

D.O.
3.   The <u>doorman</u> <u>opened</u> the door.

H.   Helping (Auxiliary) Verbs:

Directions: List the twenty-three helping verbs.

d<u>o</u>_____   h<u>as</u>_____   m<u>ay</u>_____   c<u>ould</u>_____   c<u>an</u>_____   i<u>s</u>_____   w<u>ere</u>_____

d<u>oes</u>_____   h<u>ave</u>_____   m<u>ight</u>_____   sh<u>ould</u>_____   sh<u>all</u>_____   am_____   be_____

d<u>id</u>_____   h<u>ad</u>_____   m<u>ust</u>_____   w<u>ould</u>_____   will_____   a<u>re</u>_____   b<u>eing</u>_____

w<u>as</u>_____   b<u>een</u>_____

I.   Action?:

Directions: Write <u>Yes</u> if the boldfaced verb shows action. Write <u>No</u> if
the boldfaced verb does not show action.

1.   __**Yes**__   Miss Land **handed** me a pencil.

2.   __**Yes**__   Mom **looked** at her shopping list.

3.   __**No**__   This shirt **looks** dirty.

278

G. State of Being:

Directions: Underline the subject once and the verb twice. Label the
             direct object - D.O.

Remember: The direct object receives the action of the verb.

                              D.O.
Example: Her <u>mom</u> <u>paints</u> cars.   The **object** her mom paints is *cars*.

1. She packs her lunch.

2. Gary blew bubbles.

3. The doorman opened the door.

H. Helping (Auxiliary) Verbs:

Directions: List the twenty-three helping verbs.

d_____   h_____   m_____   c_____   c_____   i____   w_____

d_____   h_____   m_____   sh____   sh____   a____   b_____

d_____   h_____   m_____   w_____   w_____   a____   b_____

                                                        w____   b_____

I. Action?:

Directions: Write <u>Yes</u> if the boldfaced verb shows action. Write <u>No</u> if
             the boldfaced verb does not show action.

1. _____   Miss Land **handed** me a pencil.

2. _____   Mom **looked** at her shopping list.

3. _____   This shirt **looks** dirty.   279

J.   Regular or Irregular:

Directions: Write the past and past participle in the blank. Then, answer the question.

Review: (to jump) Yesterday, we ____**jumped**____ rope.

I had ____**jumped**____ ten minutes before missing.

To jump is a regular verb if you added *ed.* Is *to jump* a regular or an irregular verb? ____**regular**____

Directions: Write RV in the blank if the verb is regular. Write IV if the verb is irregular.

1. __**RV**__ to slap   3. __**IV**__ to break   5. __**RV**__ to cry

2. __**IV**__ to ride   4. __**IV**__ to ring   6. __**IV**__ to sit

K.   Irregular Verbs:

Directions: Cross out any prepositional phrase(s). Underline the subject once and the verb or verb phrase twice.

1.   Our balloons have (**burst**, busted).

2.   Max may have (went, **gone**) with his grandpa.

3.   Mrs. Gant must have (**written**, wrote) to the mayor.

4.   You should have (did, **done**) your homework before dinner.

5.   Has Millie ever (gave, **given**) you a birthday card?

280

J. Regular or Irregular:

Directions: Write the past and past participle in the blank. Then, answer the question.

Review: (to jump)   Yesterday, we _____ rope.

I had _____ ten minutes before missing.

To jump is a regular verb if you added *ed.* Is *to jump* a regular or an irregular verb? _____

Directions: Write <u>RV</u> in the blank if the verb is regular. Write <u>IV</u> if the verb is irregular.

1. _____ to slap   3. _____ to break   5. _____ to cry

2. _____ to ride   4. _____ to ring   6. _____ to sit

K. Irregular Verbs:

Directions: Cross out any prepositional phrase(s). Underline the subject once and the verb or verb phrase twice.

1.   Our balloons have (burst, busted).

2.   Max may have (went, gone) with his grandpa.

3.   Mrs. Gant must have (written, wrote) to the mayor.

4.   You should have (did, done) your homework before dinner.

5.   Has Millie ever (gave, given) you a birthday card?

L. Tenses:

Directions: Write the tense of the boldfaced verb.

Remember: The tenses are ***present***, ***past***, and ***future***.

1. _____**future**_____   Tonight, I **shall bake** cookies.

2. _____**past**_____   A bell **rang**.

3. _____**present**_____   Connie **rides** her horse every day.

4. _____**past**_____   The workers **poured** concrete.

M.   Subject/Verb Agreement:

Directions: Circle the correct verb.

1.   I (**like**, likes) to play games.

2.   Some flowers (**open**, opens) only during the day.

3.   Pam and her friend (draws, **draw**) cartoons.

4.   Each ~~of your buttons~~ (**is**, are) missing.

N.   Common and Proper Noun:
Directions: Write a proper noun for each common noun.
ANSWERS WILL VARY.

1.   lake -_____**Laurel Lake**_____   3.   state -_____**Minnesota**_____

2.   person -_____**Jack**_____   4.   store -_____**Country Store**_____

L. Tenses:

Directions: Write the tense of the boldfaced verb.

Remember: The tenses are ***present***, ***past***, and ***future***.

1. _____   Tonight, I **shall bake** cookies.

2. _____   A bell **rang**.

3. _____   Connie **rides** her horse every day.

4. _____   The workers **poured** concrete.

M. Subject/Verb Agreement:

Directions: Circle the correct verb.

1. I (like, likes) to play games.

2. Some flowers (open, opens) only during the day.

3. Pam and her friend (draws, draw) cartoons.

4. Each of your buttons (is, are) missing.

N. Common and Proper Noun:

Directions: Write a proper noun for each common noun.

1. lake -_____   3. state -_____

2. person -_____   4. store - _____

O. Common or Proper Noun:

Directions: Write <u>C</u> if the noun is common; write <u>P</u> if the noun is proper.

1. __**C**__ BIRD   3. __**C**__ COUNTRY   5. __**C**__ VAN

2. __**C**__ PARROT   4. __**P**__ AMERICA   6. __**P**__ UTAH

P. Singular and Plural Nouns:

Directions: Write the plural.

1. latch - _____**latches**_____   10. curb - _____**curbs**_____

2. name - _____**names**_____   11. box - _____**boxes**_____

3. dish - _____**dishes**_____   12. gulf - _____**gulfs**_____

4. glass - _____**glasses**_____   13. deer - _____**deer**_____

5. mouse - _____**mice**_____   14. ox - _____**oxen**_____

6. potato - _____**potatoes**_____   15. child - _____**children**_____

7. goose - _____**geese**_____   16. flea - _____**fleas**_____

8. story - _____**stories**_____   17. play - _____**plays**_____

9. calf - _____**calves**_____   18. moose - _____**moose**_____

Name_____   **Cumulative Review**
Adjectives

Date_____

O. Common or Proper Nouns:

Directions: Write C if the noun is common. Write P if the noun is proper.

1. _____ BIRD   3. _____ COUNTRY   5. _____ VAN

2. _____ PARROT   4. _____ AMERICA   6. _____ UTAH

P. Singular and Plural Nouns:

Directions: Write the plural.

1. latch - _____

2. name - _____

3. dish - _____

4. glass - _____

5. mouse - _____

6. potato - _____

7. goose - _____

8. story - _____

9. calf - _____

10. curb - _____

11. box - _____

12. gulf - _____

13. deer - _____

14. ox - _____

15. child - _____

16. flea - _____

17. play - _____

18. moose - _____

Q.   Possessive Nouns:

Directions: Write the possessive.

1.   a pet belonging to Kyle - _____**Kyle's pet**_____

2.   cats belonging to Mr. Bond - _____**Mr. Bond's cats**_____

3.   a ball shared by four girls - _____**girls' ball**_____

4.   a hotel room shared by more than one woman - **women's hotel room**

R.   Noun Identification:

Directions: Circle any nouns.

Remember: A noun names a person, place, or thing.
Look for "things" you can see.

1.   Three **cows** stood by an old **fence.**

2.   **Bob** and his **dad** run in the **park.**

3.   **Karen** put **bread** into the **toaster.**

4.   Your **ring** and **bracelet** are on the **chair.**

5.   A **basket** of **strawberries** is by our front **door.**

Q. Possessive Nouns:

   Directions: Write the possessive.

1. a pet belonging to Kyle - _____

2. cats belonging to Mr. Bond - _____

3. a ball shared by four girls - _____

4. a hotel room shared by more than one woman - _____

R.   Noun Identification:

   Directions: Circle any nouns.

   Remember: A noun names a person, place, or thing.
               Look for "things" you can see.

1. Three cows stood by an old fence.

2. Bob and his dad run in the park.

3. Karen put bread into the toaster.

4. Your ring and bracelet are on the chair.

5. A basket of strawberries is by our front door.

Name_____ **Cumulative Test**
Adjectives

Date_____

Note to Teacher: **Although this test is four pages, it requires very little writing. Students should not need more than twenty minutes to complete it.**

A. Directions: Cross out the prepositional phrase in each sentence. Then, underline the subject once and the verb twice.

1. A <u>fox</u> <u>lives</u> ~~in that hole~~.

2. Two <u>cars</u> and a <u>truck</u> <u>pulled</u> ~~into the driveway~~.

3. <u>(You)</u> <u>Put</u> the broom ~~by the back door~~.

4. <u>Did</u> <u>you</u> <u>write</u> your name ~~above the date~~?

5. <u>Craig</u> <u>packed</u> boxes and <u>set</u> them ~~on a wagon~~.

B. Directions: Write the contraction in the space provided.

1. I will - _____**I'll**_____   4. we are - _____**we're**_____

2. is not - _____**isn't**_____   5. cannot - _____**can't**_____

3. what is - _____**what's**_____   6. they are - _____**they're**_____

C. Directions: Circle the correct word.

1. I don't know if (**it's**, its) time to eat.

2. (**You're**, Your) a good basketball player.

3. (**They're**, There, Their) not ready.

4. You (can, **may**) get a drink.

5. Cassie and Dora want to bring (they're, there, **their**) dog along.
288

A. Directions: Cross out the prepositional phrase in each sentence.
                                Then, underline the subject once and the verb twice.

1.   A fox lives in that hole.

2.   Two cars and a truck pulled into the driveway.

3.   Put the broom by the back door.

4.   Did you write your name above the date?

5.   Craig packed boxes and set them on a wagon.

B. Directions: Write the contraction in the space provided.

1.   I will - _____   4.   we were - _____

2.   is not - _____   5.   cannot - _____

3.   what is - _____   6.   they are - _____

C. Directions: Circle the correct word.

1.   I don't know if (it's, its) time to eat.

2.   (You're, Your) a good basketball player.

3.   (They're, There, Their) not ready.

4.   You (can, may) get a drink.

5.   Cassie and Dora want to bring (they're, there, their) dog along.

D. Directions: Write <u>Yes</u> if the boldfaced verb shows action. Write <u>No</u> if the boldfaced verb does not show action.

1. **Yes**   Heidi **swings** the bat too soon.

2. **No**   This bread **tastes** stale.

E. Directions: Circle the correct verb.

1. The hamster (**runs**, run) around in its cage.

2. Roses (**bloom**, blooms) for many months.

3. Ned and I (**hike**, hikes) nearly every Saturday.

F. Directions: Write <u>RV</u> if the verb is regular and <u>IV</u> if the verb is irregular.

1.   **IV**   to find   2.   **RV**   to live   3.   **RV**   to join

G. Directions: Underline the verb phrase twice.
    Reminder: Underlining the subject once may help you to find the verb phrase.

1. They **had chosen** white roses for their wedding.

2. These crackers **are broken** into many pieces.

3. I **have** not **received** my package.

H. Directions: Circle the correct verb.

1. She has (wrote, **written**) us a note.

2. That business has (**given**, give) coupons to its best customers.

290

D. Directions: Write <u>Yes</u> if the boldfaced verb shows action. Write <u>No</u> if the boldfaced verb does not show action.

1. _____ Heidi **swings** the bat too soon.

2. _____ This bread **tastes** stale.

E. Directions: Circle the correct verb.

1. The hamster (runs, run) around in its cage.

2. Roses (bloom, blooms) for many months.

3. Ned and I (hike, hikes) nearly every Saturday.

F. Directions: Write <u>RV</u> if the verb is regular and <u>IV</u> if the verb is irregular.

1. _____ to find   2. _____ to live   3. _____ to join

G. Directions: Underline the verb phrase twice.
   Reminder: Underlining the subject once may help you to find the verb phrase.

1. They had chosen white roses for their wedding.

2. These crackers are broken into many pieces.

3. I have not received my package.

H. Directions: Circle the correct verb.

1. She has (wrote, written) us a note.

2. That business has (given, give) coupons to its best customers.

291

3. The ladies have (**shaken**, shook) hands.

4. Several toys had been (broke, **broken**).

5. They had (drank, **drunk**) too much lemonade.

6. She has (**sung**, sang) for our President.

7. Her keys had been (stole, **stolen**).

8. You should have (brang, **brought**) your video games.

9. Miss Jones has (rode, **ridden**) in a helicopter.

10. Which was (**chosen**, chose) as the winner?

I. Directions: Write the tense (*present, past,* or *future*) of the boldfaced verb.

1. _____**present**_____ Loran often **sleeps** in a tent.

2. _____**past**_____ Both horses **galloped** fast.

3. _____**future**_____ He **will pick** you up at the airport .

4. _____**present**_____ They **gather** firewood each fall.

J. Directions: Write <u>C</u> if the noun is common. Write <u>P</u> if the noun is proper.

1. __**C**__ CITY   3. __**P**__ DALLAS

2. __**C**__ NEWSPAPER   4. __**C**__ CANARY

3. The ladies have (shaken, shook) hands.

4. Several toys had been (broke, broken).

5. They had (drank, drunk) too much lemonade.

6. She has (sung, sang) for our President.

7. Her keys had been (stole, stolen).

8. You should have (brang, brought) your video games.

9. Miss Jones has (rode, ridden) in a helicopter.

10. Which was (chosen, chose) as the winner?

I. Directions: Write the tense (*present*, *past*, or *future*) of the boldfaced verb.

1. _____ Loran often **sleeps** in a tent.

2. _____ Both horses **galloped** fast.

3. _____ He **will pick** you up at the airport.

4. _____ They **gather** firewood each fall.

J. Directions: Write <u>C</u> if the noun is common. Write <u>P</u> if the noun is proper.

1. _____ CITY   3. _____ DALLAS

2. _____ NEWSPAPER   4. _____ CANARY

K. Directions: Write the plural of each noun.

1. pass - _____**passes**_____   6. friend - _____**friends**_____

2. pan - _____**pans**_____   7. bee - _____**bees**_____

3. lady - _____**ladies**_____   8. eyelash - _____**eyelashes**_____

4. tomato - _____**tomatoes**_____   9. elf - _____**elves**_____

5. child - _____**children**_____   10. ray - _____**rays**_____

L. Directions: Write the possessive.

1. a book belonging to Hannah - _____**Hannah's book**_____

2. a room shared by two boys - _____**boys' room**_____

3. a meeting held for more than one man - _____**men's meeting**_____

4. checkers belonging to Chris - _____**Chris's checkers**_____

M. Directions: Circle any nouns in each sentence.

1. A **motorcycle** is sitting in the **driveway**.

2. **Jerry** put **milk** in his **bowl** of **cereal**.

3. Several **babies** slept on **towels** at the **beach**.

4. A **policeman** raised his **hand** and blew his **whistle**.

294

K. Directions: Write the plural of each noun.

1. pass - _____

2. pan - _____

3. lady - _____

4. tomato - _____

5. child - _____

6. friend - _____

7. bee - _____

8. eyelash - _____

9. elf - _____

10. ray - _____

L. Directions: Write the possessive.

1.   a book belonging to Hannah - _____

2.   a room shared by two boys - _____

3.   a meeting held for more than one man - _____

4.   checkers belonging to Chris - _____

M. Directions: Circle any nouns in each sentence.

1. A motorcycle is sitting in the driveway.

2. Jerry put milk in his bowl of cereal.

3. Several babies slept on towels at the beach.

4. A policeman raised his hand and blew his whistle.   295

Date_____

And, **but**, and **or** usually join two or more other words. They are called

conjunctions.

      Examples: Ed **and** Tim are brothers.

                Do you want mashed potatoes **or** a baked potato?

                I like carrots **but** not celery.

🐢 🐢 🐢 🐢 🐢 🐢 🐢 🐢 🐢 🐢 🐢 🐢 🐢 🐢 🐢 🐢 🐢 🐢

A.   Directions: Write **and** on the dotted lines and fill in the blank.
ANSWERS WILL VARY.

1. pizza **a n d** _____**coke**_____

2. bacon **a n d** _____**eggs**_____

3. up **a n d** _____**down**_____

4. in **a n d** _____**out**_____

5. knife, fork, **a n d** _____**spoon**_____

6. eyes, nose, **a n d** _____**ears**_____

B.   Fill in the blank with **or** or **but**.

1. You may stay ____**or**____ leave.

2. She cut her leg, ____**but**____ it's healing.

3. He wants tea ____**or**____ coffee.

4. I'll wait, ____**but**____ you must hurry.

Date_____

And, **but**, and **or** usually join two or more other words. They are called

conjunctions.

> Examples: Ed **and** Tim are brothers.
>
> Do you want mashed potatoes **or** a baked potato?
>
> I like carrots **but** not celery.

🐢 🐢 🐢 🐢 🐢 🐢 🐢 🐢 🐢 🐢 🐢 🐢 🐢 🐢 🐢 🐢 🐢 🐢

A.   Directions: Write <u>and</u> on the dotted lines and fill in the blank.

1. pizza **a** _ _ _____

2. bacon **a** _ _ _____

3. up **a** _ _ _____

4. in **a** _ _ _____

5. knife, fork, **a** _ _ _____

6. eyes, nose, **a** _ _ _____

B.   Fill in the blank with <u>or</u> or <u>but</u>.

1. You may stay _____ leave.

2. She cut her leg, _____ it's healing.

3. He wants tea _____ coffee.

4. I'll wait, _____ you must hurry.   297

Words that express emotion are called interjections.

      Examples: Yippee! I'm the winner!

                 Wow! My new bike is great!

Sometimes, interjections will have two or more words.

      Examples: Oh no! I can't believe I did that!

                 Boo hiss! We have to leave!

A special punctuation mark called an exclamation point is placed after an interjection.

🐢 🐢 🐢 🐢 🐢 🐢 🐢 🐢 🐢 🐢 🐢 🐢 🐢 🐢 🐢 🐢 🐢

A.   Directions: Write an interjection and an exclamation point on the line provided.

ANSWERS WILL VARY.

1.   ___**Far out!**___ George caught the ball!

2.   ___**Yeah!**___ Dad is buying us ice cream cones!

3.   ___**Yes!**___ We won!

B.   Directions: Circle any interjection.

1.   **Drats!** I'm not allowed to go!

2.   This milk is sour! **Yuck!**

3.   **Yikes!** Look out!

4.   **Hurrah!** Our team beat the Redbirds!

Name_____ **INTERJECTIONS**

Date_____

Words that express emotion are called interjections.

      Examples: Yippee! I'm the winner!

                Wow! My new bike is great!

Sometimes, interjections will have two or more words.

      Examples: Oh no! I can't believe I did that!

                Boo hiss! We have to leave!

A special punctuation mark called an exclamation point is placed after an interjection.

🐢 🐢 🐢 🐢 🐢 🐢 🐢 🐢 🐢 🐢 🐢 🐢 🐢 🐢 🐢 🐢 🐢 🐢

A.   Directions: Write an interjection and an exclamation point on the line provided.

1.   _____George caught the ball!

2.   _____Dad is buying us ice cream cones!

3.   _____We won!

B.   Directions: Circle any interjection.

1.   Drats! I'm not allowed to go!

2.   This milk is sour! Yuck!

3.   Yikes! Look out!

4.   Hurrah! Our team beat the Redbirds!

TO THE TEACHER: **Please read this page carefully before teaching the adverb unit.**

Adverbs can be very confusing. This chapter is simply a cursory introduction to them. I recommend that you introduce each concept separately. Be sure that students comprehend that adverbs usually modify verbs.

Because the **goal of grammar** is to help us speak and write correctly, the idea that a word usually has an adjective form and an adverb form is extremely important. We want students not only to understand that *I drive slow* is incorrect, but also to know **why** *I drive slowly* is correct.

You will note that more pages have been devoted to teaching *how* than to teaching other concepts. We need to ascertain that students comprehend the difference between adjectives and adverbs mentioned in the previous paragraph. Errors in writing and speaking occur most frequently in this area. Only one lesson has been provided for *when*, *where*, and *to what extent*; these are simply introduced in this text. More thorough teaching of these concepts occurs in ensuing texts:

> Easy Grammar: Grade 4
> Easy Grammar: Grade 5
> Easy Grammar: Grade 6
> Easy Grammar Plus

Teaching *to what extent*:

> Most adverbs modify verbs. However, adverbs that tell *to what extent* often modify adjectives and other adverbs. You must decide if your students are ready to determine what part of speech the adverb modifies. At this level, I don't think it's necessary. However, I do advise having students **memorize** the seven adverbs that commonly tell *to what extent*.

The **unit review** and the **adverb test** separate out identifying adverbs that tell *how, when*, *where*, and *to what extent*. This promotes student success.

NEITHER A CUMULATIVE REVIEW NOR A CUMULATIVE TEST HAS BEEN PROVIDED AT THE END OF THIS UNIT. Because the adverb unit is relatively short, placing another lengthy cumulative review so soon might overwhelm students. A complete cumulative review including both adjectives and adverbs will occur at the end of the pronoun unit.

ADVERBS

🐢 **Adverbs can tell how someone does or did something.**
   Justin swung the bat smoothly.

someone	**did**	**how**
Justin	swung	smoothly

Swung is the verb.   ***Smoothly*** tells *how* Justin swung the bat.

🐢 **Adverbs can tell how something does (did) something.**
   The kite dips quickly in the wind.

something	**did**	**how**
kite	dips	quickly

Dips is the verb.   ***Quickly*** tells *how* the kite dips in the wind.

Most adverbs that tell *how* go over to (modify) a verb and end in **ly**.
However, some do not. *Fast*, *hard*, and *well* tell *how* and do not end in **ly**.

🐢🐢🐢🐢🐢🐢🐢🐢🐢🐢🐢🐢🐢🐢🐢🐢🐢🐢

ANSWERS WILL VARY.
A.   Directions: Write a word that tells *how*. That word is an adverb.

1. He sings _____**well**_____ .   4. A bird chirped _____**merrily**_____ .

2. They played __**happily**__ .   5. She runs _____**fast**_____ .

3. I sneezed ____**softly**____ .   6. The wind blew ____**strongly**____ .

B.   Directions: Write a verb before the boldfaced adverb.

1. The drummer _____**played**_____ **loudly.**

2. The man and woman ____**shouted**____ **angrily.**

3. Vonnie ____**danced**____ **happily.**

302

Name_____

Date_____

🐢 **Adverbs can tell how someone does or did something.**
Justin swung the bat smoothly.

someone	**did**	**how**
Justin	swung	smoothly

Swung is the verb. **Smoothly** tells *how* Justin swung the bat.

🐢 **Adverbs can tell how something does (did) something.**
The kite dips quickly in the wind.

something	**did**	**how**
kite	dips	quickly

Dips is the verb. **Quickly** tells *how* the kite dips in the wind.

Most adverbs that tell *how* go over to (modify) a verb and end in **ly**.
However, some do not. *Fast, hard,* and *well* tell *how* and do not end in ly.

🐢 🐢 🐢 🐢 🐢 🐢 🐢 🐢 🐢 🐢 🐢 🐢 🐢 🐢 🐢 🐢 🐢 🐢 🐢

A.   Directions: Write a word that tells *how*. That word is an adverb.

1.   He sings _____.

2.   They played _____.

3.   I sneezed _____.

4.   A bird chirped _____.

5.   She runs _____.

6.   The wind blew _____.

B.   Directions: Write a verb before the boldfaced adverb.

1.   The drummer _____ **loudly.**

2.   The man and woman _____ **angrily.**

3.   Vonnie _____ **happily.**

Note to Teacher: I recommend that you do this page orally. Before doing part B, review crossing out prepositional phrases to find subject and verb. Discuss each sentence, stressing that the adverb modifies a verb.

🐢**Adverbs can tell *how*.**

A.   Directions: Fill in the blank.

Example: The girls played jacks quietly.

Quietly tells _____**how**_____ the girls __**played jacks**__ .

1.   Susan answered calmly.

Calmly tells _____**how**_____ Susan __**answered**_____ .

2.   Water tumbled swiftly over rocks.

Swiftly tells _____**how**_____ the water __**tumbled over rocks**____ .

3.   Dick yells loudly for his team.

Loudly tells _____**how**_____ Dick __**yells for his team**_____ .

4.   They cleaned their room well.

Well tells _____**how**_____ they __**cleaned their room**_____ .

B.   Directions: Circle the adverb in each sentence. Then, draw a line to the verb it goes over to (modifies).

ADVERBS ARE IN BOLDFACED ITALICS.
Note: Crossing out prepositional phrases will help you. An adverb that tells *how* will not usually be in a prepositional phrase.

1.   The winner **smiled** *cheerfully* ~~at us~~.

2.   She **sat** ~~on the old chair~~ *carefully*.

3.   A car **slid** *dangerously* ~~around the curve~~.

304

🐢 **Adverbs can tell *how*.**

A. Directions: Fill in the blank.

   Example: The girls played jacks quietly.

   Quietly tells _____**how**_____ the girls __**played jacks**__.

1.   Susan answered calmly.

   Calmly tells _____Susan _____.

2.   Water tumbled swiftly over rocks.

   Swiftly tells _____ the water _____.

3.   Dick yells loudly for his team.

   Loudly tells _____Dick _____.

4.   They cleaned their room well.

   Well tells _____they _____.

B. Directions: Circle the adverb in each sentence. Then, draw a line to the
                   verb it goes over to (modifies).

**Note: Crossing out prepositional phrases will help you. An
adverb that tells *how* will not usually be in a prepositional phrase.**

1.   The winner smiled cheerfully at us.

2.   She sat on the old chair carefully.

3.   A car slid dangerously around the curve.

305

🐢 An adjective, as you have learned, describes a noun.

Jim is a **loud** drummer.

> **Loud** is an adjective that describes drummer.

🐢 The adverb form of <u>loud</u> is **loudly**. <u>Loudly</u> tells *how* Jim plays.

Incorrect: Jim plays the drums loud.
Correct: Jim plays the drums **loudly**.

ADJECTIVE	**ADVERB**
slow	slowly
kind	kindly
angry	angrily

🐢🐢🐢🐢🐢🐢🐢🐢🐢🐢🐢🐢🐢🐢🐢🐢🐢🐢🐢

A.   Directions: Write the adverb form of each adjective:

1. quick - **quickly**   4. shy - **shyly**

2. careless - **carelessly**   5. hopeful - **hopefully**

3. firm - **firmly**   6. tight - **tightly**

B.   Directions: Write the adverb form of the adjective in parenthesis ( ).

1.   (playful)   The kitten chased the ball of yarn **playfully**.

2.   (polite)   We always answer **politely**.

3.   (loose)   His shirt fits **loosely**.

4.   (neat)   Val folds towels **neatly**.

5.   (cautious)   The driver approached the light **cautiously**.

306

Name_____   **ADVERBS**
                                               How?
Date_____

🐢 **An adjective, as you have learned, describes a noun.**

   Jim is a **loud** drummer.

   Loud is an adjective that describes drummer.

🐢 The adverb form of <u>loud</u> is **loudly**. <u>Loudly</u> tells *how* Jim plays.

   Incorrect: Jim plays the drums loud.
   Correct: Jim plays the drums **loudly**.

ADJECTIVE	**ADVERB**
slow	slowly
kind	kindly
angry	angrily

🐢🐢🐢🐢🐢🐢🐢🐢🐢🐢🐢🐢🐢🐢🐢🐢🐢🐢🐢

A.   Directions: Write the adverb form of each adjective:

1. quick - _____   4. shy - _____

2. careless - _____   5. hopeful - _____

3. firm - _____   6. tight - _____

B.   Directions: Write the adverb form of the adjective in parenthesis ( ).

1. (playful)   The kitten chased the ball of yarn _____.

2. (polite)   We always answer _____.

3. (loose)   His shirt fits _____.

4. (neat)   Val folds towels _____.

5. (cautious)   The driver approached the light _____.

307

It is important to use the correct adverb form in our speaking and writing.

ADJECTIVE	**ADVERB**
slow	slowly

The following sentence is incorrect: **I talk slow.**

I am a slow talker.   *Slow* describes talker.

Slow is an adjective. *Slow* cannot tell how I talk.

Correct: I talk slowly.

However, there are several words that are the same in both adjective and adverb forms:

Examples:
     adjective   adverb
     Ken is a **fast** runner.   He runs **fast**.
     adjective   adverb
     Lori is a **hard** hitter.   She hits **hard**.

🐢 🐢 🐢 🐢 🐢 🐢 🐢 🐢 🐢 🐢 🐢 🐢 🐢 🐢 🐢 🐢 🐢

Directions: Write the adverb form of each adjective.

1.   (light)   The nurse pressed _____**lightly**_____ on the man's arm.

2.   (fast)   That trains travels _____**fast**_____.

3.   (tearful)   The child answered _____**tearfully**_____.

4.   (hard)   Rick slammed the door too _____**hard**_____.

5.   (bright)   The sun shines _____**brightly**_____.

6.   (serious)   Her father spoke _____**seriously**_____ about the accident.

308

It is important to use the correct adverb form in our speaking and writing.

| **ADJECTIVE** | **ADVERB** |
| slow | slowly |

The following sentence is incorrect: **I talk slow.**

I am a slow talker.   *Slow* describes talker.

Slow is an adjective. *Slow* cannot tell how I talk.

Correct: I talk slowly.

However, there are several words that are the same in both adjective and adverb forms:

Examples:

adjective	adverb
Ken is a **fast** runner.	He runs **fast**.
adjective	adverb
Lori is a **hard** hitter.	She hits **hard**.

🐢 🐢 🐢 🐢 🐢 🐢 🐢 🐢 🐢 🐢 🐢 🐢 🐢 🐢 🐢 🐢 🐢 🐢 🐢 🐢

Directions: Write the adverb form of each adjective.

1.   (light)   The nurse pressed _____ on the man's arm.

2.   (fast)   That trains travels _____.

3.   (tearful)   The child answered _____.

4.   (hard)   Rick slammed the door too _____.

5.   (bright)   The sun shines _____.

6.   (serious)   Her father spoke _____ about the accident.

🐢 **Adverbs can tell when something happens (happened).**

Example: Yesterday, Julia fished for two hours.

Yesterday tells when Julia fished.

Most adverbs that tell *when* **go over to (modify) a verb.**

Some adverbs that tell *when* are:

now	late	always	sometimes	yesterday
then	later	never	early	today
soon	when	forever	earlier	tomorrow
sooner	first	again	daily	tonight

There are others. Simply decide if any word in the sentence tells *when*.

🐢 🐢 🐢 🐢 🐢 🐢 🐢 🐢 🐢 🐢 🐢 🐢 🐢 🐢 🐢 🐢 🐢 🐢 🐢

ANSWERS WILL VARY.

A.   Directions: Write an adverb that tells *when*.

1.   Shelley _____**never**_____ swims.

2.   They arrived _____**late**_____.

3.   Patsy _____**always**_____ whispers.

4.   _____**Tonight**_____, I shall stay up late.

5.   You may go _____**now**_____.

B.   Directions: Write a verb in each sentence.
Students may write additional words with the verb. For example, #3 may
read: *When will you stop that?*

1.   We are _____**diving**_____ today.

2.   May I _____**leave**_____ soon?

3.   **When** will you _____**stop**_____?

310

🐢 **Adverbs can tell when something happens (happened).**

Example: Yesterday, Julia fished for two hours.

Yesterday tells when Julia fished.

Most adverbs that tell *when* **go over to (modify) a verb.**

Some adverbs that tell *when* are:

now	late	always	sometimes	yesterday
then	**later**	**never**	**early**	**today**
soon	**when**	**forever**	**earlier**	**tomorrow**
sooner	**first**	**again**	**daily**	**tonight**

There are others. Simply decide if any word in the sentence tells *when.*

🐢 🐢 🐢 🐢 🐢 🐢 🐢 🐢 🐢 🐢 🐢 🐢 🐢 🐢 🐢 🐢 🐢 🐢 🐢

A.   Directions: Write an adverb that tells *when.*

1.   Shelley _____ swims.

2.   They arrived _____ .

3.   Patsy _____ whispers.

4.   _____ , I shall stay up late.

5.   You may go _____ .

B.   Directions: Write a verb in each sentence.

1.   We are _____ **today**.

2.   May I _____ **soon**?

3.   **When** will you _____ ?   311

🐢 **Adverbs can tell where.**

Example: Come here.

Here tells *where* you should come.

Most adverbs that tell *where* usually **go over to (modify) a verb**.
Some adverbs that tell *where* are:

here	**everywhere**	**in**	**up**
there	**anywhere**	**out**	**down**
where	**somewhere**	**inside**	**around**

There are others. Simply decide if any **word** in the sentence tells *where*.

🐢 🐢 🐢 🐢 🐢 🐢 🐢 🐢 🐢 🐢 🐢 🐢 🐢 🐢 🐢 🐢 🐢 🐢 🐢
ANSWERS WILL VARY.
A.   Directions: Write an adverb that tells *where*.

1.   Look _____**here**_____ .

2.   Stand _____**up**_____ .

3.   I want to go _____**somewhere**_____ .

4.   Come _____**in**_____ .

5.   Have you searched _____**everywhere**_____ for your money?

B.   Directions: Write a verb in each sentence.

1.   They _____**moved**_____ here.

2.   William _____**wants**_____ out.

3.   She _____**lay**_____ down.
312

Name_____

Date_____

🐢 **Adverbs can tell where.**

Example: Come here.

Here tells *where* you should come.

Most adverbs that tell *where* usually **go over to (modify) a verb.**
Some adverbs that tell *where* are:

here	**everywhere**	**in**	**up**
there	**anywhere**	**out**	**down**
where	**somewhere**	**inside**	**around**

There are others. Simply decide if any **word** in the sentence tells *where.*

🐢 🐢 🐢 🐢 🐢 🐢 🐢 🐢 🐢 🐢 🐢 🐢 🐢 🐢 🐢 🐢 🐢 🐢

A.   Directions: Write an adverb that tells *where.*

1.   Look _____.

2.   Stand _____.

3.   I want to go _____.

4.   Come _____.

5.   Have you searched _____ for your money?

B.   Directions: Write a verb in each sentence.

1.   They _____ **here**.

2.   William _____**out**.

3.   She _____ **down**.

313

Name_____

Date_____

ADVERBS
To What Extent?

<u>**Note to Teacher: Be sure that you discuss the words, *quit*, *quiet*, and *quite*. Students find these confusing.**</u>

🐢 **Adverbs can tell to what extent.**

There are seven adverbs that usually tell *to what extent:* **not, so, very, too, quite, rather,** and **somewhat.**

Examples:	She is **not** happy.	This is **quite** good.
	I am **so** hot!	It's **rather** windy.
	I am **somewhat** sad.	I'm **too** tired.
	Her cousin is **very** talented.	

There are other words that tell *to what extent.* Look for words such as *unusually* or *extremely*.

🐢 🐢 🐢 🐢 🐢 🐢 🐢 🐢 🐢 🐢 🐢 🐢 🐢 🐢 🐢 🐢 🐢 🐢 🐢

Directions: Circle any adverbs that tell *to what extent.*

1. The dog was **not** friendly.

2. I am **so** busy.

3. Her hair is **very** pretty.

4. This soup is **too** cold.

5. She is **quite** sick.

6. This road is **rather** curvy.

7. I'm **somewhat** worried.

8. Mrs. Land is **extremely** funny.

314

Name_____

Date_____

🐢 **Adverbs can tell to what extent.**

There are seven adverbs that usually tell *to what extent:* **not, so, very, too, quite, rather,** and **somewhat.**

Examples: She is **not** happy.   This is **quite** good.

I am **so** hot!   It's **rather** windy.

I am **somewhat** sad.   I'm **too** tired.

Her cousin is **very** talented.

There are other words that tell *to what extent.* Look for words such as *unusually* or *extremely.*

🐢 🐢 🐢 🐢 🐢 🐢 🐢 🐢 🐢 🐢 🐢 🐢 🐢 🐢 🐢 🐢 🐢 🐢 🐢

Directions: Circle any adverbs that tell *to what extent.*

1.   The dog was not friendly.

2.   I am so busy.

3.   Her hair is very pretty.

4.   This soup is too cold.

5.   She is quite sick.

6.   This road is rather curvy.

7.   I'm somewhat worried.

8.   Mrs. Land is extremely funny.

315

Name_____   **ADVERBS**

WORKBOOK PAGE 142   **Degrees**

Date_____

<u>**Note to Teacher: Be sure that students understand the importance of using a dictionary. I recommend that you have students look up a word such as *early* to see how the dictionary includes it.**</u>

🐢**Adverbs can make comparisons.**

The comparative form compares **two** things.

Example: *I* run **faster** than my *brother*.

🐢There are three ways to form the comparative form:
1. Add **<u>er</u>** to most one-syllable adverbs.

fast - faster

2. Add **<u>more</u>** before most two or more syllable adverbs.

cheerfully - more cheerfully

Some two-syllable words add **<u>er</u>**.

early - earlier

Use a dictionary to check if <u>er</u> should be added. **If the dictionary does not say *adv. er*, use <u>more</u>.**

3. Some adverbs totally change form.

well - better

🐢 🐢 🐢 🐢 🐢 🐢 🐢 🐢 🐢 🐢 🐢 🐢 🐢 🐢 🐢 🐢 🐢 🐢 🐢

Directions: Write the correct form of the boldfaced adverb.

1. James talks **fast**.
    However, his sister talks _____**faster**_____.

2. Candy writes **neatly**.
    However, her dad writes _____**more neatly**_____.

3. They didn't play ball **well** today.
    They played _____**better**_____yesterday.

316

🐢**Adverbs can make comparisons.**

The comparative form compares **two** things.

Example: *I* run **faster** than my *brother.*

🐢There are three ways to form the comparative form:
1.   Add **er** to most one-syllable adverbs.

fast - faster

2.   Add **more** before most two or more syllable adverbs.

cheerfully - more cheerfully

Some two-syllable words add **er**.

early - earlier

Use a dictionary to check if er should be added. **If the dictionary does not say *adv. er*, use more.**

3.   Some adverbs totally change form.

well - better

🐢 🐢 🐢 🐢 🐢 🐢 🐢 🐢 🐢 🐢 🐢 🐢 🐢 🐢 🐢 🐢 🐢 🐢

Directions: Write the correct form of the boldfaced adverb.

1.   James talks **fast**.
      However, his sister talks _____.

2.   Candy writes **neatly**.
      However, her dad writes _____.

3.   They didn't play ball **well** today.
      They played _____ yesterday.   317

🐢 **Adverbs can make comparisons.**

The superlative form compares **three or more** things.

Example: I run fastest of all my friends.

🐢 There are three ways to form the superlative form:
    1. Add **est** to most one-syllable adverbs.

fast - fastest

    2. Add **most** before most two or more syllable adverbs.

cheerfully - most cheerfully

Some two-syllable words add **est**.

early - earliest

Use a dictionary to check if <u>est</u> should be added. **If the dictionary does not say *adv. est*, use <u>most</u>.**

    3. Some adverbs totally change form.

well - best

🐢 🐢 🐢 🐢 🐢 🐢 🐢 🐢 🐢 🐢 🐢 🐢 🐢 🐢 🐢 🐢 🐢 🐢 🐢

Directions: Write the correct form of the boldfaced adverb.

1. Troy throws the ball **high** in the air.
    In fact, on his team, he throws it _____**highest**_____.

2. During her first show, she danced **beautifully**.
    She danced _____**most beautifully**_____ during her third show.

3. Their group did **well** in the finals.
    They did _____**best**_____ during the sixth game.

318

🐢 **Adverbs can make comparisons.**

The superlative form compares **three or more** things.

Example: I run fastest of all my friends.

🐢 There are three ways to form the superlative form:
1. Add **est** to most one-syllable adverbs.

fast - fastest

2. Add **most** before most two or more syllable adverbs.

cheerfully - most cheerfully

Some two-syllable words add **est**.

early - earliest

Use a dictionary to check if <u>est</u> should be added. **If the dictionary does not say *adv. est*, use <u>most</u>.**

3. Some adverbs totally change form.

well - best

🐢 🐢 🐢 🐢 🐢 🐢 🐢 🐢 🐢 🐢 🐢 🐢 🐢 🐢 🐢 🐢 🐢 🐢 🐢

Directions: Write the correct form of the boldfaced adverb.

1. Troy throws the ball **high** in the air.
    In fact, on his team, he throws it _____.

2. During her first show, she danced **beautifully**.
    She danced _____ during her third show.

3. Their group did **well** in the finals.
    They did _____ during the sixth game.

🐢 **The comparative form compares *two* things.**

    1.   Add **er** to most one-syllable adverbs.

    2.   Add **more** before most two or more syllable adverbs.
        However, some two-syllable words add **er**.

    3.   Some adverbs totally change form.

🐢 **The superlative form compares *three or more* things.**

    1.   Add **est** to most one-syllable adverbs.

    2.   Add **most** before most two or more syllable adverbs.
        However, some two-syllable words add **est**.

    3.   Some adverbs totally change form.

🐢 🐢 🐢 🐢 🐢 🐢 🐢 🐢 🐢 🐢 🐢 🐢 🐢 🐢 🐢 🐢 🐢 🐢 🐢

Directions: Circle the correct form.

1.   This red toy car goes (**faster**, fastest) than the white one.

2.   Alice works (**more cheerfully**, most cheerfully) than her friend.

3.   Kermie tried (harder, **hardest**) on his third try.

4.   The children sang (**better**, best) during their second performance.

5.   I did my second lesson (**more carefully**, most carefully) than my first.

6.   Barbara pitched the ball (harder, **hardest**) the third time.

7.   Is Venus (closer, **closest**) of all the planets?

8.   Her truck runs (**more smoothly**, most smoothly) than our car.
320

🐢 **The comparative form compares *two* things.**

    1.   Add **er** to most one-syllable adverbs.

    2.   Add **more** before most two or more syllable adverbs.
         However, some two-syllable words add **er**.

    3.   Some adverbs totally change form.

🐢 **The superlative form compares *three or more* things.**

    1.   Add **est** to most one-syllable adverbs.

    2.   Add **most** before most two or more syllable adverbs.
         However, some two-syllable words add **est**.

    3.   Some adverbs totally change form.

🐢 🐢 🐢 🐢 🐢 🐢 🐢 🐢 🐢 🐢 🐢 🐢 🐢 🐢 🐢 🐢 🐢 🐢

Directions: Circle the correct form.

1.   This red toy car goes (faster, fastest) than the white one.

2.   Alice works (more cheerfully, most cheerfully) than her friend.

3.   Kermie tried (harder, hardest) on his third try.

4.   The children sang (better, best) during their second performance.

5.   I did my second lesson (more carefully, most carefully) than my first.

6.   Barbara pitched the ball (harder, hardest) the third time.

7.   Is Venus (closer, closest) of all the planets?

8.   Her truck runs (more smoothly, most smoothly) than our car.   321

ADVERBS
Double Negatives

<u>Note to Teacher:</u>   <u>Correcting double negatives is difficult for students</u>
<u>who have heard them constantly and have internalized them as</u>
<u>"sounding" correct. The more students "hear" correct usage, the more</u>
<u>likely they will be to internalize it.</u>
No, **not** (**n't**), **never**, **none**, **nobody**, and **nothing** are negative words.

<u>Do not use more than one negative word in the same sentence.</u>

Example: Wrong: I do**n't** want **nothing**.

Right: I want **nothing**.

or

I do**n't** want anything.

However, if <u>no</u> is used to answer a question, another negative word may be
used in the sentence:

Have you found your baseball glove?

No, I have **not** begun to look for it.

🐢 🐢 🐢 🐢 🐢 🐢 🐢 🐢 🐢 🐢 🐢 🐢 🐢 🐢 🐢 🐢 🐢 🐢

A.   Directions: Unscramble these negative words.

1.   gintohn - _____**nothing**_____   4.   oenn - _____**none**_____

2.   reven - _____**never**_____   5.   on - _____**no**_____

3.   otn - _____**not**_____   6.   bdoyon - _____**nobody**_____

B.   Directions: Circle the correct word.

1.   I don't want (none, **any**).

2.   Carl doesn't have (**anybody**, nobody) with him.

3.   They never have (no, **any**) extra pennies.

4.   Jordan cannot drink (**anything**, nothing) with sugar.

322

No, **not (n't)**, **never**, **none**, **nobody**, and **nothing** are negative words.

Do not use more than one negative word in the same sentence.

Example: Wrong: I do**n't** want **nothing**.

Right: I want **nothing**.

or

I do**n't** want anything.

However, if <u>no</u> is used to answer a question, another negative word may be used in the sentence.

Have you found your baseball glove?

No, I have **not** begun to look for it.

A.   Directions: Unscramble these negative words.

1.   gintohn - _____   4.   oenn - _____

2.   reven - _____   5.   on - _____

3.   otn - _____   6.   bdoyon - _____

B.   Directions: Circle the correct word.

1.   I don't want (none, any).

2.   Carl doesn't have (anybody, nobody) with him.

3.   They never have (no, any) extra pennies.

4.   Jordan cannot drink (anything, nothing) with sugar.

A. Adverbs:

   Directions: Write the adverb form of the word.

1. happy - _____**happily**_____   3. wise - _____**wisely**_____

2. sweet - _____**sweetly**_____   4. tearful - _____**tearfully**_____

B.   Adverbs That Tell How:

   Directions: Fill in the blank.

1. My dad is a light sleeper.

   He sleeps _____**lightly**_____.

2. They wrote correct answers.

   They answered _____**correctly**_____.

3. Karla is a bold speaker.

   She spoke _____**boldly**_____ against the law.

C.   Adverbs That Tell How:

   Directions: Circle the adverb that tells *how*.

1. The light shone **brightly**.

2. Mack can jump **high**.

3. That dog barks **loudly**.

4. I erase **carefully**.

5. We play cards **well**.

324

A. Adverbs:

Directions: Write the adverb form of the word.

1. happy -_____   3. wise - _____

2. sweet - _____   4. tearful - _____

B. Adverbs That Tell How:

Directions: Fill in the blank.

1. My dad is a light sleeper.

He sleeps _____.

2. They wrote correct answers.

They answered _____.

3. Karla is a bold speaker.

She spoke _____ against the law.

C. Adverbs That Tell How:

Directions: Circle the adverb that tells *how*.

1. The light shone brightly.

2. Mack can jump high.

3. That dog barks loudly.

4. I erase carefully.

5. We play cards well.   325

D.   Adverbs That Tell When:

   Directions: Circle the adverb that tells *when.*

1.   He rises **earlier** on Sunday.

2.   Do that **again**.

3.   **Sometimes**, Ben sleeps in a tent.

4.   Linda **always** writes thank you cards.

5.   Let's go to a hockey game **tonight**.

E.   Adverbs That Tell Where:

   Directions: Circle the adverb that tells *where.*

1.   I can go **nowhere** today.

2.   The man stood **up**.

3.   **Where** is my ball?

4.   The fawn lay **down** ~~by his mother~~.

5.   Their cousins visit **here** ~~in June~~.

326

D. Adverbs That Tell When:

Directions: Circle the adverb that tells *when*.

1. He rises earlier on Sunday.

2. Do that again.

3. Sometimes, Ben sleeps in a tent.

4. Linda always writes thank you cards.

5. Let's go to a hockey game tonight.

E. Adverbs That Tell Where:

Directions: Circle the adverb that tells *where*.

1. I can go nowhere today.

2. The man stood up.

3. Where is my ball?

4. The fawn lay down by his mother.

5. Their cousins visit here in June.

F.   Adverbs That Tell to What Extent:

Directions: Circle the adverb that tells *to what extent.*

1. Toby's friend is **so** serious.

2. My uncle drives **very** slowly.

3. The dog is **too** large for his doghouse.

4. Her arms are **somewhat** burned.

5. The teacher gave me a **rather** strange look.

G.   Degrees of Adverbs:

Directions: Circle the correct form.

1. She speaks English (**more plainly**, most plainly) than German.

2. He writes (**better**, best) with his right hand.

3. Marie rides her bike (faster, **fastest**) of all her friends.

4. Her collie barks (oftener, **more often**) than her neighbor's poodle.

5. Shawn glided (more steadily, **most steadily**) of all the surfers.

F.   Adverbs That Tell to What Extent:

   Directions: Circle the adverb that tells *to what extent.*

1. Toby's friend is so serious.

2.   My uncle drives very slowly.

3.   The dog is too large for his doghouse.

4.   Her arms are somewhat burned.

5.   The teacher gave me a rather strange look.

G.   Degrees of Adverbs:

   Directions: Circle the correct form.

1. She speaks English (more plainly, most plainly) than German.

2.   He writes (better, best) with his right hand.

3.   Marie rides her bike (faster, fastest) of all her friends.

4.   Her collie barks (oftener, more often) than her neighbor's poodle.

5.   Shawn glided (more steadily, most steadily) of all the surfers.

Name_____   **Adverb Test**

Date_____

A.   Directions: Circle the adverb that tells *how*:

1.   The car stopped **suddenly**.

2.   Beth kicks the soccer ball **hard**.

B.   Directions: Circle the adverb that tells *when*:

1.   I'll do that **later**.

2.   **Now**, let's decide.

C.   Directions: Circle the adverb that tells *where*:

1.   I can't find my brush **anywhere**.

2.   Please come **in**.

D.   Directions: Circle the adverb that tells *to what extent*:

1.   Our trash is **quite** full.

2.   This book is **very** interesting.

E.   Directions: Circle the correct adverb form.

1.   The small monkey chatters (**more noisily**, most noisily) than the larger one.

2.   Brian swam (faster, **fastest**) in his third lap.

3.   Grandpa comes to the park (**more often**, oftener) than his friend.

330

A.   Directions: Circle the adverb that tells *how*:

1.   The car stopped suddenly.

2.   Beth kicks the soccer ball hard.

B.   Directions: Circle the adverb that tells *when*:

1.   I'll do that later.

2.   Now, let's decide.

C.   Directions: Circle the adverb that tells *where*:

1.   I can't find my brush anywhere.

2.   Please come in.

D.   Directions: Circle the adverb that tells *to what extent*:

1.   Our trash is quite full.

2.   This book is very interesting.

E.   Directions: Circle the correct adverb form.

1.   The small monkey chatters (more noisily, most noisily) than the larger one.

2.   Brian swam (faster, fastest) in his third lap.

3.   Grandpa comes to the park (more often, oftener) than his friend.

Name_____ **SENTENCE TYPES**

WORKBOOK PAGE 149

Date_____

<u>Note to Teacher:</u>   **Be sure that students comprehend that imperative sentences give a command and that** *please* **is frequently used. Although the spelling of each sentence type may be difficult at this level, students, most certainly, are capable of** *copying* **the correct spelling. Instruct them to do so.**

There are **four** types of sentences.

    🐢A **declarative** sentence makes a <u>statement</u>. It ends in a *period*.

       This candy bar melted.

    🐢An **interrogative** sentence asks a <u>question</u>. It ends with a *question mark*.

       Has the candy bar melted?

    🐢An **imperative** sentence gives a <u>command</u>. It ends with a *period*.

       Give me that candy bar.

    🐢An **exclamatory sentence** <u>shows emotion</u>.   It ends with an *exclamation point.*

       Yuck! This candy bar is melted!

🐢 🐢 🐢 🐢 🐢 🐢 🐢 🐢 🐢 🐢 🐢 🐢 🐢 🐢 🐢 🐢 🐢 🐢

Directions: Write the sentence type.

1.   Pass the mustard.   _____**imperative**_____

2.   May I read your poem?   _____**interrogative**_____

3.   We passed the test!   _____**exclamatory**_____

4.   Mort got a speeding ticket.   _____**declarative**_____

5.   Don't touch that, please.   _____**imperative**_____

6.   Her arm was broken in two places.   _____**declarative**_____

332

There are **four** types of sentences.

   🐢A **declarative** sentence makes a <u>statement</u>. It ends in a *period*.

      This candy bar melted.

   🐢An **interrogative** sentence asks a <u>question</u>. It ends with a *question mark*.

      Has the candy bar melted?

   🐢An **imperative** sentence gives a <u>command</u>. It ends with a *period*.

      Give me that candy bar.

   🐢An **exclamatory sentence** <u>shows emotion</u>. It ends with an *exclamation point.*

      Yuck! This candy bar is melted!

🐢 🐢 🐢 🐢 🐢 🐢 🐢 🐢 🐢 🐢 🐢 🐢 🐢 🐢 🐢 🐢 🐢 🐢 🐢

Directions: Write the sentence type.

1. Pass the mustard. _____

2. May I read your poem? _____

3. We passed the test! _____

4. Mort got a speeding ticket. _____

5. Don't touch that, please. _____

6. Her arm was broken in two places. _____

WORKBOOK PAGE 150
Date_____
Note to Teacher: Check this page very carefully. If students are confused, it should be evident here. Also, be sure that students end each sentence with proper punctuation.

There are **four** types of sentences.

    🐢A **declarative** sentence makes a <u>statement</u>. It ends in a ***period***.

          Jodi ate the chips.

    🐢An **interrogative** sentence asks a <u>question</u>. It ends with a ***question mark***.

          Has Jodi eaten all the chips?

    🐢An **imperative** sentence gives a <u>command</u>. It ends with a ***period***.

          Try these onion chips.

    🐢An **exclamatory sentence** <u>shows emotion</u>.   It ends with an ***exclamation point***.

          These chips taste terrible!

🐢 🐢 🐢 🐢 🐢 🐢 🐢 🐢 🐢 🐢 🐢 🐢 🐢 🐢 🐢 🐢 🐢 🐢

Directions: Write a sentence for each type.
ANSWERS WILL VARY.
1.   declarative: **This icicle is ten inches long.**

2.   interrogative: **How do you spell your last name?**

3.   imperative: **Seal this envelope.**

4.   exclamatory: **Our pizza just arrived!**

334

Name_____   **SENTENCE TYPES**

Date_____

There are **four** types of sentences.

    🐢A **declarative** sentence makes a <u>statement</u>. It ends in a ***period***.

        Jodi ate the chips.

    🐢An **interrogative** sentence asks a <u>question</u>. It ends with a **question mark**.

        Has Jodi eaten all the chips?

    🐢An **imperative** sentence gives a <u>command</u>. It ends with a ***period***.

        Try these onion chips.

    🐢An **exclamatory sentence** <u>shows emotion</u>. It ends with an **exclamation point.**

        These chips taste terrible!

🐢 🐢 🐢 🐢 🐢 🐢 🐢 🐢 🐢 🐢 🐢 🐢 🐢 🐢 🐢 🐢 🐢 🐢

Directions: Write a sentence for each type.

1.   declarative: _____

2.   interrogative: _____

3.   imperative: _____

4.   exclamatory: _____

TO THE TEACHER:

Pronouns are difficult. Be patient with your students.

Personal pronouns have been limited to their use as subject, object of the preposition, and direct object.

Be sure to do most of the pages concerning compound pronouns orally. The purpose is to use the "finger trick" and operate by sound. (Yes, determining by sound is acceptable here!)

Possessive pronouns have been included; however, antecedents have not. (These will be introduced in other texts.) A review of its/it's, their/they're/there, and your/you're is included as part of possessive skills.

I have not included interrogative pronouns; these appear in <u>Easy Grammar: Grade 4</u>. Reflexive pronouns, demonstrative pronouns, and indefinite pronouns are introduced in at other levels.

Pronouns

Pronouns take the place of nouns.

<u>NOUN</u>	<u>PRONOUN</u>
Tara	she
Marco	he
book	it

Subject pronouns usually serve as the subject of a sentence. These include **I**, **he**, **she**, **we**, **they**, **who**, **you**, and **it**. Subject pronouns are also called nominative pronouns.

        Examples: **Kala** likes to camp.
                      She likes to camp.

                      Mano and **Van** are friends.
                      They are friends.

🐢 🐢 🐢 🐢 🐢 🐢 🐢 🐢 🐢 🐢 🐢 🐢 🐢 🐢 🐢 🐢 🐢 🐢

Directions: In part A, write a person's name. In part B, write a pronoun for the name. In the double underlined part, finish the sentence.

        Example: A. _____**Leah**_____ is my friend.

                  B. _____**She**_____ likes <u>to brush her dogs.</u>

ANSWERS WILL VARY.

1.   A. _____**Juanita**_____ is my friend.

     B. _____**She**_____ lives <u>**in a townhouse.**</u>

2.   A. My name is ___**Neema**___ .

     B. ____**I**____ am <u>**a good athlete.**</u>

3.   A. Two people I know are ___**Rana**___ and ___**Chiko**___ .

     B. ____**They**____ like <u>**to fish in the ocean.**</u>

Name_____

Date_____

Pronouns take the place of nouns.

<u>NOUN</u>	<u>PRONOUN</u>
Tara	she
Marco	he
book	it

Subject pronouns usually serve as the subject of a sentence. These include **I**, **he**, **she**, **we**, **they**, **who**, **you**, and **it**. Subject pronouns are also called nominative pronouns.

Examples: **Kala** likes to camp.
She likes to camp.

Mano and **Van** are friends.
They are friends.

🐢 🐢 🐢 🐢 🐢 🐢 🐢 🐢 🐢 🐢 🐢 🐢 🐢 🐢 🐢 🐢 🐢 🐢

Directions: In part A, write a person's name. In part B, write a pronoun for the name. In the double underlined part, finish the sentence.

Example: A.   _____**Leah**_____ is my friend.

B.   _____**She**_____ likes _to brush her dogs._

1.   A.   _____ is my friend.

B.   _____ lives _____

2.   A.   My name is _____.

B.   _____ am _____

3.   A.   Two people I know are _____ and _____.

B.   _____ like _____

Pronouns take the place of nouns.

Subject pronouns usually serve as the subject of a sentence. These include

I, **he**, **she**, **we**, **they**, **who**, **you**, and **it**.

> Example: **Hank** has a new bike.
> **He** keeps it in the garage.

<u>Important</u>: If you are talking about yourself, use the pronoun, **I**, at or near the beginning of the sentence.

> Example: During the storm, **I** stayed inside.

> When referring to yourself and another person, say the other person's name first.

> Example: Jean and **I** made cloth dolls.

Do not say Jean and me or me and Jean.

🐢🐢🐢🐢🐢🐢🐢🐢🐢🐢🐢🐢🐢🐢🐢🐢🐢🐢

Directions: On the line provided, write each sentence correctly.

1.   My mom and me like potato chips.

_____**My mom and I like potato chips.**_____

2.   I and my sister play the flute.

_____**My sister and I play the flute.**_____

3.   Me and my friend want to go to recess.

_____**My friend and I want to go to recess.**_____

4.   Their dad and me play catch.

_____**Their dad and I play catch.**_____

340

Pronouns take the place of nouns.

Subject pronouns usually serve as the subject of a sentence. These include

I, **he**, **she**, **we**, **they**, **who**, **you**, and **it**.

> Example: **Hank** has a new bike.
> **He** keeps it in the garage.

Important: If you are talking about yourself, use the pronoun, **I**, at or near
the beginning of the sentence.

> Example: During the storm, **I** stayed inside.

When referring to yourself and another person, say the other
person's name first.

> Example: Jean and **I** made cloth dolls.

Do not say Jean and me or me and Jean.

🐢 🐢 🐢 🐢 🐢 🐢 🐢 🐢 🐢 🐢 🐢 🐢 🐢 🐢 🐢 🐢 🐢 🐢 🐢

Directions: On the line provided, write each sentence correctly.

1.   My mom and me like potato chips.

_____

2.   I and my sister play the flute.

_____

3.   Me and my friend want to go to recess.

_____

4.   Their dad and me play catch.

_____

Pronouns take the place of nouns.

Subject pronouns are **I**, **he**, **she**, **we**, **they**, **who**, **you**, and **it**.

They serve as the subject of a sentence.

Examples: **I** like to play in the sand.

H e joined a club.

She braids her hair.

Yesterday, **we** went grocery shopping.

They often watch television.

Who wants ice cream?

You need to earn extra money.

It is 5:00.

Directions: Circle the correct pronoun.

1.   (**We**, Us) gave our dog a bath.

2.   May (me, **I**) play, too?

3.   Yesterday, (**they**, them) went to a baseball game.

4.   During lunch, (him, **he**) sits by himself.

5.   (Her, **She**) laughs often.

6.   Tonight, Bud and (me, **I**) are going to make dinner.

342

Pronouns take the place of nouns.

Subject pronouns are **I**, **he**, **she**, **we**, **they**, **who**, **you**, and **it**.

They serve as the subject of a sentence.

Examples: **I** like to play in the sand.

He joined a club.

She braids her hair.

Yesterday, **we** went grocery shopping.

They often watch television.

Who wants ice cream?

You need to earn extra money.

It is 5:00.

🐢 🐢 🐢 🐢 🐢 🐢 🐢 🐢 🐢 🐢 🐢 🐢 🐢 🐢 🐢 🐢 🐢 🐢 🐢

Directions: Circle the correct pronoun.

1.   (We, Us) gave our dog a bath.

2.   May (me, I) play, too?

3.   Yesterday, (they, them) went to a baseball game.

4.   During lunch, (him, he) sits by himself.

5.   (Her, She) laughs often.

6.   Tonight, Bud and (me, I) are going to make dinner.

Object pronouns are **me**, **him**, **her**, **us**, **them**, **whom**, **you**, and **it**.
They can serve as an ***object of the preposition***.

🐢 **Remember:** **An object of the preposition is the word that comes** <u>after</u> **a preposition.**

Take this *to* your dad.

To is a preposition.

To your dad is a prepositional phrase.

Dad is the last word of the prepositional phrase.

Dad is the <u>object of the preposition</u>.

Use **me**, **him**, **her**, **us**, **them**, **whom**, **you**, or **it** after a preposition.

Example: Jenny went shopping *with* **Dawn**.
Jenny went shopping *with* **her**.

🐢 🐢 🐢 🐢 🐢 🐢 🐢 🐢 🐢 🐢 🐢 🐢 🐢 🐢 🐢 🐢 🐢

Directions: Place an <u>X</u> above the preposition. Then, circle the correct pronoun.
Prepositions are in boldfaced italics.

1.   This present is *from* (**me**, I).

2.   You may sit *by* (we, **us**).

3.   Uncle Sunny talked *to* (**her**, she).

4.   The letter is *for* (they, **them**).

5.   Tanya rode bikes *with* (**him**, he).

6.   An airplane flew *over* (**us**, we).
344

Object pronouns are **me**, **him**, **her**, **us**, **them**, **whom**, **you**, and **it**.
They can serve as an *object of the preposition*.

🐢 **Remember: An object of the preposition is the word that**
   comes <u>after</u> a preposition.

> Take this *to* your dad.

>> *To* is a preposition.

>> *To your dad* is a prepositional phrase.

>> **Dad** is the last word of the prepositional phrase.

>> **Dad** is the <u>object of the preposition.</u>

Use **me**, **him**, **her**, **us**, **them**, **whom**, **you**, or **it** after a preposition.

> Example: Jenny went shopping *with* **Dawn**.
>   Jenny went shopping *with* **her**.

🐢 🐢 🐢 🐢 🐢 🐢 🐢 🐢 🐢 🐢 🐢 🐢 🐢 🐢 🐢 🐢 🐢 🐢

Directions: Place an <u>X</u> above the preposition. Then, circle the correct
   pronoun.

1.   This present is from (me, I).

2.   You may sit by (we, us).

3.   Uncle Sunny talked to (her, she).

4.   The letter is for (they, them).

5.   Tanya rode bikes with (him, he).

6.   An airplane flew over (us, we).

Object pronouns are **me**, **him**, **her**, **us**, **them**, **whom**, **you**, and **it**.
They can serve as a **_direct object_**.

🐢 **Remember:** **A direct object receives the action of the verb.**

The child hit Peter.   The **object** the child hit was *Peter*.
The child hit **him** on the leg.

Doris planted a tree.   The **object** Doris planted was a tree.
Doris planted **it** last Monday.

Use **me**, **him**, **her**, **us**, **them**, **whom**, **you**, or **it** as a direct object.

Example: Mr. Cline met **Stan** and **Bobby** in Canada.
              Mr. Cline met **them** in Canada.

🐢 🐢 🐢 🐢 🐢 🐢 🐢 🐢 🐢 🐢 🐢 🐢 🐢 🐢 🐢 🐢 🐢

Directions: In part A, underline the subject once and the verb twice.
              Label the direct object - D.O. In part B, write a pronoun for the
              word labeled as a direct object.

D.O.
1. A. <u>Rob</u> <u><u>sees</u></u> Eileen often.

    B. Rob sees ____**her**____ often.
D.O.
2. A. <u>Micah</u> <u><u>pushed</u></u> Todd down.

    B. Micah pushed ____**him**____ down.
D.O.
3. A. The <u>customer</u> <u><u>dropped</u></u> a quarter.

    B. The customer dropped ____**it**____.
D.O.
4. A. <u>Everyone</u> <u><u>likes</u></u> **ANSWERS WILL VARY**. (Write your name in the blank.)

    B. Everyone likes ____**me**____.

346

Object pronouns are **me**, **him**, **her**, **us**, **them**, **whom**, **you**, and **it**.
They can serve as a *direct object*.

🐢 **Remember: A direct object receives the action of the verb.**

The child hit Peter.   The **object** the child hit was *Peter*.
The child hit **him** on the leg.

Doris planted a tree.   The **object** Doris planted was a tree.
Doris planted   **it**   last Monday.

Use **me**, **him**, **her**, **us**, **them**, **whom**, **you**, or **it** as a direct object.

> Example: Mr. Cline met **Stan** and **Bobby** in Canada.
> Mr. Cline met **them** in Canada.

🐢 🐢 🐢 🐢 🐢 🐢 🐢 🐢 🐢 🐢 🐢 🐢 🐢 🐢 🐢 🐢 🐢 🐢

Directions: In part A, underline the subject once and the verb twice.
Label the direct object - <u>D.O.</u> In part B, write a pronoun for the
word labeled as a direct object.

1.   A.   Rob sees Eileen often.

     B.   Rob sees _____ often.

2.   A.   Micah pushed Todd down.

     B.   Micah pushed _____ down.

3.   A.   The customer dropped a quarter.

     B.   The customer dropped _____.

4.   A.   Everyone likes _____. (Write your name in the blank.)

     B.   Everyone likes _____.

WORKBOOK PAGE 156

Date_____

Note to Teacher: Teach a lesson about compounds and use the finger trick before doing this page. Do this page and the ensuing one orally so that students can learn how the process works.

🐢 **Sometimes, there is more than one subject in a sentence.**

Example: **Gregg** and **Annie** built a fort.

🐢 **Sometimes, there is more than one object.**

Example: The teacher walked with **Susie** and **Lance**.

PRONOUN FINGER TRICK:

If you are unsure which pronoun to use, place your finger(s) over the **first part** of the compound. Usually, the pronoun that sounds right is correct.

Example: Gregg and (she, her) built a fort.
__**She**__ built a fort.
Gregg and (her, **she**) built a fort.

Example: The teacher walked with Susie and (he, him).
The teacher walked with __**him**__.
The teacher walked with Susie and (he, **him**).

🐢🐢🐢🐢🐢🐢🐢🐢🐢🐢🐢🐢🐢🐢🐢🐢🐢🐢

Directions: Circle the correct pronoun.

Remember: **Place your finger(s) over the first part of the compound. Then, reread the sentence and choose the correct pronoun.**

1. Rebecca sits beside Tally and (I, **me**).

2. Jay and (**I**, me) went to the movies.

3. Mom and (her, **she**) enjoy bridge.

4. Has Tracy gone with Chase and (she, **him**)?

348

🐢 **Sometimes, there is more than one subject in a sentence.**

     Example: **Gregg** and **Annie** built a fort.

🐢 **Sometimes, there is more than one object.**

     Example: The teacher walked with **Susie** and **Lance**.

PRONOUN FINGER TRICK:

If you are unsure which pronoun to use, place your finger(s) over the **first part** of the compound. Usually, the pronoun that sounds right is correct.

     Example: Gregg and (she, her) built a fort.

                   She   built a fort.

            Gregg and (her, **she**) built a fort.

     Example: The teacher walked with Susie and (he, him).

            The teacher walked with   **him**.

            The teacher walked with Susie and (he, **him**).

🐢 🐢 🐢 🐢 🐢 🐢 🐢 🐢 🐢 🐢 🐢 🐢 🐢 🐢 🐢 🐢 🐢 🐢 🐢

Directions: Circle the correct pronoun.

Remember: **Place your finger(s) over the first part of the compound. Then, reread the sentence and choose the correct pronoun.**

1.   Rebecca sits beside Tally and (I, me).

2.   Jay and (I, me) went to the movies.

3.   Mom and (her, she) enjoy bridge.

4.   Has Tracy gone with Chase and (she, him)?

Name_____   **PRONOUNS**
WORKBOOK PAGE 157   Compound Pronouns
Date_____

<u>**Note to Teacher: You may wish to do this worksheet orally.   Be sure to**</u>
<u>**have students actually place fingers over the first part of the compound.**</u>
PRONOUN FINGER TRICK:

If you don't know which pronoun to use, place your finger(s) over the **first**
part of the compound. Usually, the pronoun that sounds right is correct.

Examples: They handed awards to Julie and (me, I).
They handed awards to   (**me**, I).

Krista and (we, us) will be in charge.
... (**we**, us) will be in charge.

🐢 🐢 🐢 🐢 🐢 🐢 🐢 🐢 🐢 🐢 🐢 🐢 🐢 🐢 🐢 🐢 🐢 🐢

Directions: Circle the correct pronoun.

Remember: Place your finger(s) over the first part of the
compound.   Then, reread the sentence and choose
the correct pronoun.

1.   Marsha and (**I**, me) became sick.

2.   The thief was looking at their luggage and (they, **them**).

3.   Sit behind Randy and (**me**, I).

4.   A bee buzzed around our dad and (we, **us**).

5.   Miss Stump and (**he**, him) married last spring.

6.   After the final inning, Jamie and (her, **she**) bought soda.

7.   The flowers are from Mother and (**him**, he).

8.   Next week, his dad and (them, **they**) are going to Texas.
350

PRONOUN FINGER TRICK:

If you don't know which pronoun to use, place your finger(s) over the **first part** of the compound. Usually, the pronoun that sounds right is correct.

Examples: They handed awards to Julie and (me, I).

They handed awards to   (**me**, I).

Krista and (we, us) will be in charge.

... (**we**, us) will be in charge.

Directions: Circle the correct pronoun.

Remember: Place your finger(s) over the first part of the compound. Then, reread the sentence and choose the correct pronoun.

1. Marsha and (I, me) became sick.

2. The thief was looking at their luggage and (they, them).

3. Sit behind Randy and (me, I).

4. A bee buzzed around our dad and (we, us).

5. Miss Stump and (he, him) married last spring.

6. After the final inning, Jamie and (her, she) bought soda.

7. The flowers are from Mother and (him, he).

8. Next week, his dad and (them, they) are going to Texas.

A possessive pronoun takes the place of a noun and shows ownership.

my	mine
his	
her	hers
your	yours
its	
our	ours
their	theirs

My, *his*, *her*, *your*, *its*, *our*, and *their* will come **before** a noun (or pronoun).
Mine, *hers*, *yours*, *ours*, and *theirs* will come **after** a noun (or pronoun).

Example: shoes belonging to Juan

Juan's shoes

his shoes

🐢 🐢 🐢 🐢 🐢 🐢 🐢 🐢 🐢 🐢 🐢 🐢 🐢 🐢 🐢 🐢 🐢 🐢 🐢

Directions: Write a possessive pronoun on the line.

1.   Craig has black hair, and _____**his**_____ hair is curly.

2.   Gigi owns a parakeet, but _____**her**_____ parakeet is not yellow.

3.   Mr. and Mrs. Pod fly to Reno because _____**their**_____ son lives there.

4.   Ike said, "I like to dive, and _____**my**_____ favorite spot is Lake Erie."

5.   The lion roared and twitched _____**its**_____ tail.

6.   Look down. _____**Your**_____ shoelaces are loose.

7.   This is not your book. It is _____**mine/hers/his/theirs**_____ .

352

Name_____

Date_____

A possessive pronoun takes the place of a noun and shows ownership.

my	**mine**
his	
her	**hers**
your	**yours**
its	
our	**ours**
their	**theirs**

My, *his*, *her*, *your*, *its*, *our*, and *their* will come **before** a noun (or pronoun).
Mine, *hers*, *yours*, *ours*, and *theirs* will come **after** a noun (or pronoun).

Example: shoes belonging to Juan

Juan's shoes

his shoes

🐢 🐢 🐢 🐢 🐢 🐢 🐢 🐢 🐢 🐢 🐢 🐢 🐢 🐢 🐢 🐢 🐢 🐢

Directions: Write a possessive pronoun on the line.

1.   Craig has black hair, and _____ hair is curly.

2.   Gigi owns a parakeet, but _____ parakeet is not yellow.

3.   Mr. and Mrs. Pod fly to Reno because _____ son lives there.

4.   Ike said, "I like to dive, and _____ favorite spot is Lake Erie."

5.   The lion roared and twitched _____ tail.

6.   Look down. _____ shoelaces are loose.

7.   This is not your book. It is _____.

353

Name_____
WORKBOOK PAGE 159
Date_____

PRONOUNS
Its, It's
Your, You're
Their, There, They're

Note to Teacher: Although this is a review, some students have trouble. Be sure to first teach how to separate a contraction into two words and read the sentence again.

Incorrect:	I like you're coat.
	I like you are coat.
Correct:	I like your coat.

One of the most frequent errors is "Your nice." Give students ample time to write (positive) sentences to each other so that they can use the "You're nice" pattern.

🐢 *Its* **is a possessive pronoun.**

The dog wagged *its* tail.

If you can use *its*, ask *its what?* In this case, *its tail*

🐢 *Your* **is a possessive pronoun.**

Your dinner is getting cold.

If you can use *your*, ask *your what?* In this case, *your dinner.*

🐢 **Their is a possessive pronoun.**

Their parents are nice.

If you can use *their*, ask *their what?* In this case, *their parents.*

Remember, their is spelled <u>the + ir</u>.

There is an adverb telling where. *They're* is a contraction for *they are.*

🐢 🐢 🐢 🐢 🐢 🐢 🐢 🐢 🐢 🐢 🐢 🐢 🐢 🐢 🐢 🐢 🐢 🐢 🐢

Directions: Circle the correct word.

1. (Your, **You're**) very lucky.

2. Gigi has (**your**, you're) jacket.

3. Someone stole (**their**, they're, there) car.

4. A purse fell over on (**its**, it's) side.

5. (Its, **It's**) probably true.

6. I wonder if (their, **they're**, there) leaving today.

7. He believes that (your, **you're**) not feeling well.

8. Have you ever been (their, they're, **there**)?
354

🐢 *Its* **is a possessive pronoun.**
                    The dog wagged *its* tail.
If you can use *its*, ask *its what?* In this case, *its tail.*

🐢 *Your* **is a possessive pronoun**.
                    Your dinner is getting cold.
If you can use *your*, ask *your what?* In this case, *your dinner.*

🐢 **Their is a possessive pronoun.**
                    Their parents are nice.
If you can use *their*, ask *their what?* In this case, *their parents.*

          Remember, their is spelled <u>the + ir.</u>
There is an adverb telling where. *They're* is a contraction for *they are.*

🐢 🐢 🐢 🐢 🐢 🐢 🐢 🐢 🐢 🐢 🐢 🐢 🐢 🐢 🐢 🐢 🐢 🐢 🐢

Directions: Circle the correct word.

1.   (Your, You're) very lucky.

2.   Gigi has (your, you're) jacket.

3.   Someone stole (their, they're, there) car.

4.   A purse fell over on (its, it's) side.

5.   (Its, It's) probably true.

6.   I wonder if (their, they're, there) leaving today.

7.   He believes that (your, you're) not feeling well.

8.   Have you ever been (their, they're, there)?

Name_____

WORKBOOK PAGE 160

Date_____

PRONOUNS
Its, It's
Your, You're
Their, There, They're

Note to Teacher: You may wish to do at least half of this page orally. Students should be able to separate the contraction or if the possessive is used, tell what the pronoun modifies (as in #3, *its top*).

Directions: Circle the correct word.

1. (Its, **It's**) a close race.

2. This salsa is spicy, but (its, **it's**) not too hot.

3. The desk is new, yet (**its**, it's) top looks used.

4. (**Your**, You're) peanut butter sandwich is on the counter.

5. (Your, **You're**) always so quiet.

6. Does she know about (**your**, you're) plans?

7. (Their, **They're**, There) making pancakes.

8. (Their, They're, **There**) are no pencils in this box.

9. (**Their**, They're, There) cousins are from Denver.

10. An elephant lifted (**its**, it's) head and trumpeted.

11. (Your, **You're**) the only one who can help me.

12. I like (**your**, you're) checked wallpaper.

13. She asked if (**their**, they're, there) uncle golfs.

14. He doesn't know if (their, **they're**, there) leaving tomorrow.

15. The bank opens (**its**, it's) doors at nine o'clock.

356

Name_____

Date_____

Directions: Circle the correct word.

1.   (Its, It's) a close race.

2.   This salsa is spicy, but (its, it's) not too hot.

3.   The desk is new, yet (its, it's) top looks used.

4.   (Your, You're) peanut butter sandwich is on the counter.

5.   (Your, You're) always so quiet.

6.   Does she know about (your, you're) plans?

7.   (Their, They're, There) making pancakes.

8.   (Their, They're, There) are no pencils in this box.

9.   (Their, They're, There) cousins are from Denver.

10.   An elephant lifted (its, it's) head and trumpeted.

11.   (Your, You're) the only one who can help me.

12.   I like (your, you're) checked wallpaper.

13.   She asked if (their, they're, there) uncle golfs.

14.   He doesn't know if (their, they're, there) leaving tomorrow.

15.   The bank opens (its, it's) doors at nine o'clock.

Note to Teacher: **Although this review is four pages, it should not take long for students to complete it. However, pages have again been set up with name and date so that the pages can be completed over many days, if desired.**

A.   Subject Pronouns:

Subject pronouns usually serve as the subject of a sentence.
Subject pronouns include **I**, **he**, **she**, **we**, **they**, **you**, and **it**.

Directions: In part A, write a person's name. In part B, write a pronoun for the name. In the double underlined part, finish the sentence.

Example: A. _____**Les**_____ is a fireman.

B. _____**He**_____ works _in San Diego._

ANSWERS WILL VARY.

1.   A. _____**Mr. Krick**_____ is my principal.

B. _____**He**_____ is _very smart._

2.   A. _____**Brittany**_____ and I are friends.

B. _____**We**_____ like _to put puzzles together._

B.   Using I:

Directions: Rewrite the sentence correctly.

1.   My friend and me go to the park.

_____**My friend and I go to the park.**_____

2.   Me and my dog chase each other.

_____**My dog and I chase each other.**_____

358

A. Subject Pronouns:

Subject pronouns usually serve as the subject of a sentence.
Subject pronouns include **I**, **he**, **she**, **we**, **they**, **you**, and **it**.

Directions: In part A, write a person's name. In part B, write a
pronoun for the name. In the double underlined part,
finish the sentence.

Example: A. _____**Les**_____ is a fireman.

B. _____**He**_____ works _in San Diego._

1. A. _____ is my principal.

B. _____ is _____

2. A. _____ and I are friends.

B. _____ like _____

B. Using I:

Directions: Rewrite the sentence correctly.

1. My friend and me go to the park.

_____

2. Me and my dog chase each other.

_____

Date_____

C.   Object Pronouns - Object of the Preposition:

Object pronouns can serve as an object of the preposition. Object pronouns include **me**, **him**, **her**, **us**, **them**, **you**, and **it**.

Directions: Place an X above the preposition. Then, circle the correct pronoun.
PREPOSITIONS ARE IN BOLDFACED ITALICS.

1.   The waiter stared *at* (she, **her**).

2.   A stranger walked *toward* (we, **us**).

3.   You may enter *after* (I, **me**).

4.   A laughing child put a bug *on* (**him**, he).

D.   Object Pronouns - Direct Object:

Object pronouns can serve as a direct object. Object pronouns include **me**, **him**, **her**, **us**, **them**, **you**, and **it**.

Directions: In part A, underline the subject once and the verb twice.
Label the direct object - <u>D.O.</u> In part B, write a pronoun for the word labeled as a direct object.
                         D.O.
1.   A.   A <u>wasp</u> <u>stung</u> Helen.

     B.   A wasp stung _____**her**_____.
                        D.O.   **D.O.**
2.   A.   His <u>remark</u> <u>hurt</u> Allan and his sister.

     B.   His remark hurt ____**them**____.
                        D.O.   **D.O.**   ANSWERS WILL VARY.
3.   A.   The <u>teacher</u> <u>likes</u> Darla and ____**Pearl**____. *(Write your name.)*

     B.   The teacher likes ____**us**____.

C.   Object Pronouns - Object of the Preposition:

Object pronouns can serve as an object of the preposition. Object pronouns include **me**, **him**, **her**, **us**, **them**, **you**, and **it**.

> Directions: Place an X above the preposition. Then, circle the correct pronoun.

1.   The waiter stared at (she, her).

2.   A stranger walked toward (we, us).

3.   You may enter after (I, me).

4.   A laughing child put a bug on (him, he).

D.   Object Pronouns - Direct Object:

Object pronouns can serve as a direct object. Object pronouns include **me, him**, **her**, **us**, **them**, **you**, and **it**.

Directions: In part A, underline the subject once and the verb twice.
Label the direct object - D.O. In part B, write a pronoun for the word labeled as a direct object.

1.   A.   A wasp stung Helen.

 B.   A wasp stung _____.

2.   A.   His remark hurt Allan and his sister.

 B.   His remark hurt _____.

3.   A.   The teacher likes Darla and _____. (*Write your name.*)

 B.   The teacher likes _____.

E.   Subject or Object Pronouns:

   Directions: Circle the correct pronoun.

1.   Corey slapped (**me**, I) on the back.

2.   No, don't pick (he, **him**) up!

3.   During her break, (**she**, her) reads.

4.   A man reached above (we, **us**) for his hat.

5.   Miss Lane gave directions to (they, **them**).

6.   Do (**we**, us) need an umbrella today?

F.   Compound Pronouns:

   Directions: Circle the correct pronoun.

🐢 **Remember: Place your finger(s) over the first part of the compound.   Then, reread the sentence and choose the correct pronoun.**

1.   A porter carried bags for our parents and (we, **us**).

2.   The Jensens and (them, **they**) are having a picnic.

3.   Martha and (**I**, me) rode a pony.

4.   Do you want to ride with Nicky and (I, **me**)?
                         plays   (In using the finger trick, s̲ must be added to the verb.)

5.   Shannon and (**he**, him) play bingo.

362

E. Subject or Object Pronouns:

Directions: Circle the correct pronoun.

1. Corey slapped (me, I) on the back.

2. No, don't pick (he, him) up!

3. During her break, (she, her) reads.

4. A man reached above (we, us) for his hat.

5. Miss Lane gave directions to (they, them).

6. Do (we, us) need an umbrella today?

F. Compound Pronouns:

Directions: Circle the correct pronoun.

🐢 **Remember: Place your finger(s) over the first part of the compound. Then, reread the sentence and choose the correct pronoun.**

1. A porter carried bags for our parents and (we, us).

2. The Jensens and (them, they) are having a picnic.

3. Martha and (I, me) rode a pony.

4. Do you want to ride with Nicky and (I, me)?

5. Shannon and (he, him) play bingo.

G.   Possessive Pronouns:

A possessive pronoun takes the place of a noun and shows ownership.
My (mine), his, her (hers), your (yours), its, our (ours), and **their (theirs)** are possessive pronouns.

Directions: Write a possessive pronoun on the line.

1.   I am having fun, and _____**my**_____ day is going well.

2.   You need to take _____**your**_____ dish to the sink.

3.   Several cows lay in the field. _____**Their**_____ calves grazed nearby.

4.   My sister and I made a toy boat, and _____**our**_____ father painted it.

H.   Its/It's, Your/You're, Their/They're/There:

Directions: Circle the correct word.

1.   (Its, **It's**) becoming cloudy.

2.   Do I have (**your**, you're) phone number?

3.   (**Their**, They're, There) kitten sleeps in a box.

4.   Tomorrow, (their, **they're**, there) climbing a mountain.

5.   The rat had a string caught in (**its**, it's) foot.

6.   (Your, **You're**) the leader of our team.

364

G.   Possessive Pronouns:

A possessive pronoun takes the place of a noun and shows ownership.
My (mine), his, her (hers), your (yours), its, our (ours), and **their (theirs)** are possessive pronouns.

   Directions: Write a possessive pronoun on the line.

1.   I am having fun, and _____ day is going well.

2.   You need to take _____ dish to the sink.

3.   Several cows lay in the field. _____ calves grazed nearby.

4.   My sister and I made a toy boat, and _____ father painted it.

H.   Its/It's, Your/You're, Their/They're/There:

   Directions: Circle the correct word.

1.   (Its, It's) becoming cloudy.

2.   Do I have (your, you're) phone number?

3.   (Their, They're, There) kitten sleeps in a box.

4.   Tomorrow, (their, they're, there) climbing a mountain.

5.   The rat had a string caught in (its, it's) foot.

6.   (Your, You're) the leader of our team.   365

Name_____

Date_____

A.   Directions: Circle the correct pronoun.

1.   His team played against (we, **us**).

2.   (**She**, Her) has come alone.

3.   Their mother sat beside (I, **me**).

4.   Miss Plank tutors (they, **them**) on Saturday.

5.   At the end of June, (**we**, us) go to a baseball camp.

6.   His partner told (he, **him**) about the case.

7.   (**They**, Them) have bought hot dogs for lunch.

8.   Jill and (me, **I**) want to take piano lessons.

9.   Are the cookies from (she, **her**)?

10.   Between innings, Roy and (**he**, him) walked around.

B.   Directions: Circle the correct word.

1.   Someone said that (its, **it's**) beginning to snow.

2.   Are the windows in (**your**, you're) van rolled down?

3.   The Hunts take (**their**, they're, there) dogs to the park.

4.   (Your, **You're**) the first to hear the news.

5.   Don't stop them. (Their, **They're**, There) in a hurry.

A. Directions: Circle the correct pronoun.

1. His team played against (we, us).

2. (She, Her) has come alone.

3. Their mother sat beside (I, me).

4. Miss Plank tutors (they, them) on Saturday.

5. At the end of June, (we, us) go to a baseball camp.

6. His partner told (he, him) about the case.

7. (They, Them) have bought hot dogs for lunch.

8. Jill and (me, I) want to take piano lessons.

9. Are the cookies from (she, her)?

10. Between innings, Roy and (he, him) walked around.

B. Directions: Circle the correct word.

1. Someone said that (its, it's) beginning to snow.

2. Are the windows in (your, you're) van rolled down?

3. The Hunts take (their, they're, there) dogs to the park.

4. (Your, You're) the first to hear the news.

5. Don't stop them. (Their, They're, There) in a hurry.   367

TO THE TEACHER:

The **capitalization** and **punctuation** units have been placed after the pronoun cumulative reviews and tests.

EXTREMELY IMPORTANT:

You may wish to wait to do the cumulative reviews and tests **after** you have completed capitalization and punctuation. Allowing more time before reviewing grammar concepts has its positive and negative aspects. In doing the reviews and tests **before** capitalization and punctuation, the material will be fresher in the students' minds and thus the material should be reinforced again. However, if your goal is to gain a perspective on how much has been learned so that you can go back and reteach parts that have not been understood, completing the reviews after capitalization and punctuation would be best.

TO THE TEACHER: **EXTREMELY IMPORTANT**

The cumulative review for the end of the pronoun unit has been separated into three parts:

A.   The first part on pages **370-377** covers **prepositions, subjects,** and **verbs.**

   A **test** for the first part is on pages *392-397* (3 test pages).

B.   The second part on pages **378-385** covers **nouns** and **adjectives.**

   A **test** for the second part is on pages *398-401* (2 test pages).

C.   The third part on pages **386-391** covers **conjunctions, interjections, sentence types,** and **adverbs.**

   A **test** for the third part is on pages *402-405* (2 test pages).

ABOUT THE CUMULATIVE TESTS:

In most cases, the cumulative tests do not include subskills. For example, students have not been asked to list the twenty-three helping verbs. Mastery of these will be reflected in underlining verb phrases. Also, students have not been required to delete prepositional phrases or to determine subject and verb phrase when circling the past participle form. Although I believe that this practice helps (and was included in the cumulative review), it has not been required on the test. You may wish to instruct students to use the process on pages 396-397, part F. Also, because sentence types were introduced so late in this text, an explanation of the types has been included on the cumulative test.

A. **Prepositions and Verb Phrases:**

Directions: Cross out any prepositional phrase(s). Underline the subject once and the verb or verb phrase twice.

Remember: **helping verb(s) + main verb = verb phrase**
may have gone = may have gone

1. A stray <u>cat</u> <u><u>is sitting</u></u> ~~on our patio~~.

2. <u>They</u> <u><u>must have left</u></u> ~~before the end of the tennis match~~.

3. ~~During our picnic~~, <u>John</u> <u><u>did</u></u> **not** <u><u>help</u></u> ~~with the cooking~~.

4. <u>(You)</u> <u><u>Save</u></u> the water ~~in this cup for me~~.

B. **Compound Subject and Compound Verb:**

Directions: Cross out any prepositional phrase(s). Underline the subject once and the verb or verb phrase twice.

Remember: **The subject or verb will not be a word in a prepositional phrase.**

1. <u>Paper</u> and <u>pencils</u> <u><u>are</u></u> ~~on a table by the speaker~~.

2. A <u>child</u> <u><u>leaned</u></u> ~~over the railing~~ and <u><u>tossed</u></u> a coin ~~into the water~~.

C. **Can/May:**

Directions: Circle the correct word.

1. (Can, **May**) I go to the bathroom?

2. I (**can**, may) understand your problem.

A.   Prepositions and Verb Phrases:

Directions: Cross out any prepositional phrase(s). Underline the
subject once and the verb or verb phrase twice.

Remember: **helping verb(s) + main verb = verb phrase**
may have   gone   = may have gone

1.   A stray cat is sitting on our patio.

2.   They must have left before the end of the tennis match.

3.   During our picnic, John did not help with the cooking.

4.   Save the water in this cup for me.

B.   Compound Subject and Compound Verb:

Directions: Cross out any prepositional phrase(s). Underline the
subject once and the verb or verb phrase twice.

Remember: **The subject or verb will not be a word in a prepositional
phrase.**

1.   Paper and pencils are on a table by the speaker.

2.   A child leaned over the railing and tossed a coin into the water.

C.   Can/May:

Directions: Circle the correct word.

1.   (Can, May) I go to the bathroom?

2.   I (can, may) understand your problem.

371

D.   Contractions:

Directions: Write the contraction in the space provided.

1. were not - _____**weren't**_____   8. I will - _____**I'll**_____

2. where is - _____**where's**_____   9. cannot - _____**can't**_____

3. we are - _____**we're**_____   10. will not - _____**won't**_____

4. should not - _____**shouldn't**_____   11. they are - _____**they're**_____

5. you will - _____**you'll**_____   12. that is - _____**that's**_____

6. did not - _____**didn't**_____   13. I have - _____**I've**_____

7. you are - _____**you're**_____   14. does not - _____**doesn't**_____

E.   Direct Objects:

Directions: Underline the subject once and the verb twice. Label the
               direct object - D.O.

D.O.
1. That <u>dentist</u> <u>gives</u> toothbrushes.

D.O.
2. Our <u>dog</u> <u>buried</u> a bone.

D.O.
3. <u>We</u> <u>wash</u> our car every Saturday.

D.   Contractions:

Directions: Write the contraction in the space provided.

1. were not - _____   8. I will - _____

2. where is - _____   9. cannot - _____

3. we are - _____   10. will not - _____

4. should not - _____   11. they are - _____

5. you will - _____   12. that is - _____

6. did not - _____   13. I have - _____

7. you are - _____   14. does not - _____

E.   Direct Objects:

Directions: Underline the subject once and the verb twice. Label the
direct object - <u>D.O.</u>

1. That dentist gives toothbrushes.

2. Our dog buried a bone.

3. We wash our car every Saturday.

F.   Action?:

Directions: Write <u>Yes</u> if the boldfaced verb shows action.   Write <u>No</u> if the boldfaced verb does not show action.

1.   __**Yes**__   The boy **looked** everywhere for his glasses.

2.   __**No**__   You **look** very pleased with yourself.

G.   Regular or Irregular:

Directions: Write <u>RV</u> in the blank if the verb is regular.   Write <u>IV</u> if the verb is irregular.

1.   __**IV**__   to shake   2.   __**IV**__   to bring   3.   __**RV**__   to need

H.   Helping (Auxiliary) Verbs:

Directions: Write the twenty-three helping verbs.

__**do, does, did, has, have, had, may, might, must, should, would,**__

__**could, shall, will, can, is, am, are, was, were, be, being, been**__

I.   Subject/Verb Agreement:

Directions: Circle the correct verb.

1.   My cat (meow, **meows**) softly.

2.   Those birds (**drink**, drinks) from our birdbath.

3.   I (**stay**, stays) inside after dinner.

374

F. Action?:

Directions: Write <u>Yes</u> if the boldfaced verb shows action. Write <u>No</u> if the boldfaced verb does not show action.

1. _____   The boy **looked** everywhere for his glasses.

2. _____   You **look** very pleased with yourself.

G.   Regular or Irregular:

Directions: Write <u>RV</u> in the blank if the verb is regular. Write <u>IV</u> if the verb is irregular.

1. _____ to shake   2. _____ to bring   3. _____ to need

H.   Helping (Auxiliary) Verbs:

Directions: Write the twenty-three helping verbs.

_____

_____

I.   Subject/Verb Agreement:

Directions: Circle the correct verb.

1. My cat (meow, meows) softly.

2. Those birds (drink, drinks) from our birdbath.

3. I (stay, stays) inside after dinner.

J.   Irregular Verbs:

Directions: Cross out any prepositional phrase(s). Underline the
subject once and the verb or verb phrase twice.

1.   The football <u>game has</u> (began, <u>begun</u>).

2.   The <u>canoe must have</u> (<u>sunk</u>, sank).

3.   <u>Allie should have</u> (saw, <u>seen</u>) the comet!

4.   <u>Have you</u> (<u>worn</u>, wore) your new shoes?

5.   <u>I could have</u> (took, <u>taken</u>) the bus.

6.   <u>Dad has</u> **not** (got, <u>gotten</u>) the mail.

7.   <u>Mrs. Hand should have</u> (ran, <u>run</u>) ~~for governor~~.

8.   The taxi <u>cab has</u> finally (came, <u>come</u>).

K.   Tenses:

Directions: Write the tense of the boldfaced verb.

Remember: The tenses are *present*, *past*, and *future*.

1.   _____**present**_____   His mom **lifts** weights.

2.   _____**past**_____   We **found** someone's wallet.

3.   _____**future**_____   Franny **will fly** to Tulsa tomorrow.
376

J.   Irregular Verbs:

Directions: Cross out any prepositional phrase(s). Underline the subject once and the verb or verb phrase twice.

1.   The football game has (began, begun).

2.   The canoe must have (sunk, sank).

3.   Allie should have (saw, seen) the comet!

4.   Have you (worn, wore) your new shoes?

5.   I could have (took, taken) the bus.

6.   Dad has not (got, gotten) the mail.

7.   Mrs. Hand should have (ran, run) for governor.

8.   The taxi cab has finally (came, come).

K.   Tenses:

Directions: Write the tense of the boldfaced verb.

Remember: The tenses are *present*, *past*, and *future*.

1.   _____   His mom **lifts** weights.

2.   _____   We **found** someone's wallet.

3.   _____   Franny **will fly** to Tulsa tomorrow.

377

A.   Common and Proper Nouns:

Directions: Write a proper noun for each common noun.
ANSWERS WILL VARY.

1.   town -_____**Hanover**_____   3.   country -_____**Japan**_____

2.   actor -_____**John Wayne**_____   4.   ocean -_____**Arctic Ocean**_____

B.   Common or Proper Nouns:

Directions: Write <u>C</u> if the noun is common. Write <u>P</u> if the noun is proper.

1.   __**C**__   COMB   3.   __**C**__   BUBBLE GUM 5.   __**C**__   HOUND

2.   __**P**__   RED SEA   4.   __**C**__   COMPUTER   6.   __**P**__   SUSAN

C.   Singular and Plural Nouns:

Directions: Write the plural.

1.   bush - _____**bushes**_____   6.   flame - _____**flames**_____

2.   crutch - _____**crutches**_____   7.   mix - _____**mixes**_____

3.   pain - _____**pains**_____   8.   goose - _____**geese**_____

4.   elf - _____**elves**_____   9.   day - _____**days**_____

5.   deer - _____**deer**_____   10. rodeo - _____**rodeos**_____

378

A.   Common and Proper Nouns:

Directions: Write a proper noun for each common noun.

1.   town -_____   3.   country -_____

2.   actor -_____   4.   ocean - _____

B.   Common or Proper Nouns:

Directions: Write C if the noun is common.   Write P if the noun is proper.

1.   _____ COMB   3.   _____ BUBBLE GUM 5.   _____ HOUND

2.   _____ RED SEA   4.   _____ COMPUTER   6.   _____ SUSAN

C.   Singular and Plural Nouns:

Directions: Write the plural.

1.   bush - _____   6.   flame - _____

2.   crutch - _____   7.   mix - _____

3.   pain - _____   8.   goose - _____

4.   elf - _____   9.   day - _____

5.   deer - _____   10. rodeo - _____

379

D. Possessive Nouns:

Directions: Write the possessive.

1. shoes belonging to David - _____ **David's shoes** _____

2. a locker shared by two girls - _____ **girls' locker** _____

3. a store owned by more than one man - **men's store** _____

4. goldfish owned by Wendy - _____ **Wendy's goldfish** _____

E. Noun Identification:

Directions: Circle any nouns.

🐢 Remember: **A noun names a person, place, or thing.**
Look for "things" you can see.

1. A **groundhog** ran across the **road**.

2. **Bess** bought a **puppy** for her **brother**.

3. A **car** and **boat** are parked by their **house**.

4. His **family** goes to **Kansas** in a **jet**.

5. **Grandma** keeps her **watch** in a tiny **dish** by her **bed**.

380

D. Possessive Nouns:

Directions: Write the possessive.

1. shoes belonging to David - _____

2. a locker shared by two girls - _____

3. a store owned by more than one man - _____

4. goldfish owned by Wendy -_____

E. Noun Identification:

Directions: Circle any nouns.

🐢 **Remember:** **A noun names a person, place, or thing.**
Look for "things" you can see.

1. A groundhog ran across the road.

2. Bess bought a puppy for her brother.

3. A car and boat are parked by their house.

4. His family goes to Kansas in a jet.

5. Grandma keeps her watch in a tiny dish by her bed.

F.   Adjectives (Describing Words):

Directions: Write two describing words for each noun.
ANSWERS WILL VARY.

1. _____**fancy**_____   _____**lace**_____   bedspread

2. _____**little**_____   _____**red**_____   wagon

3. _____**pretty**_____   _____**flowered**_____   dress

G.   A, An, and The:

Directions: Write *a* or *an* before each word or group of words.

1. __**an**__ army   4. __**an**__ octopus

2. __**a**__ coat   5. __**an**__ inch

3. __**an**__ elm tree   6. __**a**__ chocolate shake

H.   Limiting Adjectives:

Directions: Fill in the blank.

1. __**A**__ , __**an**__ , and __**the**__ are articles that are adjectives.
ANSWERS WILL VARY.

2.   Write an example of a number used as an adjective: __**eleven**__ horses.

3.   Unscramble these adjectives that tell how many:

   a. laresve - __**several**__   c. yanm - __**many**__

   b. moes - __**some**__   d. wfe - __**few**__

F.   Adjectives (Describing Words):

Directions: Write two describing words for each noun.

1.   _____   _____ bedspread

2.   _____   _____ wagon

3.   _____   _____ dress

G.   A, An, and The:

Directions: Write *a* or *an* before each word or group of words.

1.   _____ army   4.   _____ octopus

2.   _____ coat   5.   _____ inch

3.   _____ elm tree   6.   _____ chocolate shake

H.   Limiting Adjectives:

Directions: Fill in the blank.

1.   _____, _____, and _____ are articles that are adjectives.

2.   Write an example of a number used as an adjective: _____ horses.

3.   Unscramble these adjectives that tell how many:

   a. laresve - _____   c. yanm - _____

   b. moes - _____   d. wfe -_____   383

I.   Identifying Adjectives:

Directions: Circle each adjective.

🐢 **Remember:**   *A*, *an*, and *the* are adjectives.

Numbers and words like *some*, *several*, *few*,
many, *no*, and *any* can be limiting adjectives.
Most adjectives are describing words.

1.   **A puffer** fish swam in **the blue** water.

2.   **Two large** sheep grazed in **an open** field.

3.   I like **banana** splits with **chopped** nuts.

4.   Have **any yellow** birds flown by?

J.   Degrees of Adjectives:

Directions: Circle the correct form.

1.   Elaine is (**taller**, tallest) than her mother.

2.   He is the (heavier, **heaviest**) triplet.

3.   Your funny story is (interestinger, **more interesting**) than my scary
one.

4.   This puppy is (more loveable, **most loveable**) of the litter.

5.   Of the two radios, the blue one has (**better**, best) sound.

384

I. Identifying Adjectives:

Directions: Circle each adjective.

🐢**Remember:**   *A*, *an*, and *the* are adjectives.

Numbers and words like *some*, *several*, *few*,

many, *no*, and *any* can be limiting adjectives.

Most adjectives are describing words.

1. A puffer fish swam in the blue water.

2. Two large sheep grazed in an open field.

3. I like banana splits with chopped nuts.

4. Have any yellow birds flown by?

J. Degrees of Adjectives:

Directions: Circle the correct form.

1. Elaine is (taller, tallest) than her mother.

2. He is the (heavier, heaviest) triplet.

3. Your funny story is (interestinger, more interesting) than my scary one.

4. This puppy is (more loveable, most loveable) of the litter.

5. Of the two radios, the blue one has (better, best) sound.   385

A.   Conjunctions:

Directions: Write <u>conj.</u> above each conjunction.

conj.
1.   Meg **or** her friend will take you to the airport.

conj.   **conj.**
2.   You may go, **but** take your brother **and** sister.

B.   Interjections:

Directions: Write <u>intj.</u> above each interjection.

intj.
1.   **Wow!** You are very strong!

intj.
2.   I can do it! **Yeah!**

C.   Sentence Types:

Directions: Write the sentence type.

Remember: A **declarative** sentence makes a *statement.*
An **interrogative** sentence asks a *question.*
An **imperative** sentence gives a *command.*
An **exclamatory sentence** *shows emotion.*

1.   _____**interrogative**_____   Who left?

2.   _____**declarative**_____   He left.

3.   _____**imperative**_____   Please leave.

4.   _____**exclamatory**_____   Yippee! We're leaving!

386

A. Conjunctions:

Directions: Write <u>conj.</u> above each conjunction.

1.   Meg or her friend will take you to the airport.

2. You may go, but take your brother and sister.

B. Interjections:

Directions: Write <u>intj.</u> above each interjection.

1. Wow! You are very strong!

2. I can do it!   Yeah!

C. Sentence Types:

Directions: Write the sentence type.

Remember: A **declarative** sentence makes a *statement.*
An **interrogative** sentence asks a *question.*
An **imperative** sentence gives a *command.*
An **exclamatory sentence** *shows emotion.*

1. _____   Who left?

2. _____   He left.

3. _____   Please leave.

4. _____   Yippee! We're leaving!

D. **Adverbs That Tell How**:

Directions: Fill in the blank.

1. Angie is a soft talker.

    She talks ___**softly**_____.

2. His face had a wide smile.

    He smiled ___**widely**_____.

E. **Adverbs That Tell How**:

Directions: Circle the adverb that tells *how*.

1. The host laughed **loudly**.

2. Corbin works **harder** in the evening.

3. The little girl looked **sadly** at her father.

F. **Adverbs That Tell When**:

Directions: Circle the adverb that tells *when*.

1. We must do it **now**.

2. **Tonight**, I hope to see a shooting star.

3. Mrs. Robb visits her mother **daily**.

4. I **never** put sugar on my cereal.

388

D.   Adverbs That Tell How:

Directions: Fill in the blank.

1.   Angie is a soft talker.

She talks _____.

2.   His face had a wide smile.

He smiled _____.

E.   Adverbs That Tell How:

Directions: Circle the adverb that tells *how*.

1.   The host laughed loudly.

2.   Corbin works harder in the evening.

3.   The little girl looked sadly at her father.

F.   Adverbs That Tell When:

Directions: Circle the adverb that tells *when*.

1.   We must do it now.

2.   Tonight, I hope to see a shooting star.

3.   Mrs. Robb visits her mother daily.

4.   I never put sugar on my cereal.

G. Adverbs That Tell Where:

Directions: Circle the adverb that tells *where*.

1. Stay **there**.

2. **Where** are you going?

3. Please come **inside**.

H. Adverbs That Tell to What Extent:

Directions: Circle the adverb that tells *to what extent*.

1. He answered **very** rudely.

2. This ball has become **rather** flat.

3. You swim **quite** well.

I. Degrees of Adverbs:

Directions: Circle the correct form.

1. She hit the ball (**harder**, hardest) during her second time at bat.

2. I write (**more sloppily**, most sloppily) with my left hand.

3. Rob draws animals (**better**, weller) than people.

4. The banker spoke (more kindly, **most kindly**) to his third client.

5. Michael skates (**more rapidly**, most rapidly) than his older brother.

G. Adverbs That Tell Where:

Directions: Circle the adverb that tells *where*.

1. Stay there.

2. Where are you going?

3. Please come inside.

H. Adverbs That Tell to What Extent:

Directions: Circle the adverb that tells *to what extent*.

1. He answered very rudely.

2. This ball has become rather flat.

3. You swim quite well.

I. Degrees of Adverbs:

Directions: Circle the correct form.

1. She hit the ball (harder, hardest) during her second time at bat.

2. I write (more sloppily, most sloppily) with my left hand.

3. Rob draws animals (better, weller) than people.

4. The banker spoke (more kindly, most kindly) to his third client.

5. Michael skates (more rapidly, most rapidly) than his older brother. 391

Name_____

Date_____

A. Directions: Cross out any prepositional phrase(s). Underline the
                 subject once and the verb or verb phrase twice.
                 Label the direct object - <u>D.O.</u> in sentences 4, 5, and 6.

1. <u>Herb</u> <u>works</u> ~~on a farm~~ ~~during the summer~~.

2. <u>Daisies</u> and <u>roses</u> <u>have been placed</u> ~~in a vase~~.

3. (You) <u>Step</u> ~~into the tub~~ ~~of warm water~~.
                         D.O.

4. <u>Todd</u> <u>sands</u> and <u>paints</u> furniture ~~for his uncle~~.
                         D.O.

5. <u>We</u> <u>could</u> **not** <u>attend</u> the wedding.
                         D.O.

6. <u>Rita</u> <u>must have given</u> her ring ~~to her sister~~.

B. Directions: Circle the correct verb.

1. He (**can**, may) dive well.

2. You (can, **may**) check out this library book.

3. (Can, **May**) Mrs. Storm take your coat?

4. His posters (**shine**, shines) in the dark.

5. A bear (**lives**, live) in those woods.

6. I (**clean**, cleans) my room each week.

7. Jay and his sister (**like**, likes) to sled.

392

A.   Directions: Cross out any prepositional phrase(s). Underline the
                     subject once and the verb or verb phrase twice.
                     Label the direct object - <u>D.O.</u> in sentences 4, 5, and 6.

1.   Herb works on a farm during the summer.

2.   Daisies and roses have been placed in a vase.

3.   Step into the tub of warm water.

4.   Todd sands and paints furniture for his uncle.

5.   We could not attend the wedding.

6.   Rita must have given her ring to her sister.

B.   Directions: Circle the correct verb.

1.   He (can, may) dive well.

2.   You (can, may) check out this library book.

3.   (Can, May) Mrs. Storm take your coat?

4.   His posters (shine, shines) in the dark.

5.   A bear (lives, live) in those woods.

6.   I (clean, cleans) my room each week.

7.   Jay and his sister (like, likes) to sled.

C.   Directions: Write the contraction.

1. I am - _____**I'm**_____   8. are not - _____**aren't**_____

2. that is - _____**that's**_____   9. who is - _____**who's**_____

3. you will - _____**you'll**_____   10. will not - _____**won't**_____

4. would not - _**wouldn't**_____   11. cannot - _____**can't**_____

5. they are - _____**they're**_____   12. we are - _____**we're**_____

6. she is - _____**she's**_____   13. is not - _____**isn't**_____

7. does not - ____**doesn't**_____   14. I will - _____**I'll**_____

D.   Directions: Write <u>Yes</u> if the boldfaced verb shows action. Write <u>No</u> if
                 the boldfaced verb does not show action.

1. ___**Yes**___   Her book **fell** to the floor.

2. ___**No**____   I **feel** sick.

3. ___**Yes**___   A large owl often **sits** on that branch.

E.   Directions: Write <u>RV</u> in the blank if the verb is regular. Write <u>IV</u> if the
                 verb is irregular.

1. ___**IV**___ to speak   2. ___**RV**___ to crawl   3. ___**IV**___ to keep

C. Directions: Write the contraction.

1. I am - _____

2. that is - _____

3. you will - _____

4. would not - _____

5. they are - _____

6. she is - _____

7. does not - _____

8. are not - _____

9. who is - _____

10. will not - _____

11. cannot - _____

12. we are - _____

13. is not - _____

14. I will - _____

D. Directions: Write <u>Yes</u> if the boldfaced verb shows action. Write <u>No</u> if the boldfaced verb does not show action.

1. _____ Her book **fell** to the floor.

2. _____ I **feel** sick.

3. _____ A large owl often **sits** on that branch.

E. Directions: Write <u>RV</u> in the blank if the verb is regular. Write <u>IV</u> if the verb is irregular.

1. _____ to speak   2. _____ to crawl   3. _____ to keep

F.   Directions: Circle the correct verb.

1.   The dam has (busted, **burst**).

2.   I could have (**swum**, swam) longer.

3.   Have you ever (ran, **run**) in a relay race?

4.   Jude must have (stole, **stolen**) third base!

5.   I have never (**seen**, saw) a puffin.

6.   Has the telephone (rang, **rung**)?

7.   You should have (rode, **ridden**) your bike.

8.   Shirley may not have (**taken**, took) the right bus.

9.   He has (went, **gone**) to a movie with his dad.

10. Someone must have (**drunk**, drank) my milk.

G.   Directions: Write the tense (*present*, *past*, or *future*) of the boldfaced verb.

1. _____**past**_____   I **hid** your present.

2. _____**present**_____   Jimmy **saves** pennies.

3. _____**future**_____   Ken **will type** his paper tomorrow.

4. _____**present**_____   They sometimes **sleep** outside.

396

F.   Directions: Circle the correct verb.

1.   The dam has (busted, burst).

2.   I could have (swum, swam) longer.

3.   Have you ever (ran, run) in a relay race?

4.   Jude must have (stole, stolen) third base!

5.   I have never (seen, saw) a puffin.

6.   Has the telephone (rang, rung)?

7.   You should have (rode, ridden) your bike.

8.   Shirley may not have (taken, took) the right bus.

9.   He has (went, gone) to a movie with his dad.

10.   Someone must have (drunk, drank) my milk.

G.   Directions: Write the tense (*present, past,* or *future*) of the boldfaced verb.

1.   _____   I **hid** your present.

2.   _____   Jimmy **saves** pennies.

3.   _____   Ken **will type** his paper tomorrow.

4.   _____   They sometimes **sleep** outside.

Name_____   **Cumulative Test**
                                          Pronouns
Date_____

A.   Directions: Write <u>C</u> if the noun is common.   Write <u>P</u> if the noun is proper.

1.   __**C**__   RIVER   3.   __**P**__   GLENN   5.   __**C**__   BUILDING

2.   __**P**__   SNAKE RIVER 4.   __**C**__   BOY   6.   __**C**__   TOWER

B.   Directions: Write the plural.

1.   match - _____**matches**_____   6.   play - _____**plays**_____

2.   guppy - _____**guppies**_____   7.   deer - _____**deer**_____

3.   eye - _____**eyes**_____   8.   mouse - _____**mice**_____

4.   rash - _____**rashes**_____   9.   box - _____**boxes**_____

5.   child - _____**children**_____   10.   tomato - _____**tomatoes**_____

C.   Directions: Circle any nouns.

1.   The **man** carried a **stick** and a **cane**.

2.   **Derek** baked **brownies** and **cookies**.

3.   Her **parents** visited **friends** in **Texas**.

4.   Does **Ginger** have a **ticket** for the **show**?
398

A.   Directions: Write C if the noun is common. Write P if the noun is proper.

1. _____ RIVER   3. _____ GLENN   5. _____ BUILDING

2. _____ SNAKE RIVER   4. _____ BOY   6. _____ TOWER

B.   Directions: Write the plural.

1. match - _____   6. play - _____

2. guppy - _____   7. deer - _____

3. eye - _____   8. mouse - _____

4. rash - _____   9. box - _____

5. child - _____   10. tomato - _____

C.   Directions: Circle any nouns.

1.   The man carried a stick and a cane.

2.   Derek baked brownies and cookies.

3.   Her parents visited friends in Texas.

4.   Does Ginger have a ticket for the show?

D. Directions: Write the possessive.

1. a car belonging to Nancy - _____**Nancy's car**_____

2. a room shared by two boys - _____**boys' room**_____

3. the president of a club - _____**club's president**_____

4. a swing used by more than one child - ___**children's swing**___

E. Directions: Circle any adjectives.

1. **The** lynx is **an** animal with **a short** tail.

2. **A** dolphin has **a long** body and **many** teeth.

3. Latina has **straight red** hair and **big blue** eyes.

4. I ate **two juicy** plums and **several sour** grapes.

F. Directions: Circle the correct form.

1. This bat is the (lighter, **lightest**) of the three.

2. Your dad is (**quieter**, quietest) than your mom.

3. Of all the children, Andy is (more loving, **most loving**).

4. Is a cobra (**more harmful**, most harmful) than a rattlesnake?

400

D. Directions: Write the possessive.

1. a car belonging to Nancy - _____

2. a room shared by two boys - _____

3. the president of a club - _____

4. a swing used by more than one child - _____

E. Directions: Circle any adjectives.

1. The lynx is an animal with a short tail.

2. A dolphin has a long body and many teeth.

3. Latina has straight red hair and big blue eyes.

4. I ate two juicy plums and several sour grapes.

F. Directions: Circle the correct form.

1. This bat is the (lighter, lightest) of the three.

2. Your dad is (quieter, quietest) than your mom.

3. Of all the children, Andy is (more loving, most loving).

4. Is a cobra (more harmful, most harmful) than a rattlesnake?

A. Directions: Write <u>conj.</u> above each conjunction.
Write <u>intj.</u> above each interjection.

   intj.   **conj.**
1. **Yippee!** Vicki **or** Luke finished first!

      conj.   **conj.**
2. Brook **and** her son left, **but** they forgot their cards.

B. Directions: Write the sentence type.

Remember: A **declarative** sentence makes a *statement.*
An **interrogative** sentence asks a *question.*
An **imperative** sentence gives a *command.*
An **exclamatory** sentence *shows emotion.*

1. _____**declarative**_____   A panda lives in China.

2. _____**exclamatory**_____   Let's go!

3. _____**interrogative**_____   What do you want?

4. _____**imperative**_____   Please put this in your room.

C. Directions: Circle the adverb that tells *how.*

1. The boy fell **limply** across his bed.

2. Her aunt talked **excitedly** about her trip.

3. Mr. and Mrs. Scribber bowl **well**.
402

A. Directions: Write <u>conj.</u> above each conjunction.
                   Write <u>intj.</u> above each interjection.

1. Yippee! Vicki or Luke finished first!

2. Brook and her son left, but they forgot their cards.

B. Directions: Write the sentence type.

Remember: A **declarative** sentence makes a *statement.*
                 An **interrogative** sentence asks a *question.*
                 An **imperative** sentence gives a *command.*
                 An **exclamatory sentence** *shows emotion.*

1. _____ A panda lives in China.

2. _____ Let's go!

3. _____ What do you want?

4. _____ Please put this in your room.

C. Directions: Circle the adverb that tells *how.*

1. The boy fell limply across his bed.

2. Her aunt talked excitedly about her trip.

3. Mr. and Mrs. Scribber bowl well.

D.   Directions: Circle the adverb that tells *when*.

1.   I'll catch up with you **later**.

2.   **First**, I must close the door.

3.   **Yesterday**, Bruce visited his uncle.

4.   What happened **then**?

E.   Directions: Circle the adverb that tells *where*.

1.   The dog wants to go **out**.

2.   Have you seen Laura **anywhere**?

3.   I want to stay **home**.

F.   Directions: Circle the adverb that tells *to what extent*.

1.   The man was **too** sleepy to drive.

2.   That comic strip is **so** funny.

3.   You're **very** welcome.

G.   Directions: Circle the correct form.

1.   Sam runs (faster, **fastest**) in his neighborhood.

2.   She looked (more closely, **most closely**) at the third picture.

3.   I drive (**more slowly**, most slowly) than my son.

4.   His thumb was hurt (**more seriously**, most seriously) than his index finger.

404

D.   Directions: Circle the adverb that tells *when*.

1.   I'll catch up with you later.

2.   First, I must close the door.

3.   Yesterday, Bruce visited his uncle.

4.   What happened then?

E.   Directions: Circle the adverb that tells *where*.

1.   The dog wants to go out.

2.   Have you seen Laura anywhere?

3.   I want to stay home.

F.   Directions: Circle the adverb that tells *to what extent*.

1.   The man was too sleepy to drive.

2.   That comic strip is so funny.

3.   You're very welcome.

G.   Directions: Circle the correct form.

1.   Sam runs (faster, fastest) in his neighborhood.

2.   She looked (more closely, most closely) at the third picture.

3.   I drive (more slowly, most slowly) than my son.

4.   His thumb was hurt (more seriously, most seriously) than his index
     finger.   405

TO THE TEACHER:

Capitalization can be **difficult**. You will note from the *Scope and Sequence* that basic items have been included.

To help students learn, rules have been placed at the top of each page. Sentences that use **only** those rules have been provided on that page. The exception to this is capitalizing the first word of a sentence. Practice worksheets have been included to reinforce rules 1-13 and 14-22. After all rules have been taught (including those for not capitalizing), worksheets using all rules have been provided for practice.

If you are teaching capitalization before the noun unit, be sure to explain common and proper nouns. Students need to comprehend that proper nouns are capitalized.

BE SURE TO READ EACH RULE AND DISCUSS IT WITH YOUR STUDENTS. In fact, I recommend that you provide **familiar** examples. For instance, when discussing capitalizing business names, use local businesses. Solicit student examples. (Students love to share the names of businesses where their parents work.) **Write examples on the board or on a transparency.** It's important that students "see" the words capitalized.

As you progress through the unit, I suggest that you briefly **review** previous rules. You need not write all of the examples when reviewing.

I recommend a *Daily Grams: Guided Review Aiding Mastery Skills - Grade 3.* These include 180 daily reviews, and number 1 is always a capitalization review. Daily practice and review will help to promote mastery learning.

Capitalization

WORKBOOK PAGE 176
Date_____

Note to Teacher: **Be sure to discuss placing periods with abbreviations.**

Rule 1:   **Capitalize a person's name.**

         Examples: Leela

                     Jonah Boyd

Rule 2:   **Capitalize initials.**

         Examples: Pippa **A.** Begay

                     T. C. Bota

Rule 3:   **Capitalize a title with a name.**

         Examples: Uncle Carlos   Miss C. Como

                     Grandma Wong   Doctor Cohen

Rule 4:   **Capitalize the pronoun *I*.**

Rule 5:   **Capitalize the first word of a sentence.**

🐢 🐢 🐢 🐢 🐢 🐢 🐢 🐢 🐢 🐢 🐢 🐢 🐢 🐢 🐢 🐢 🐢 🐢 🐢

Directions: Write your answer on the line.
ANSWERS WILL VARY.

1.   Write your first, middle, and last name.   **Royce Paul Adams**

2.   Write your first name with your middle initial.   **Royce P.**

3.   Write your three initials.   **R. P. A.**

4.   Write your aunt's name or uncle's name with the title.   **Aunt Trudy**

5.   Answer this question in a complete sentence: *What is your favorite*

       food?   **My favorite food is lobster.**

6.   Write a complete sentence using the pronoun *I*.

         My sister and I like to write children's books.

Name_____ **CAPITALIZATION**

Date_____

Rule 1:   **Capitalize a person's name.**

Examples: **Leela**
Jonah **B**oyd

Rule 2:   **Capitalize initials.**

Examples: **P**ippa **A. B**egay
T. C. Bota

Rule 3:   **Capitalize a title with a name.**

Examples: **U**ncle **C**arlos   **Miss C. C**omo
Grandma **W**ong   **D**octor **C**ohen

Rule 4:   **Capitalize the pronoun *I*.**

Rule 5:   **Capitalize the first word of a sentence.**

🐢 🐢 🐢 🐢 🐢 🐢 🐢 🐢 🐢 🐢 🐢 🐢 🐢 🐢 🐢 🐢 🐢 🐢 🐢 🐢

Directions: Write your answer on the line.

1.   Write your first, middle, and last name. _Ashiyn Koy 4/a ch_

2.   Write your first name with your middle initial. _Ashiyn K._

3.   Write your three initials. _A. K. U._

4.   Write your aunt's name or uncle's name with the title. _Renee Linda_

5.   Answer this question in a complete sentence: *What is your favorite*
food? _I like PIZZA!_

6.   Write a complete sentence using the pronoun *I.*
I like vet stuff.

Name_____   **CAPITALIZATION**

WORKBOOK PAGE 177

Date_____

<u>Note to Teacher: In #4, you may wish to share about planting trees on</u>
<u>Arbor Day.</u>

Rule 6:   Capitalize days of the week.

            Examples: Sunday   Thursday

Rule 7:   Capitalize months of the year.

            Examples: March   September

Rule 8:   Capitalize holidays.

            Examples: Memorial Day   Presidents' Day

Rule 9:   Capitalize special days.

            Examples: Father's Day   Valentine's Day

🐢 🐢 🐢 🐢 🐢 🐢 🐢 🐢 🐢 🐢 🐢 🐢 🐢 🐢 🐢 🐢 🐢 🐢

Directions: Write your answer on the line.

1.   Write the days of the week. ____**Sunday**____, ____**Monday**____,

    ____**Tuesday**____, ____**Wednesday**____, ____**Thursday**____,

    ____**Friday**____, and ____**Saturday**____.

ANSWERS WILL VARY.

2.   Write the name of your favorite month. ____**December**____

3.   Write the name of your favorite holiday. ____**Memorial Day**____

4.   Write the name of the special day on this list that you like best:

        St. Patrick's Day   Valentine's Day
        Ground Hog's Day.   Arbor Day

    ____**Ground Hog's Day**____

5.   My favorite day is ____**Monday**____ because **I play soccer.**

410

Date_____

Rule 6: **Capitalize days of the week.**

Examples: **S**unday **T**hursday

Rule 7: **Capitalize months of the year.**

Examples: **M**arch **S**eptember

Rule 8: **Capitalize holidays.**

Examples: **M**emorial **D**ay **P**residents' **D**ay

Rule 9: **Capitalize special days.**

Examples: **F**ather's **D**ay **V**alentine's **D**ay

🐢🐢🐢🐢🐢🐢🐢🐢🐢🐢🐢🐢🐢🐢🐢🐢🐢🐢🐢

Directions: Write your answer on the line.

1. Write the days of the week. _____Sun_____, _____Mon_____,
_____tue_____, _____Wend_____, _____Thur_____,
_____Fri_____, and _____Sat_____.

2. Write the name of your favorite month. _____August_____

3. Write the name of your favorite holiday. _____Christmas_____

4. Write the name of the special day on this list that you like best:

    St. **P**atrick's **D**ay   **V**alentine's **D**ay
    Ground **H**og's **D**ay.   **A**rbor **D**ay

                V D

_____

5. My favorite day is _____ because _____

_____

Name_____   **CAPITALIZATION**

WORKBOOK PAGE 178

Date_____

<u>Note to Teacher:</u>   <u>You may wish to do a map study of roadways, towns,</u>
<u>states, and countries before teaching this lesson.</u>

Rule 10:   **Capitalize the names of streets, roads, avenues,**
                 drives, lanes, highways, trails, turnpikes, and other
                 roadways.

Examples:	Redwood Street	Lincoln Highway
	Bull Road	Pioneer Trail
	Cooper Avenue	Everett Turnpike
	Castle Drive	Swope Parkway
	Park Lane	Range Boulevard

Capitalize <u>directions</u> when they appear with a name of a roadway.

South State Street

Rule 11:   **Capitalize the name of a town or city.**

Examples: Bendersville   Jackson

Rule 12:   **Capitalize the name of a state.**

Examples: Maryland   Idaho

Rule 13:   **Capitalize the name of a country.**

Examples: China   France

🐢 🐢 🐢 🐢 🐢 🐢 🐢 🐢 🐢 🐢 🐢 🐢 🐢 🐢 🐢 🐢 🐢 🐢

Directions: Write your answer on the line.

ANSWERS WILL VARY.

1.   Write the name of your country.   _____**United States**_____

2.   Write the name of your state.   _____**Wisconsin**_____

3.   Write the name of your town or city.   _____**Talmo**_____

4.   Write the name of a street or other roadway.   **New Holland Turnpike**

5.   Write the name of a state you would like to visit.   _____**Missouri**_____

412

Rule 10: **Capitalize the names of streets, roads, avenues, drives, lanes, highways, trails, turnpikes, and other roadways.**

Examples: **Redwood Street**   **Lincoln Highway**
Bull Road   **Pioneer Trail**
Cooper Avenue   **Everett Turnpike**
Castle Drive   **Swope Parkway**
Park Lane   **Range Boulevard**

Capitalize <u>directions</u> when they appear with a name of a roadway.

South State Street

Rule 11: **Capitalize the name of a town or city.**
Examples: **Bendersville**   **Jackson**

Rule 12: **Capitalize the name of a state.**
Examples: **Maryland**   **Idaho**

Rule 13: **Capitalize the name of a country.**
Examples: **China**   **France**

🐢 🐢 🐢 🐢 🐢 🐢 🐢 🐢 🐢 🐢 🐢 🐢 🐢 🐢 🐢 🐢 🐢 🐢 🐢

Directions: Write your answer on the line.

1. Write the name of your country. ___U. S. A.___

2. Write the name of your state. ___Pennsylvainyo___

3. Write the name of your town or city. ___chanbers___

4. Write the name of a street or other roadway. ___Arbutis DR___

5. Write the name of a state you would like to visit. ___Florda___

413

Directions: Write the capital letter above any word that needs to be
capitalized.

1.   **Does Randy** live on **Coco Avenue**?

2.   **In August**, I went to **Alabama**.

3.   **Did Uncle Harry** buy a new car?

4.   **I** gave **Cindy** candy on **Valentine's Day.**

5.   **His** cousin lives in **Macon**, **Georgia**.

6.   **Brian** and **I** went to the library on **Penn Street**.

7.   **Becky A. Smith** moved to **Elk City**.

8.   **Her** aunt is coming on the third **Tuesday** in **April**.

9.   **On Memorial Day**, his family went to **Mexico**.

10.   **Did Dr. Hamel** move his office to **East Dell Street**?

11.   **Last Saturday, Mr. Sites** visited **Ash, North Carolina**.

12.   **During Christmas** vacation, he always goes to **Canada**.

13.   **We** will visit **Grandma Metz** on **Wednesday** or **Thursday**.

14.   **Our** new address is 20 **Linx Lane, Akron, Ohio** 44333.

15.   **Are Sandy** and **I** invited to your **St. Patrick's Day** party?

Name_____ **CAPITALIZATION**

Date_____

Directions: Write the capital letter above any word that needs to be
              capitalized.

1. does randy live on coco avenue?

2. in august, I went to alabama.

3. did uncle harry buy a new car?

4. i gave cindy candy on valentine's day.

5. his cousin lives in macon, georgia.

6. brian and i went to the library on penn street.

7. becky a. smith moved to elk city.

8. her aunt is coming on the third tuesday in april.

9. on memorial day, his family went to mexico.

10. did dr. hamel move his office to east dell street?

11. last saturday, mr. sites visited ash, north carolina.

12. during christmas vacation, he always goes to canada.

13. we will visit grandma metz on wednesday or thursday.

14. Our new address is 20 linx lane, akron, ohio 44333.

15. are sandy and i invited to your st. patrick's day party?

Rule 14:   **Capitalize the name of a school or college.**

Examples: Sky View School   Ball College

Rule 15:   **Capitalize the name of a library or hospital.**

Examples: Adams County Library
Fountain Valley Hospital

Rule 16:   **Capitalize the name of a store, a restaurant, or another business.**

Examples: Tang's Grocery
Mon Ton Department Store
Sesame Restaurant
Gotta Go Travel Agency
Reno Construction Company
Music Box Theater

If *in*, *to*, *for*, *of*, or other prepositions of four or less letters appear as part of the name, do <u>not</u> capitalize them. Also, do <u>not</u> capitalize *a*, *an*, *the*, *and*, *but*, *nor,* and *or* unless they are the first or last word.
Jack and Jill Shop
Food with a Flair Restaurant

🐢 🐢 🐢 🐢 🐢 🐢 🐢 🐢 🐢 🐢 🐢 🐢 🐢 🐢 🐢 🐢 🐢 🐢 🐢

Directions: Write your answer on the line.
ANSWERS WILL VARY.

1.   Write the name of your favorite school. **Desert Elementary School**

2.   Write the name of a college. **York Junior College**

3.   Write the name of a library in your town. **Liberty Library**

4.   Write the name of a hospital in your area. **Hershey Medical Center**

5.   Write the name of a store in your area. **Regency Hardware Store**
416

Rule 14: **Capitalize the name of a school or college.**

Examples: Sky View School   Ball College

Rule 15: **Capitalize the name of a library or hospital.**

Examples: Adams County Library
Fountain Valley Hospital

Rule 16: **Capitalize the name of a store, a restaurant, or another business.**

Examples: Tang's Grocery
Mon Ton Department Store
Sesame Restaurant
Gotta Go Travel Agency
Reno Construction Company
Music Box Theater

If *in*, *to*, *for*, *of*, or other prepositions of four or less letters appear as part of the name, do <u>not</u> capitalize them. Also, do <u>not</u> capitalize *a*, *an*, *the*, *and*, *but*, *nor*, and *or* unless they are the first or last word.
Jack and Jill Shop
Food with a Flair Restaurant

Directions: Write your answer on the line.

1. Write the name of your favorite school. _____

2. Write the name of a college. _____

3. Write the name of a library in your town. _____

4. Write the name of a hospital in your area. _____

5. Write the name of a store in your area. _____

Rule 17:   **Capitalize the name of a language.**

Examples: **E**nglish   **S**panish

Rule 18:   **Capitalize the first word of a direct quotation.**   (A direct quotation is when someone says something.)

Example: Richard asked,   "**W**here are my jeans?"

Rule 19:   **Capitalize the first word in a line of poetry.**
These are lines from a poem entitled "At Home" by Christina Rossetti.

Examples: **M**ix a pancake,
Stir a pancake,

Rule 20:   **Capitalize the first word of a greeting in a letter.**

Example: **D**ear Zak,

Rule 21:   **Capitalize the first word of a closing in a letter.**

Example: **S**incerely yours,

🐢 🐢 🐢 🐢 🐢 🐢 🐢 🐢 🐢 🐢 🐢 🐢 🐢 🐢 🐢 🐢 🐢 🐢 🐢

Directions: Write your answer on the line.
ANSWERS WILL VARY.

1.   The language I speak is _____**English**_____.

2.   Write something you have said: I said, _____**"I like school."**_____

3.   Write the second line of this poem:

Jack and Jill went up the hill,
To fetch a pail of water._____

Sentence 4 is a good place to note that a comma will go after the greeting of a letter.
4.   Write a greeting of a letter beginning with *dear*.   **Dear Brenda,**_____

Sentence 5 is a good place to note that a comma will go after the closing of a letter.
5.   Write the closing of a letter beginning with *your*. _____**Your cousin,**_____
418

Rule 17:   **Capitalize the name of a language.**

Examples: **E**nglish   **S**panish

Rule 18:   **Capitalize the first word of a direct quotation.** (A direct quotation is when someone says something.)

Example: Richard asked, "**W**here are my jeans?"

Rule 19:   **Capitalize the first word in a line of poetry.**
These are lines from a poem entitled "At Home" by Christina Rossetti.

Examples: **M**ix a pancake,
Stir a pancake,

Rule 20:   **Capitalize the first word of a greeting in a letter.**

Example: **D**ear Zak,

Rule 21:   **Capitalize the first word of a closing in a letter.**

Example: **S**incerely yours,

Directions: Write your answer on the line.

1.   The language I speak is _____.

2.   Write something you have said: I said, " _____."

3.   Write the second line of this poem:

Jack and Jill went up the hill,

_____

4.   Write a greeting of a letter beginning with *dear*. _____

5.   Write the closing of a letter beginning with *your*. _____

Note to Teacher: Students may not understand *university*. This page uses rules 14-22. However, #4 includes capitalizing a name.

Directions: Write the capital letter above any word that needs to be capitalized.

1. **We** ate breakfast at **Golden Nugget Cafe**.

2. **My** brother attends **Arizona State University.**

3. **The** lady checked out a **Spanish** book from **Mesa Public Library**.

4.   **My** dear friend,

     Here are the pictures of our vacation.

          Your friend,
          Amy

5. **These** are my favorite lines from a poem:

     You dance to the music of a lonely fife,
     And I march to the beat of a distant drum.

6. **She** said, "**Let's** listen to the radio."

7.   **Has Spar High School** opened yet?

8.   **Grandma** entered **York Hospital** for tests.

9.   **They** work at **Winston General Store**.

10.   **Is** your neighbor studying **French** at **Scottsdale Junior College**?

11. **Her** dad works for **Blair Insurance Agency**.

12. **Our** family went out to eat at **Silver Swan Restaurant**.

420

Name_____   **CAPITALIZATION**

Date_____

Directions: Write the capital letter above any word that needs to be
              capitalized.

1.   we ate breakfast at golden nugget cafe.

2.   my brother attends arizona state university.

3.   the lady checked out a spanish book from mesa public library.

4.   my dear friend,

         here are the pictures of our vacation.

                    your friend,
                    amy

5.   these are my favorite lines from a poem:
         you dance to the music of a lonely fife,
         and I march to the beat of a distant drum.

6.   she said, "let's listen to the radio."

7.   has spar high school opened yet?

8.   grandma entered york hospital for tests.

9.   they work at winston general store.

10. is your neighbor studying french at scottsdale junior college?

11. her dad works for blair insurance agency.

12. our family went out to eat at silver swan restaurant.

421

Name_____   **CAPITALIZATION**

WORKBOOK PAGE 183

Date_____

<u>**Note to Teacher: Explain major divisions in rule 22.**</u>

Rule 22:   **Capitalize Roman numerals, the major divisions and the first word in an outline.**

Example: **I.** Mammals
                    A. Whales
                    B. Dolphins and porpoises

Rule 23:   **Capitalize the first word, the last word, and all important words in titles. Do *not* capitalize *a, an, the, and, but, or, nor*, or prepositions of four or less letters unless they are the first or the last word.**

Examples: <u>Prayer</u>
                     "<u>Silent Night</u>"
                     <u>Birth of Liberty</u>
                     <u>Eight Little Pigs</u>
                     "<u>A Truck for Willie</u>"
                     <u>The Cat Who Went to Paris</u>

A.   Directions: Capitalize this outline.

   I. History

         A.   American history

         B.   World history

B.   Directions: Capitalize these titles.

   1. **"Thirteen"**

   2. <u>**My Country**</u>

   3. <u>**Deer** of the **World**</u>

   4. <u>**The Iron Horse**</u>

422

Rule 22: **Capitalize Roman numerals, the major divisions and the first word in an outline.**

Example: **I.** **Mammals**
           A. **Whales**
           B. **Dolphins and porpoises**

Rule 23: **Capitalize the first word, the last word, and all important words in titles. Do *not* capitalize *a, an, the, and, but, or, nor,* or prepositions of four or less letters unless they are the first or the last word.**

Examples: <u>**Prayer**</u>
        "**Silent Night**"
        <u>**Birth of Liberty**</u>
        <u>**Eight Little Pigs**</u>
        "**A Truck for Willie**"
        <u>**The Cat Who Went to Paris**</u>

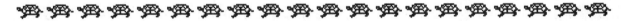

A. Directions: Capitalize this outline.

   i. history

      a. american history

      b. world history

B. Directions: Capitalize these titles.

   1. "thirteen"

   2. <u>my country</u>

   3. <u>deer of the world</u>

   4. <u>the iron horse</u>   423

Rule 24: **Capitalize the name of a particular building.**

Examples: church, temple, or synagogue - **Temple Beth Emeth**
tower - **Little Roundtop Tower**
house - **Dobbin House**
museum - **Thomas Edison Museum**
lighthouse - **Bodie Island Lighthouse**
airport - **Deer Valley Airport**

Rule 25: **Capitalize the name of a particular place.**

stream - **Potato Creek**	island - **Cedar Island**
lake - **Liberty Lake**	desert - **Sonoran Desert**
river - **Wabash River**	forest - **Turtle Mt. State Forest**
sea - **Salton Sea**	park - **Yellowstone National Park**
ocean - **Atlantic Ocean**	hill(s) - **Fox Hill**
beach - **Bonita Beach**	mountain(s) - **Ozark Mountains**

🐢 🐢 🐢 🐢 🐢 🐢 🐢 🐢 🐢 🐢 🐢 🐢 🐢 🐢 🐢 🐢 🐢 🐢 🐢

Directions: Write the capital letter above any word that needs to be capitalized.

1. **Have** you been to **Flathead Lake**?

2. **Does** the **Heard Museum** have paintings?

3. **We** have visited **Reedy Island**.

4. **Their** family attends **Sacred Heart Church**.

5. **They** went to **Bear Mountain State Park** yesterday.

6. **Is Rye Beach** on the **Atlantic Ocean**?

424

Rule 24:   **Capitalize the name of a particular building.**

Examples: church, temple, or synagogue - Temple **B**eth **E**meth
tower - **L**ittle **R**oundtop **T**ower
house - **D**obbin **H**ouse
museum - **T**homas **E**dison **M**useum
lighthouse - **B**odie **I**sland **L**ighthouse
airport - **D**eer **V**alley **A**irport

Rule 25:   **Capitalize the name of a particular place.**

stream - **P**otato **C**reek	island - **C**edar **I**sland
lake - **L**iberty **L**ake	desert - **S**onoran **D**esert
river - **W**abash **R**iver	forest - **T**urtle **M**t. **S**tate **F**orest
sea - **S**alton **S**ea	park - **Y**ellowstone **N**ational **P**ark
ocean - **A**tlantic **O**cean	hill(s) - **F**ox **H**ill
beach - **B**onita **B**each	mountain(s) - **O**zark **M**ountains

🐢 🐢 🐢 🐢 🐢 🐢 🐢 🐢 🐢 🐢 🐢 🐢 🐢 🐢 🐢 🐢 🐢 🐢 🐢

Directions: Write the capital letter above any word that needs to be capitalized.

1.   have you been to flathead lake?

2.   does the heard museum have paintings?

3.   we have visited reedy island.

4.   Their family attends sacred heart church.

5.   they went to bear mountain state park yesterday.

6.   is rye beach on the atlantic ocean?

Name_____   **DO NOT CAPITALIZE**

WORKBOOK PAGE 185

Date_____

Note to Teacher: Although proper adjectives have not been included in this text, you may wish to discuss them briefly so that students can better understand rule 3.

Rule 1:   Do not capitalize seasons of the year.

spring   summer   winter   fall (autumn)

Rule 2:   Do not capitalize directions.

north   south   east   west

However, capitalize these when they appear as part of a place name.

Patty lives at 882 **North** Ocean View Drive.

Rule 3:   Do not capitalize foods, games, plants, or animals.

food - apple pie
game - tag
plant - daisy
animal - muskrat

However, if a country's name appears with it, capitalize the country but not the food, game, plant, or animal.

food - **M**exican rice   (Mexico)
game - **C**hinese checkers   (China)
plant - **B**ermuda grass   (Bermuda)
animal - **G**erman shepherd   (Germany)

🐢🐢🐢🐢🐢🐢🐢🐢🐢🐢🐢🐢🐢🐢🐢🐢🐢🐢🐢

Directions: Write your answer on the line.

ANSWERS WILL VARY.

1.   A game I like is _____**rummy**_____.

2.   The direction I live from the closest town is _____**east**_____.

3.   My favorite season of the year is _____**summer**_____.

4.   My favorite food is _____**celery**_____.

5.   My favorite animal is a _____**dog**_____.

426

Name_____   **DO NOT CAPITALIZE**

Date_____

Rule 1:   **Do not capitalize seasons of the year.**

spring   summer   winter   fall (autumn)

Rule 2:   **Do not capitalize directions.**

north   south   east   west

However, capitalize these when they appear as part of a place name.

Patty lives at 882 **North** Ocean View Drive.

Rule 3:   **Do not capitalize foods, games, plants, or animals.**

food - apple pie
game - tag
plant - daisy
animal - muskrat

However, if a country's name appears with it, capitalize the country <u>but not the food, game, plant, or animal</u>.

food - **M**exican rice   (Mexico)
game - **C**hinese checkers   (China)
plant - **B**ermuda grass   (Bermuda)
animal - **G**erman shepherd   (Germany)

🐢 🐢 🐢 🐢 🐢 🐢 🐢 🐢 🐢 🐢 🐢 🐢 🐢 🐢 🐢 🐢 🐢 🐢 🐢

Directions: Write your answer on the line.

1.   A game I like is _____.

2.   The direction I live from the closest town is _____.

3.   My favorite season of the year is _____.

4.   My favorite food is _____.

5.   My favorite animal is a _____.   427

Directions: Write the capital letter above any word that needs to be
               capitalized.

1. **Let's** go to the **Catskill Mountains** in **July**.

2. **The** country of **Mexico** is south of **Arizona**.

3. **Sheldon Museum** was built in 1829.

4. **Dear Paula,**

         Yesterday, we went to **Garfield Park** in **Chicago**.

                    Your friend,

                    Mandy

5. **The Gotland Islands** are in the **Baltic Sea**.

6. **Dave** asked, "**Why** don't you learn **French**?"

7. **On Thanksgiving, I** attended **Hope Baptist Church**.

8. Capitalize these titles:

    a. **"Trouble"**

    b. **Eva's Story**

    c. **Butterflies** and **Moths**

    d. **Read** with **Me**

CAPITALIZATION
Review

Directions: Write the capital letter above any word that needs to be capitalized.

1.   let's go to the catskill mountains in july.

2.   the country of mexico is south of arizona.

3.   sheldon museum was built in 1829.

4.   dear paula,

        yesterday, we went to garfield park in chicago.

                your friend,

                mandy

5.   the gotland islands are in the baltic sea.

6.   dave asked, "why don't you learn french?"

7.   on thanksgiving, i attended hope baptist church.

8.   Capitalize these titles:

     a.   "trouble"

     b.   <u>eva's story</u>

     c.   <u>butterflies and moths</u>

     d.   <u>read with me</u>

Directions: Write the capital letter above any word that needs to be capitalized.

1.   **Karen** takes classes at **Wheaton College**.

2.   **Last Friday**, they fished at **Mirror Lake**.

3.   **Does** your mom shop at **Marsh Country Store**?

4.   **She** likes these two lines from a poem by **G**ene **F**owler:

   I carry boulders across the day

   From the field to the ridge.

5.   **Is Sugar Loaf Mountain** in **New Hampshire**?

6.   **Someone** gave a tulip tree to **Chambersburg Hospital**.

7.   Capitalize this outline:

   I.   Movies

   A.   Comedies

   B.   Scary movies

8.   **In August, Uncle Ralph** will visit **Iowa**.

9.   **Does Little Lost River** flow into the **Pacific Ocean**?

10.   **Next Tuesday, Doctor Roy P. Lamb** will speak to us.

Name_____   **CAPITALIZATION**
                                          Review
Date_____

Directions: Write the capital letter above any word that needs to be
              capitalized.

1.   karen takes classes at wheaton college.

2.   last friday, they fished at mirror lake.

3.   does your mom shop at marsh country store?

4.   she likes these two lines from a poem by gene fowler:

          i carry boulders across the day

          from the field to the ridge.

5.   is sugar loaf mountain in new hampshire?

6.   someone gave a tulip tree to chambersburg hospital.

7.   Capitalize this outline:

          i.   movies

              a.   comedies

              b.   scary movies

8.   in august, uncle ralph will visit iowa.

9.   does little lost river flow into the pacific ocean?

10.   next tuesday, doctor roy p. lamb will speak to us.

Directions: Write the capital letter above any word that needs to be
capitalized.

1. **The Mohawk Trail** is in **New York**.

2. **My** brother read <u>**Flying** the **Mail**</u>.

3. **He** and I leave **National Airport** on **Sunday**.

4. **Last** winter, **Mark** camped by **Miller Creek**.

5. **Amba** attends **Sunrise Elementary School**.

6. **Juan** asked, "**Are** you taking your dog?"

7. **We** celebrate **Veterans' Day** in **November**.

8. **My** dear cousin,

     We are going to **Crater National Park** tomorrow!

        Love,
        Lani

9. **Have** you been to the **Henry Ford Museum**?

10. **We** ate at **Food King** after checking out books at **Peoria Library**.

11. **On Thursday, July** 16, the couple married at **Holy Trinity Greek**

   Cathedral.

12. **His** address is 22 **Ridge Street, Gettysburg, Pennsylvania**
17325.

Directions: Write the capital letter above any word that needs to be
              capitalized.

1.   the mohawk trail is in new york.

2.   my brother read <u>flying the mail</u>.

3.   he and i leave national airport on sunday.

4.   last winter, mark camped by miller creek.

5.   amba attends sunrise elementary school.

6.   juan asked, "are you taking your dog?"

7.   we celebrate veterans' day in november.

8.   my dear cousin,

          we are going to crater national park tomorrow!

                              love,

                              lani

9.   have you been to the henry ford museum?

10. we ate at food king after checking out books at peoria library.

11. on thursday, july 16, the couple married at holy trinity greek cathedral.

12. his address is 22 ridge street, gettysburg, pennsylvania   17325.

Name_____ **Capitalization Test**

Date_____

Directions: Write the capital letter above any word that needs to be capitalized.

1. **Is Whitefish Lake** in **Minnesota**?

2. **Last Sunday, I** took my dogs to **Riverside Park**.

3. **His** new address will be 2 **West Ash Lane**.

4. **Kamet Mountain** is in the country of **India**.

5. **Franco** will attend **Sunset Middle School** in **August**.

6. **William A. Chase** works for **Hampton Shoe Company**.

7. **Dena** said, "**You'll** want to visit **Ozark National Forest**."

8. **The Betsy Ross House** is in the city of **Philadelphia**.

9. **Did Aunt Ali** make cherry cake for **Valentine's Day**?

10. **These** two lines of poetry were in my **English** book:

      Mama's shiny purple coat
      Giant-sized shoulder bag to tote

11. **Dear Rick**,

    Tonight, our family will go sailing on the **Pacific Ocean**.

                    Friends forever,
                    Brody

12. **Mom** found a book named **<u>The Best of Baking</u>** at **Buckeye Library**.

Date_____

Directions: Write the capital letter above any word that needs to be capitalized.

1.   is whitefish lake in minnesota?

2.   last sunday, i took my dogs to riverside park.

3.   his new address will be 2 west ash lane.

4.   kamet mountain is in the country of india.

5.   franco will attend sunset middle school in august.

6.   william a. chase works for hampton shoe company.

7.   dena said, "you'll want to visit ozark national forest."

8.   the betsy ross house is in the city of philadelphia.

9.   did aunt ali make cherry cake for valentine's day?

10.   these two lines of poetry were in my english book:
         mama's shiny purple coat
         giant-sized shoulder bag to tote

11.   dear rick,

      tonight, our family will go sailing on the pacific ocean.

                              friends forever,
                              brody

12.   mom found a book named the best of baking at buckeye library.

TO THE TEACHER:

Punctuation rules appear at the top of the page. This allows students to reread the rules easily when doing the practice sheet at the bottom of the page. An **additional practice** has been provided on pages 444 - 445 to review periods and apostrophes. Another one on pages 452 - 453 has been provided after commas. A third practice sheet on pages 460 - 461 has been provided after quotation marks and underlining. After all concepts have been taught, **review worksheets** have been added.

Please note that **not all rules** for each concept have been included. For example, under comma usage, the rule for using a comma after a subordinate clause is not part of the unit. This rule, of course, is too difficult at this level. Higher level rules appear in the following *Easy Grammar* texts:

> *Easy Grammar: Grades 4*
> *Easy Grammar: Grade 5*
> *Easy Grammar: Grade 6*
> *Easy Grammar Plus*

Be sure to **TEACH** each rule and **DISCUSS** it with your students before reading it in the text. Provide your **own examples** whenever possible. **Dry erase boards** on which students can write examples and add punctuation as you are teaching are ideal here. Active participation is a key to learning, and it's fun!

I suggest that you do much of this unit orally with your students. On the practice worksheets, you may wish to do half of the page orally and allow students to finish the page in class. (I usually do not assign punctuation worksheets for homework.) If possible, go over the completed page immediately.

I recommend a ***Daily Grams: Guided Review Aiding Mastery Skills*** text. These include 180 daily reviews, and number 2 is always a punctuation review. This 10 minute daily practice and review will help to promote mastery learning. Levels include:

> ***Daily Grams: Guided Review Aiding Mastery Skills - Grade 3***
> ***Daily Grams: Guided Review Aiding Mastery Skills - Grade 4***
> ***Daily Grams: Guided Review Aiding Mastery Skills - Grade 5***
> ***Daily Grams: Guided Review Aiding Mastery Skills - Grade 6***
> ***Daily Grams: Guided Review Aiding Mastery Skills - Grade 7***
> ***Daily Grams: Guided Review Aiding Mastery Skills Jr./Sr. level***

Punctuation

<u>**Note to Teacher: Students need to have mastery of days of the week.**</u>

Rule 1:   **Place a period at the end of a declarative sentence.**
               (A declarative sentence makes a ***statement***.)

               Example: Her arm is broken.

Rule 2:   **Place a period at the end of an imperative sentence.**
               (An imperative sentence gives a ***command***.)

               Example: Pick that up.

Rule 3:   **Place a period after initials.**

               Example: Hope R. Lang

Rule 4:   **Place a period after an abbreviation for a day of the week.**

Sunday - Sun.   Tuesday - Tues., Tue.*   Thursday - Thurs., Thur.*
Monday - Mon.   Wednesday - Wed.   Friday - Fri.
*The first is preferred.   Saturday - Sat.

Directions: Write your answer on the line.
ANSWERS WILL VARY FOR 1-3.
1.   My friend's initials are ____**P. R. P.**____

2.   Write a declarative sentence:

     ____**We watched a program about porpoises.**____

3.   Write an imperative sentence: ____**Write your name on this paper.**

4.   Unscramble these days of the week and then write the abbreviation:

     a. ytradhsu - **Thursday** **Thurs.** c. dtausey - **Tuesday** **Tues.**

     b. tadasryu - **Saturday** **Sat.** d. yfaird - ____**Friday** **Fri.**

438

Name_____

Date_____

Rule 1: **Place a period at the end of a declarative sentence.**
(A declarative sentence makes a *statement*.)

Example: Her arm is broken.

Rule 2: **Place a period at the end of an imperative sentence.**
(An imperative sentence gives a *command*.)

Example: Pick that up.

Rule 3: **Place a period after initials.**

Example: Hope R. Lang

Rule 4: **Place a period after an abbreviation for a day of the week.**

Sunday - Sun.	Tuesday - Tues., Tue.*	Thursday - Thurs., Thur.*
Monday - Mon.	Wednesday - Wed.	Friday - Fri.
*The first is preferred.		Saturday - Sat.

Directions: Write your answer on the line.

1.   My friend's initials are _____.

2.   Write a declarative sentence:

_____

3.   Write an imperative sentence: _____

4.   Unscramble these days of the week and then write the abbreviation:

a. ytradhsu - _____ _____   c. dtausey - _____ _____

b. tadasryu - _____ _____   d. yfaird - _____ _____

439

Rule 5: **Place a period after the abbreviation for each month.**

January - Jan.	April - Apr.	October - Oct.
February - Feb.	August - Aug.	November - Nov.
March - Mar.	September - Sept.	December - Dec.

May, June, and July do not have abbreviations.

Rule 6: **Place a period after the abbreviation for titles.**

Mr. - Mister
Mrs. - title used for a married woman's name
Ms. - title that does not show if a woman is married or unmarried
Dr. - Doctor

Do not place a period after *Miss* used as a title: Miss Brown

Rule 7: **Place a period after the abbreviation for some places.**

St. - Street	Middle St.
Ave. - Avenue	91st Ave.
Ln. - Lane	Laurel Ln.
Dr. - Drive	Dunn Dr.
Rd. - Road	Tanner Road
Mt. - Mountain	Turtle Mt.
Mts. - Mountains	Pioneer Mts.

U. S. - United States or U. S. A. - United States of America

Always use a dictionary to check for correct abbreviations.

Use the two letter postal code **without a period** for state abbreviations.

NY - New York   NE - Nebraska

Directions: Write the abbreviation.
ANSWERS WILL VARY.

1.   The month I begin school is _____**Aug.**_____. Christmas is in

_____**Dec.**_____. The month which I like best is _____**Oct.**_____.

2.   a.   Judd Lane - _____**Judd Ln.**_____   c.   Mister Ling - _____**Mr. Ling**_____

     b.   United States - _____**U. S.**_____   d.   Elk Mountain - _____**Elk Mt.**_____

440

Rule 5: **Place a period after the abbreviation for each month.**

January - Jan.	April - Apr.	October - Oct.
February - Feb.	August - Aug.	November - Nov.
March - Mar.	September - Sept.	December - Dec.

May, June, and July do not have abbreviations.

Rule 6: **Place a period after the abbreviation for titles.**

Mr. - Mister
Mrs. - title used for a married woman's name
Ms. - title that does not show if a woman is married or unmarried
Dr. - Doctor

Do not place a period after *Miss* used as a title: Miss Brown

Rule 7: **Place a period after the abbreviation for some places.**

St. - Street   Middle St.
Ave. - Avenue   91st Ave.
Ln. - Lane   Laurel Ln.
Dr. - Drive   Dunn Dr.
Rd. - Road   Tanner Road
Mt. - Mountain   Turtle Mt.
Mts. - Mountains   Pioneer Mts.
U. S. - United States or U. S. A. - United States of America

Always use a dictionary to check for correct abbreviations.

Use the two letter postal code **without a period** for state abbreviations.

NY - New York   NE - Nebraska

🐢 🐢 🐢 🐢 🐢 🐢 🐢 🐢 🐢 🐢 🐢 🐢 🐢 🐢 🐢 🐢 🐢 🐢 🐢

Directions: Write the abbreviation.

1.   The month I begin school is _____. Christmas is in

_____. The month which I like best is _____.

2.   a.   Judd Lane - _____   c.   Mister Ling - _____

b.   United States - _____   d.   Elk Mountain - _____

441

Name_____   **PUNCTUATION**
WORKBOOK PAGE 191   Apostrophe (')
Date_____

Rule 1:   **Use an apostrophe in a contraction to show where a letter or letters have been left out.**

       cannot - can't   he is - he's

Rule 2:   **Use an apostrophe to show ownership.**

    A.   **If one item owns something, add ' + <u>s</u>.**

        Examples: Brad**'s** room   pen**'s** cap

    B.   **If a word is plural (more than one) and ends in <u>s</u>, add ' after the <u>s</u> to show ownership.**

        Example: dog**s'** dish   (the dish belongs to more than one dog)

    C.   **If a word is plural (more than one) and does not end in s, add ' + <u>s</u> to show ownership.**

        Examples: children**'s** room   men**'s** shirts

Directions: Write the answer in the blank.
ANSWERS WILL VARY.

1. Write your first name: ____**Lynn**____.   Name something that you

   own: ____**book**____.   Now, use *rule 2A* to write your name and

   the item that you own: ____**Lynn's book**____.

2. a. a pet belonging to a boy - ____**boy's pet**____

   b. a pet belonging to two boys - ____**boys' pet**____

   c. toys belonging to one child - ____**child's toys**____

   d. toys shared by many children - ____**children's toys**____

442

Rule 1: Use an apostrophe in a contraction to show where a letter or letters have been left out.

cannot - can't   he is - he's

Rule 2: Use an apostrophe to show ownership.

A. If one item owns something, add ' + <u>s</u>.

Examples: Brad's room   pen's cap

B. If a word is plural (more than one) and ends in <u>s</u>, add ' after the <u>s</u> to show ownership.

Example: dogs' dish   (the dish belongs to more than one dog)

C. If a word is plural (more than one) and does not end in s, add ' + <u>s</u> to show ownership.

Examples: children's room   men's shirts

Directions: Write the answer in the blank.

1. Write your first name: _____. Name something that you

own: _____. Now, use *rule 2A* to write your name and

the item that you own: _____.

2. a. a pet belonging to a boy - _____

b. a pet belonging to two boys - _____

c. toys belonging to one child - _____

d. toys shared by many children - _____

PUNCTUATION
Using Periods
and Apostrophes

A. Directions: Write the abbreviation for each day of the week.

    1. Wednesday - ____**Wed.**____   5. Thursday - ____**Thurs.**____

    2. Saturday - ____**Sat.**____   6. Monday - ____**Mon.**____

    3. Tuesday - ____**Tues.**____   7. Friday - ____**Fri.**____

    4. Sunday - ____**Sun.**____

B. Directions: Write the abbreviation for the month of the year.

    1. January - ____**Jan.**____   6. September - ____**Sept.**____

    2. February - ____**Feb.**____   7. October - ____**Oct.**____

    3. March - ____**Mar.**____   8. November - ____**Nov.**____

    4. April - ____**Apr.**____   9. December - ____**Dec.**____

    5. August - ____**Aug.**____

C. Directions: Place a period or an apostrophe where needed.

    1. I can't go with Mrs. Kline.

    2. Mike's brother lives on Fawn St.

    3. The White Mts. aren't very high.

    4. Mail this U. S. map for me.

    5. Dr. Harton talked about his three nurses' vacations.

A. Directions: Write the abbreviation for each day of the week.

   1. Wednesday - _____   5. Thursday - _____

   2. Saturday - _____   6. Monday - _____

   3. Tuesday - _____   7. Friday - _____

   4. Sunday - _____

B. Directions: Write the abbreviation for the month of the year.

   1. January - _____   6. September - _____

   2. February - _____   7. October - _____

   3. March - _____   8. November - _____

   4. April - _____   9. December - _____

   5. August - _____

C. Directions: Place a period or an apostrophe where needed.

   1. I cant go with Mrs Kline

   2. Mikes brother lives on Fawn St

   3. The White Mts arent very high

   4. Mail this U S map for me

   5. Dr Harton talked about his three nurses vacations

445

Rule 1: **Place a comma between the day and year in a date.**
Example: April 1, 1999

Rule 2: **Place a comma between the name of a day and date.**
Example: Monday, July 21, 1997

Rule 3: **Place a comma between a town or city and a state.**
Examples: Altus, Oklahoma
Nashville, Tennessee

Rule 4: **Place a comma between a city and a country.**
Example: Mexico City, Mexico

Rule 5: **In a street address, place a comma after the street and after the city.**
Do not place a comma between a state and the zip code.
Do not place a comma between the house number and a street name.

Example: I live at 12 North Easy Street, Carefree, AZ   85529.
⬆ (no comma)   ⬆ (no comma)

🐢🐢🐢🐢🐢🐢🐢🐢🐢🐢🐢🐢🐢🐢🐢🐢🐢🐢

Directions: Read each sentence and complete it.

1.   Write today's date: _____**August 22, 1997**_____.

2.   Write the day of the week and today's date: **Friday, August 22, 1997**.

3.   Write your town (city) and your state: _____**Cool, California**_____.

4.   Write your street address: _____**88 Military Lane**_____.

5.   Place commas in this address: 2 Arc Lane, Clinton, SC*   29325.
446   *the state of South Carolina

Rule 1: **Place a comma between the day and year in a date.**
Example: April 1, 1999

Rule 2: **Place a comma between the name of a day and date.**
Example: Monday, July 21, 1997

Rule 3: **Place a comma between a town or city and a state.**
Examples: Altus, Oklahoma
Nashville, Tennessee

Rule 4: **Place a comma between a city and a country.**
Example: Mexico City, Mexico

Rule 5: **In a street address, place a comma after the street and after the city.**
Do not place a comma between a state and the zip code.
Do not place a comma between the house number and a street name.

Example: I live at 12 North Easy Street, Carefree, AZ 85529.
↑ (no comma)   ↑ (no comma)

🐢 🐢 🐢 🐢 🐢 🐢 🐢 🐢 🐢 🐢 🐢 🐢 🐢 🐢 🐢 🐢 🐢 🐢 🐢

Directions: Read each sentence and complete it.

1. Write today's date: _____.

2. Write the day of the week and today's date: _____.

3. Write your town (city) and your state: _____.

4. Write your street address: _____.

5. Place commas in this address: 2 Arc Lane Clinton SC* 29325.
   *the state of South Carolina

447

Rule 6:   **Place a comma after three or more items in a series.**
          Do not place a comma after the last item in a series.
                Example: I bought pretzels, chips, and soda for our party.

                                                    ⬆ (no comma)

          Do not place a comma between two items.
                Example: celery and carrots

Rule 7:   **Place a comma after the greeting of a friendly letter.**
                Example: Dear Randy,

Rule 8:   **Place a comma after the closing of a friendly letter.**
                Example: Your friend,

Rule 9:   **Place a comma after a word like *yes* or *no* at the
          beginning of a sentence.**
                Example: No, I don't want any dessert.

🐢🐢🐢🐢🐢🐢🐢🐢🐢🐢🐢🐢🐢🐢🐢🐢🐢🐢

Directions: Read each sentence and complete it.
ANSWERS WILL VARY FOR 1-3.
1.   Write a greeting of a letter to one of your friends: ____**Dear Bobbi,**____.

2.   Write a closing of a letter to someone: ____**Love,**_____.

3.   Finish this sentence: My three best friends are **Lauren, Mary, and**

Elizabeth_____.

4.   Place commas where needed:

     a. Yes, I would like some chips and dip.

     b. Gary, Annette, and Sammy won!

448

Rule 6: **Place a comma after three or more items in a series.**
Do not place a comma after the last item in a series.

Example: I bought pretzels, chips, and soda for our party.

⬆ (no comma)

Do not place a comma between two items.
Example: celery and carrots

Rule 7: **Place a comma after the greeting of a friendly letter.**
Example: Dear Randy,

Rule 8: **Place a comma after the closing of a friendly letter.**
Example: Your friend,

Rule 9: **Place a comma after a word like *yes* or *no* at the beginning of a sentence.**

Example: No, I don't want any dessert.

🐢 🐢 🐢 🐢 🐢 🐢 🐢 🐢 🐢 🐢 🐢 🐢 🐢 🐢 🐢 🐢 🐢 🐢 🐢 🐢

Directions: Read each sentence and complete it.

1. Write a greeting of a letter to one of your friends: _____.

2. Write a closing of a letter to someone: _____.

3. Finish this sentence: My three best friends are _____

_____.

4. Place commas where needed:

   a. Yes I would like some chips and dip.

   b. Gary Annette and Sammy won!

Rule 10:   **Place a comma when speaking to someone.**

a. **If the name of the person is at the beginning of a sentence, place a comma after the person's name.**

Example: Hansel, when is your birthday?

b. **If the name of the person is at the end of a sentence, place a comma before the person's name.**

Example: I like your sweater, Jana.

Rule 11:   **Place a comma in a direct quotation.**
A direct quotation states exactly what the person says.

Example: "I'm too tired to race again," said Dena.

If the person who is talking is given first, place a comma after the person's name + *said* or *asked*.

Example: Yancy asked, "Why are you leaving?"

Directions: Place commas where needed.

1. Lani said, "Let's buy some candy."

2. Seth, will you hand me that hammer?

3. "Thanks for your help, " said Kammie.

4.   I'll be right back, Howi.

5. Mrs. Reno asked, "Where is Rose Lane?"

450

Rule 10: **Place a comma when speaking to someone.**

a. **If the name of the person is at the beginning of a sentence, place a comma after the person's name.**

Example: Hansel, when is your birthday?

b. **If the name of the person is at the end of a sentence, place a comma before the person's name.**

Example: I like your sweater, Jana.

Rule 11: **Place a comma in a direct quotation.**
A direct quotation states exactly what the person says.

Example: "I'm too tired to race again,"   said Dena.

If the person who is talking is given first, place a comma after the person's name + *said* or *asked*.

Example: Yancy asked, "Why are you leaving?"

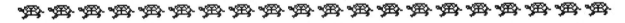

Directions: Place commas where needed.

1.   Lani said   "Let's buy some candy."

2.   Seth will you hand me that hammer?

3.   "Thanks for your help "   said Kammie.

4.   I'll be right back Howi.

5.   Mrs. Reno asked "Where is Rose Lane?"

Name_____   **PUNCTUATION**
WORKBOOK PAGE 196   **Using Commas**
Date_____

<u>**Note to Teacher:**</u>   <u>**You may need to explain that Paris is a city and**</u>
<u>**France is a country in #13**</u>.
Directions: Place commas where needed.

1.   Dear Joan,

     I'll see your next week in Florida.

         Forever friends,
         Stacey

2.   The couple was married on June 28, 1996.

3.   Yes, we want you to come with us.

4.   "A diamond is harder than an opal, "   said the teacher.

5.   Billy, this lumber is too soft.

6.   He is taking a towel, lotion, and a radio to the beach.

7.   Their aunt and uncle live in Austin, Texas.

8.   She was born on Thursday, May 20, 1982.

9.   Dottie's address is 59 Hutton Avenue, Toney, AL   35773.

10.   Gwen asked, "How is your father?"

11.   Please mail this card, Jackie.

12.   No, they aren't serving ice cream and cake.

13.   Fred, Nan, and Terry are flying to Paris, France.

452

PUNCTUATION
Using Commas

Directions: Place commas where needed.

1.   Dear Joan

      I'll see your next week in Florida.

                    Forever friends

                    Stacey

2.   The couple was married on June 28 1996.

3.   Yes we want you to come with us.

4.   "A diamond is harder than an opal "   said the teacher.

5.   Billy this lumber is too soft.

6.   He is taking a towel lotion and a radio to the beach.

7.   Their aunt and uncle live in Austin Texas.

8.   She was born on Thursday May 20 1982.

9.   Dottie's address is 59 Hutton Avenue Toney AL 35773.

10.   Gwen asked   "How is your father?"

11.   Please mail this card Jackie.

12.   No they aren't serving ice cream and cake.

13.   Fred Nan and Terry are flying to Paris France.

Note to Teacher: **You may wish to teach that when a direct quotation uses the word** *exclaim(ed),* **an exclamation point is used at the end of the quotation.**

Colon (:):

Rule: **Place a colon between the hour and minute(s) in time.**

Example: It's 2:15 P. M.

Question Mark (?):

Rule: **Place a question mark at the end of a sentence that asks a question.**

Example: Do you have any money**?**

Exclamation Point (Mark) (!):

Rule 1: **Place an exclamation point after an interjection.**

Remember: An interjection shows emotion.
An interjection is not a complete sentence.

Example: Wow!

Rule 2: **Place an exclamation point after a sentence that shows emotion.**

Example: We've finally landed!

🐢 🐢 🐢 🐢 🐢 🐢 🐢 🐢 🐢 🐢 🐢 🐢 🐢 🐢 🐢 🐢 🐢 🐢 🐢

Directions: Place a colon, question mark, or exclamation point where needed.

1.   The meeting will start at 8:00 P. M.

2.   Yeah!   We're the champs!

3.   Bob exclaimed,   "I'm allowed to go!"

4.   Does the picnic begin at 4:30 in the afternoon**?**

454

Name_____

Date_____

PUNCTUATION
Colon
Question Mark
Exclamation Point

Colon (:):

Rule: **Place a colon between the hour and minute(s) in time.**

Example: It's 2:15 P. M.

Question Mark (?):

Rule: **Place a question mark at the end of a sentence that asks a question.**

Example: Do you have any money**?**

Exclamation Point (Mark) (!):

Rule 1: **Place an exclamation point after an interjection.**

Remember: An interjection shows emotion.
An interjection is not a complete sentence.

Example: Wow!

Rule 2: **Place an exclamation point after a sentence that shows emotion.**

Example: We've finally landed!

Directions: Place a colon, question mark, or exclamation point where needed.

1. The meeting will start at 8 00 P. M.

2. Yeah   We're the champs

3. Bob exclaimed, "I'm allowed to go "

4. Does the picnic begin at 4 30 in the afternoon

455

Underlining (_):

Rule 1:   Underline the title of a book.

Example: The child's mom reads <u>Corduroy</u> to him.

Rule 2:   Underline the title of a magazine.

Example: I like <u>Bees and Bugs</u>.

Rule 3:   Underline the title of a newspaper.

Example: My uncle always reads <u>Current Times</u>.

Rule 4:   Underline the title of a movie or television show.

Example: Dad likes to watch <u>Travels with Ama</u>.

🐢 🐢 🐢 🐢 🐢 🐢 🐢 🐢 🐢 🐢 🐢 🐢 🐢 🐢 🐢 🐢 🐢

Directions: Complete each sentence.

1.   My favorite book when I was little was ___<u>**The Cat Ate My Hat**</u>___.

2.   My favorite book now is ___<u>**Baseball Pals**</u>___.

3.   My favorite movie is ___<u>**We All Sing Together**</u>___.

4.   My favorite television show is ___<u>**Ali's Friends**</u>___.

5.   The name of a magazine is ___<u>**Sunny Skies**</u>___.

6.   The name of a newspaper is ___<u>**The Auto Journal**</u>___.

456

Underlining (_):

Rule 1: **Underline the title of a book.**

Example: The child's mom reads <u>Corduroy</u> to him.

Rule 2: **Underline the title of a magazine.**

Example: I like <u>Bees and Bugs</u>.

Rule 3: **Underline the title of a newspaper.**

Example: My uncle always reads <u>Current Times</u>.

Rule 4: **Underline the title of a movie or television show.**

Example: Dad likes to watch <u>Travels with Ama</u>.

🐢 🐢 🐢 🐢 🐢 🐢 🐢 🐢 🐢 🐢 🐢 🐢 🐢 🐢 🐢 🐢 🐢 🐢

Directions: Complete each sentence.

1.   My favorite book when I was little was _____.

2.   My favorite book now is _____.

3.   My favorite movie is _____.

4.   My favorite television show is _____.

5.   The name of a magazine is _____.

6.   The name of a newspaper is _____.

Note to Teacher: Allowing students to find titles of short stories and poems in their reading book is a good idea. Also, allow students time to peruse their science and social studies texts for chapter and unit titles.

Quotation Marks (" "):

Rule 1:   **Place quotation marks around a direct quotation.**
A direct quotation is what someone says.

Example: Matt said, "Let's play basketball."

Rule 2:   **Place quotation marks around the title of a short story.**

Example: Dad read the story, "Angus and the Cat," to us.

Rule 3:   **Place quotation marks around the title of a poem.**

Example: She likes the poem, "White Season."

Rule 4:   **Place quotation marks around the title of a song.**

Example: "Don't Tell My Heart" was a popular song.

Rule 5:   **Place quotation marks around the title of a chapter.**

Example: The first chapter of our science book is "Plants."

🐢🐢🐢🐢🐢🐢🐢🐢🐢🐢🐢🐢🐢🐢🐢🐢🐢🐢🐢

Directions: Complete each sentence.
ANSWERS WILL VARY.

1.   My favorite song is _____**"The Peanut Song."**_____

2.   The name of a short story is _____**"Marika, the Snowmaiden."**_____

3.   The name of a poem is _____**"City Trees."**_____

4.   The name of a chapter in a book is _____**"My State."**_____

5.   Write something you have said: **"Texas was an independent country for nearly ten years,"** said **Miss Martin** (your name).

458

Quotation Marks (" "):

Rule 1: **Place quotation marks around a direct quotation.**
A direct quotation is what someone says.

Example: Matt said, "Let's play basketball."

Rule 2: **Place quotation marks around the title of a short story.**
Example: Dad read the story, "Angus and the Cat," to us.

Rule 3: **Place quotation marks around the title of a poem.**
Example: She likes the poem, "White Season."

Rule 4: **Place quotation marks around the title of a song.**
Example: "Don't Tell My Heart" was a popular song.

Rule 5: **Place quotation marks around the title of a chapter.**
Example: The first chapter of our science book is
"Plants."

Directions: Complete each sentence.

1.   My favorite song is _____.

2.   The name of a short story is _____.

3.   The name of a poem is _____.

4.   The name of a chapter in a book is _____.

5.   Write something you have said: _____

_____said _____ (your name).   459

PUNCTUATION
Using Quotation Marks
and Underlining

Note to Teacher: **This page is difficult; you may wish to do it orally. Also, it may be helpful to teach the concept using the following information:** (Titles of major "works" are underlined.) The title of an item that you "can receive in the mail" is underlined. For example, a book is often shipped to us at home; a magazine frequently comes by mail. Those titles are underlined. Titles of anything within a major "work" such as a poem or a short story are placed in quotation marks. You may wish to use a reading book to show that chapter titles, poems, and short stories can be found *within* a book.

Directions: Use quotation marks or underlining where needed.

1.   Kali said, "That's my coat."

2.   We watched the movie, <u>Abel's Island</u>.

3.   They sang "The Mitten Song" after lunch.

4.   Casper read the book named <u>Elmo the Pig</u>.

5.   We read the short story, "Sylvester and the Magic Pebble."

6.   He watched <u>Cooking with Kana</u> on television.

7.   We opened our science book to the chapter, "Bugs."

8.   Mother often reads the magazine, <u>Patterns</u>.

9.   My favorite poem is "Snowball Wind."

10.   "Will you carry this for me?" asked Chika.

11.   The title of my mother's favorite short story is "The Necklace."

12.   Dad read the book, <u>The Songwriters Idea Book</u>.

13.   The lady at the airport read the newspaper, <u>Spotlight News</u>.

Directions: Use quotation marks or underlining where needed.

1.   Kali said,   That's my coat.

2.   We watched the movie, Abel's Island.

3.   They sang The Mitten Song after lunch.

4.   Casper read the book named Elmo the Pig.

5.   We read the short story, Sylvester and the Magic Pebble.

6.   He watched Cooking with Kana on television.

7.   We opened our science book to the chapter, Bugs.

8.   Mother often reads the magazine, Patterns.

9.   My favorite poem is Snowball Wind.

10.   Will you carry this for me?   asked Chika.

11.   The title of my mother's favorite short story is The Necklace.

12.   Dad read the book, The Songwriters Idea Book.

13.   The lady at the airport read the newspaper, Spotlight News.

A. Periods:

Directions: Place periods where needed.

1. Mr. Dine lives on Rabbit Rd.

2. Write the abbreviation for each day of the week:

   a. Sunday - **Sun.**   c. Tuesday - **Tues.**   e. Thursday - **Thurs.**

   b. Monday - **Mon.**   d. Wednesday - **Wed.**   f. Friday - **Fri.**

                                                      g. Saturday - **Sat.**

3. Write the abbreviation for these months:

   a. January - **Jan.**   d. September - **Sept.**

   b. February - **Feb.**   e. October - **Oct.**

   c. August - **Aug.**   f. December - **Dec.**

B. Apostrophes:

Directions: Place apostrophes where needed.

1. She hasn't washed her truck.

2. Brian's dog is a German shepherd.

3. The boys' bathroom is down the hall.

4. His men's baseball team plays tonight.

462

Date_____

A. Periods:

Directions: Place periods where needed.

1. Mr Dine lives on Rabbit Rd

2. Write the abbreviation for each day of the week:

a. Sunday - _____   c. Tuesday - _____   e. Thursday - _____

b. Monday - _____   d. Wednesday - _____   f. Friday - _____

g. Saturday - _____

3. Write the abbreviation for these months:

a. January - _____   d. September - _____

b. February - _____   e. October - _____

c. August - _____   f. December - _____

B. Apostrophes:

Directions: Place apostrophes where needed.

1. She hasnt washed her truck.

2. Brians dog is a German shepherd.

3. The boys bathroom is down the hall.

4. His mens baseball team plays tonight.   463

WORKBOOK PAGE 202

Date_____

C.   Commas:

Directions: Place commas where needed.

1.   Millie lives in Chicago, Illinois.

2.   Yes, I'll be there.

3.   She likes eggs, ham, and toast for breakfast.

4.   Ted, I want to talk to you.

5.   "I'd like two slices of pizza,"   said Leslie.

6.   They met on January 1, 1995.

7.   Will you loan me your skates, Pam?

8.   His parents went to London, England.

9.   Dear Julie,

May I stay with you this weekend?

Love,

Denise

10.   Her next appointment is Friday, August 11, 2000.

11.   Their new address is 12 Bridge Street, Elkton, Maryland   21922.

Date_____

C. Commas:

Directions: Place commas where needed.

1. Millie lives in Chicago Illinois.

2. Yes I'll be there.

3. She likes eggs ham and toast for breakfast.

4. Ted I want to talk to you.

5. "I'd like two slices of pizza " said Leslie.

6. They met on January 1 1995.

7. Will you loan me your skates Pam?

8. His parents went to London England.

9. Dear Julie

   May I stay with you this weekend?

   Love

   Denise

10. Her next appointment is Friday August 11 2000.

11. Their new address is 12 Bridge Street Elkton Maryland 21922.

D.   Colons, Question Marks, and Exclamation Points:

   Directions: Place colons, question marks, or exclamation points
                 where needed.

1.   Does your grandfather plant a garden**?**

2.   Yippee!   It's recess!

3.   They arrived at 11**:** 15 A. M.

E.   Underlining and Quotation Marks:

   Directions: Underline or use quotation marks where needed.

1.   Titles:

   a.   book: <u>The Beatle Bush</u>

   b.   short story: "Here, Puppy"

   c.   movie: <u>Baby's Bedtime</u>

   d.   poem: "At the Zoo"

   e.   song: "Here's a Happy Song"

   f.   newspaper: <u>Frogtown News</u>

   g.   magazine: <u>Beaches</u>

2.   Brody said,   "It's nice to meet you."
466

D. Colons, Question Marks, and Exclamation Points:

Directions: Place colons, question marks, or exclamation points where needed.

1. Does your grandfather plant a garden

2. Yippee   It's recess

3. They arrived at 11 15 A. M.

E. Underlining and Quotation Marks:

Directions: Underline or use quotation marks where needed.

1. Titles:

    a. book: The Beatle Bush

    b. short story: Here, Puppy

    c. movie: Baby's Bedtime

    d. poem: At the Zoo

    e. song: Here's a Happy Song

    f. newspaper: Frogtown News

    g. magazine: Beaches

2. Brody said,   It's nice to meet you.

Name_____ **Punctuation Test**

Date_____

Directions: Use needed punctuation.

Remember: You have learned about periods, apostrophes, commas, colons, question marks, exclamation points, underlining, and quotation marks.

1.   Please don't sit there.

2.   Yes, the time is 9:30.

3.   Wow! We won a prize!

4.   Mary's room is painted blue.

5.   Her home is near the Green Mts. in Vermont.

6.   He read the book named Top Wing.

7.   Bobby, may I borrow your skates?

8.   They were married on Nov. 18, 1996.

9.   Dear Liz,

      I found your camera in our car. (*or* !)

          Your friend,

          Rich

10.   His favorite short story is "The Snow in Chelm."

Name_____ **Punctuation Test**

Date_____

Directions: Use needed punctuation.

Remember: You have learned about periods, apostrophes, commas, colons, question marks, exclamation points, underlining, and quotation marks.

1. Please dont sit there

2. Yes the time is 9 30

3. Wow We won a prize

4. Marys room is painted blue

5. Her home is near the Green Mts in Vermont

6. He read the book named Top Wing

7. Bobby may I borrow your skates

8. They were married on Nov 18 1996

9. Dear Liz

   I found your camera in our car

   Your friend

   Rich

10. His favorite short story is The Snow in Chelm

TO THE TEACHER:

PAGE 471 = WORKBOOK PAGE 204

It is important that you **teach** how to write formal notes.

As in all good writing, you will eventually include the basics of the **writing process**: discussing a purpose and sharing ideas (brainstorming), writing a rough draft, editing and revising, and writing a published copy. However, for the first note experience, skip the writing process and **model the format step-by-step**. This means that you visually introduce **each** step to your students. Circulate and check their work. Put students in pairs to peruse each other's work.

I am providing you with **lengthy** instruction for a note. This appears in abbreviated form for the student on the following page. Use this to model the format.

To write a formal note:

1. If desired, place the date in the upper right hand corner with the last digit of the year ending with the right margin. (I recommend that students write out the date.)

2. Skip down a line or two on the note paper to write a greeting. Since most note paper is unlined, this can be a challenge:
   a. The number of lines students skip depends on the length of their message, their handwriting size, and the size of the paper.
   b. The message should not be "bunched" at the top of the note; it should flow down the page.
   c. You may wish to have students place heavily-lined paper under their notes. This helps to space the lines evenly and prevents students from writing uphill. (You can darken the lines of regular notebook paper and make copies. Each student, then, keeps his own copy in a writing folder.)

3. The greeting should begin at the left margin.

4. The message (or body) should be indented. The general agreement in a written note is to indent five spaces. This is easy if using the salutation, *dear*, because students will begin to write below the space after the *r*.
   a. Be sure students come back out to the left margin when writing the message.
   b. Ascertain that students do not write beyond the right margin which can be discerned easily if the date has been included.

5. If the date has been used, align the closing with the written date. (If no date has been used or students have used all numbers for the date, the closing should be just to the right of the middle of the note.)

470

Writing Formal Notes:

To write a formal note:

1. If desired, place the date in the upper right hand corner (about one-half to one inch from the top) with the last digit of the year ending with your right margin.

2. Skip down a line or two on the note paper to write your greeting.

   a. The number of lines you skip depends on the length of the message, your handwriting size, and the size of the paper.

   b. The message should not be "bunched" at the top of the note but flow down the page.

3. The greeting should begin at your left margin. (Be sure to place a comma after the greeting.)

4. The message (or body) should be indented. Indent five spaces.

5. Write your closing. (Be sure to place a comma after it.)

6. Write your name directly under the first letter of your closing.

July 23, 1997	**date**
Dear Grandma,	**greeting**
Thanks for my birthday card and money. I want to use the money for a new jacket.	**message (body)**
How are you? Are you still coming to visit us at Christmas? I hope so.	
Love,	**closing**
Ginger	**signature**

TO THE TEACHER: **Friendly Letter**

PAGE 473 = WORKBOOK PAGE 205

An overview of a friendly letter appears on the ensuing page. Many friendly letter ideas are given in *Easy Grammar: Grades 4 and 5*.

If you are teaching this text to third graders, don't worry if you don't teach friendly letter as thoroughly as a formal note. If you are teaching fourth grade, you may wish to spend more time introducing its purpose and format.

As mentioned in notes, students do need to follow the writing process:
   A.   Discuss the purpose of writing and share ideas   (brainstorm)
   B.   Write a rough draft
   C.   Edit and Revise
   D.   Write the published (final) copy

However, when *introducing* friendly letter, focus on format. Provide paper for each student and visually walk them through each component. Be clear about content and placement of each line of the heading. Check each student's placement of the street address line. If you can catch an error here and correct it, much time will be saved.

I have my students write their first friendly letter to me; thus, they write *Dear Mrs. Phillips* as the greeting. I actually dictate the message (body): I am learning how to set up a friendly letter. I understand that a friendly letter has five parts: the heading, the greeting, the message or body, the closing, and the signature. I am placing this letter in my notebook so that I can look at it in the future. With a colored pencil or a highlighter, I have my students write *COPY* across the letter diagonally. (We save it in a notebook or writing folder.)

Doesn't this take a long time? Yes! Walking students through the format and checking each paper (while teaching) to ascertain that placement is correct takes time. You may want to introduce the format in two sessions. Allow me to stress how very important it is that students write it correctly the first time; it saves problems and time later.

I, personally, wait approximately two weeks before I reintroduce friendly letter format. Again, I walk the students through each part of the heading, soliciting from them what is written on each line. (Yes, I allow them to look back at their copies. However, I don't want them merely copying that. This is another learning time!) After slowly reteaching and completing heading and greeting, we actually discuss *writing with a reason* and brainstorm. (I often have students write about themselves or their experiences, i.e. a funny incident.) I ask students to write their rough draft for the message but not to write the closing. (I ask students to "free read" after checking their work.) After all students are finished with the body, I walk them through the process of aligning the closing with the heading and placing the signature directly under the closing. I do collect this letter and check the format **very carefully**. If an error has been made, I want to find it. My focus is format. When I return the letters, I set aside time to talk with each student about **any format error**. I have a **model** available so that students can see the proper format.

472

FRIENDLY LETTER

The parts of a friendly letter are the **heading**, the **greeting**, the **body (message)**, the **closing**, and the **signature**.

A three-lined **formal** heading will be used. In **informal** letters, the date is frequently the only item included. However, the formal heading is important to know.

In a formal letter, as in all formal writing, abbreviations are not used.

The **exception** to this is the postal code for states. A postal code is capitalized, and no punctuation is used.

Examples: South Dakota = SD   Oklahoma = OK
           Wyoming = WY   Michigan = MI

Friendly Letter Parts:

heading	HOUSE NUMBER AND STREET NAME CITY, STATE ZIP CODE COMPLETE DATE (not abbreviated)

greeting Dear (Person)   ,

body   The body is also called the message. It is written here. Indent at least five spaces. You may skip a line between the greeting and the body. Note that you have margins on each side of the paper.

closing   Truly yours,

signature   Your Name

MY OWN NOTES

WRITING SENTENCES

TO THE TEACHER:

This writing unit teaches students how to write items in a series. You may choose to do these lessons as a separate writing unit or to spread them over a period of weeks.

A *best practice* would be to teach the concepts in the lesson before reading and discussing the lesson with your students.

I have provided note sheets entitled "My Own Notes" for students. You may want to have students write your examples and/or their own examples on these pages. These can also be used to write examples as you review the preceding lesson.

MY OWN NOTES

A sentence expresses a complete thought. The subject of a sentence is **who** or **what** the sentence is about.

> **Example:** A little girl danced.

We are talking about a girl. *Girl* is the subject of the sentence.

ॐॐॐ

Sometimes, the sentence is about more than one thing.

> **Example:** A little girl and her sister danced.

We are talking about the girl **and** her sister. *Girl* and *sister* are the

subject of the sentence. We call this a **compound subject**.

Usually, we use **and** to join two words in a compound subject.

ॐॐॐॐॐॐॐॐॐॐ

Directions: Use **and** to join the subject of two sentences.

> **Example:**   Pedro painted a chair. Tony painted, too.

> **Pedro and Tony painted a chair.**

ANSWERS WILL VARY/REPRESENTATIVE ANSWERS:

1.   Mom played in a softball game. Dad played in a softball game.

> **Mom and Dad played in a softball game.**

_____

2.   Eggs were served for breakfast. Muffins were served for breakfast, too.

> **Eggs and muffins were served for breakfast.**

_____

478

A sentence expresses a complete thought. The subject of a sentence is **who** or **what** the sentence is about.

>   **Example:**   A little girl danced.

We are talking about a girl. *Girl* is the subject of the sentence.
>   ❧❧❧

Sometimes, the sentence is about more than one thing.

>   **Example:**   A little girl and her sister danced.

We are talking about the girl **and** her sister. *Girl* and *sister* are the

subject of the sentence. We call this a **compound subject**.

Usually, we use **and** to join two words in a compound subject.

>   ❧❧❧❧❧❧❧❧❧❧❧

Directions: Use **and** to join the subject of two sentences.

>   **Example:**   Pedro painted a chair. Tony painted, too.
>   **Pedro and Tony painted a chair.**

1. Mom played in a softball game. Dad played in a softball game.

_____

_____

2. Eggs were served for breakfast. Muffins were served for
    breakfast, too.

_____

_____

479

3. The boys ride bikes to school. The girls ride bikes to school.

       The boys and girls ride bikes to school.

4. Our grandmother baked cookies. Our grandfather baked cookies.

       Our grandmother and grandfather baked

       cookies.

5. Jan wanted to sail. Her brother wanted to sail, also.

       Jan and her brother wanted to sail.

6. Ice will melt quickly in hot weather. Ice cream will melt quickly in hot weather.

       Ice and ice cream will melt quickly in

       hot weather.

7. Lani washed cherries for a fruit salad. Moe washed cherries, too.

       Lani and Moe washed cherries for a

       fruit salad.

8. Tulips are blooming. Daisies are blooming.

       Tulips and daisies are blooming.

3. The boys ride bikes to school. The girls ride bikes to school.

_____

_____

4. Our grandmother baked cookies. Our grandfather baked cookies.

_____

_____

5. Jan wanted to sail. Her brother wanted to sail, also.

_____

_____

6. Ice will melt quickly in hot weather. Ice cream will melt quickly in hot weather.

_____

_____

7. Lani washed cherries for a fruit salad. Moe washed cherries, too.

_____

_____

8. Tulips are blooming. Daisies are blooming.

_____

_____

TO THE TEACHER:

Students have learned to join items with the conjunction, *and*. Now, they will learn to do so using the conjunction, *or*.

A *best practice* would be to teach the concepts in the lesson before reading and discussing the lesson with your students. Use your own examples. Teach with enthusiasm!

I have provided note sheets entitled "My Own Notes" for students. You may want to have students write your examples and/or their own examples on these pages. These can also be used to review the preceding lesson.

If you have never used individual *dry erase boards (white boards)* for each student to write examples, you may wish to order them. Students *love* writing examples on these erasable boards.

(Call the telephone number on the title page or on the back cover to inquire about ordering one for each of your student. You may email us at info@easygrammar.com if you wish. You will find that you can use dry erase boards in other subjects, too!)

MY OWN NOTES

Writing Sentences

Items in a Series

A sentence expresses a complete thought. The subject of a sentence is **who** or **what** the sentence is about.

> **Example:** Candy or Eric will cut the melons.

We are talking about Candy or Eric. <u>Candy</u> + <u>Eric</u> = **compound subject**. Sometimes, we use **or** to join two words in a compound subject.

࿊࿊࿊࿊࿊࿊࿊࿊࿊࿊࿊

Directions: Use **or** to join the subject of two sentences.

> **Example:** Pat made peanut butter sandwiches.
> Kim may have made peanut butter sandwiches.

> **Pat or Kim made peanut butter sandwiches.**

1. Jana won the game. Devi may have won the game.

> **Jana or Devi won the game.**

2. A neighbor built the fence. Her friend may have built the fence.

> **A neighbor or her friend built the fence.**

3. Hamburgers may be served for dinner. Tacos may be served instead.

> **Hamburgers or tacos may be served for dinner.**

4. My sister will march in a parade. My brother may take her place.

> **My sister or brother will march in a parade.**

A sentence expresses a complete thought. The subject of a sentence is **who** or **what** the sentence is about.

Example: Candy or Eric will cut the melons.

We are talking about Candy or Eric. <u>Candy</u> + <u>Eric</u> = **compound subject**. Sometimes, we use **or** to join two words in a compound subject.

ฅ ฅ ฅ ฅ ฅ ฅ ฅ ฅ ฅ ฅ ฅ ฅ

Directions: Use **or** to join the subject of two sentences.

Example: Pat made peanut butter sandwiches.
Kim may have made peanut butter sandwiches.

Pat or Kim made peanut butter sandwiches.

1. Jana won the game. Devi may have won the game.

_____

_____

2. A neighbor built the fence. Her friend may have built the fence.

_____

_____

3. Hamburgers may be served for dinner. Tacos may be served instead.

_____

_____

4. My sister will march in a parade. My brother may take her place.

_____

_____

TO THE TEACHER:

The next lesson discusses that a verb may change when subjects are combined.

Examples: Jonah **is** my brother.
Joey **is** my other brother.

_____Jonah and Joey **are** my brothers._____

Maria **plays** soccer.
Julie **plays** soccer.

_____Maria and Julie **play** soccer._____

Be sure to teach this concept very carefully!

MY OWN NOTES

The subject of a sentence is **who** or **what** the sentence is about. **Sometimes, a verb may change.**

> **Example:** Min wants a snack. Suzy wants a snack, too.

When we talk about one (singular), we use a singular verb. Each person **wants** a snack. However, when we join *Min and Suzy*, we make a compound subject. The verb must agree with the plural (more than one) subject. Therefore, Min and Suzy **want** a snack.

ﾗﾗﾗ

A verb may change form with a compound subject.

> **Example:** My foot is swollen. My ankle is also swollen.

When we talk about one (singular), we use a singular verb. When we are talking about two or more joined by **and**, we must use a verb that agrees.

> Wrong: My foot and ankle **is** swollen.

> Right: My foot and ankle **are** swollen.

ﾗﾗﾗﾗﾗﾗﾗﾗﾗﾗﾗﾗ

Directions: Use **and** to join the subjects of two sentences.

Example: Tyger likes car races. Chris likes car races, too.

> **Tyger and Chris like car races.**

1. Luis eats lunch late. Annie eats lunch late, too.

> **Luis and Annie eat lunch late.**
> _____

488

The subject of a sentence is **who** or **what** the sentence is about. **Sometimes, a verb may change.**

> **Example:** Min wants a snack. Suzy wants a snack, too.

When we talk about one (singular), we use a singular verb. Each person **wants** a snack. However, when we join *Min and Suzy*, we make a compound subject. The verb must agree with the plural (more than one) subject. Therefore, Min and Suzy **want** a snack.

৯৯৯

A verb may change form with a compound subject.

> **Example:** My foot is swollen. My ankle is also swollen.

When we talk about one (singular), we use a singular verb. When we are talking about two or more joined by **and**, we must use a verb that agrees.

> Wrong: My foot and ankle **is** swollen.

> Right: My foot and ankle **are** swollen.

৯৯৯৯৯৯৯৯৯৯৯

Directions: Use **and** to join the subjects of two sentences.

Example: Tyger likes car races. Chris likes car races, too.

Tyger and Chris like car races.

1. Luis eats lunch late. Annie eats lunch late, too.

_____

_____

2. Kirk is a model.   Lisa is a model, also.

      Kirk and Lisa are models.

3. Her mother sews costumes for our school plays. His aunt sews costumes for our school plays.

      Her mother and his aunt sew costumes

      for our school plays.

4. Their sister wants to go to a beach this summer. Their brother wants to go to a beach this summer.

      Their sister and brother want to go to a

      beach this summer.

5. Misty goes to soccer practice on Mondays. Marc goes to soccer practice on Mondays, too.

      Misty and Marc go to soccer practice on

      Mondays.

6. Mr. Liss was a pilot. His wife was a pilot, also.

      Mr. Liss and his wife were pilots.

7. Dad is standing by the door. My uncle is standing by the door, too.

      Dad and my uncle are standing by the door.

2. Kirk is a model. Lisa is a model, also.

_____

_____

3. Her mother sews costumes for our school plays. His aunt sews costumes for our school plays.

_____

_____

4. Their sister wants to go to a beach this summer. Their brother wants to go to a beach this summer.

_____

_____

5. Misty goes to soccer practice on Mondays. Marc goes to soccer practice on Mondays, too.

_____

_____

6. Mr. Liss was a pilot. His wife was a pilot, also.

_____

_____

7. Dad is standing by the door. My uncle is standing by the door, too.

_____

_____

TO THE TEACHER:

The next lesson concerns joining not only a compound subject but also other parts of speech.

Below are the examples used on pages 494-495. I have placed more information for you than I have placed on the student worksheet. Because you know your students best, you can determine if you want to include parts of speech (and in two cases, how they serve in the sentence).

Examples:	She *sang* and *whistled*.	**(verbs)**
	Mom buys *juice* and *water*.	**(nouns-direct objects)**
	He and *I* are good friends.	**(pronouns-subject)**
	Her hair is *short* and *curly*.	**(adjectives)**
	They looked *up* and *down*.	**(adverbs)**

492

MY OWN NOTES

Two items can be joined by **and**. <u>They do not have to join the subject</u> of a sentence.

> **Examples:**   She *sang* and *whistled*.
>
> Mom buys *juice* and *water*.
>
> *He* and *I* are good friends.
>
> Her hair is *short* and *curly*.
>
> They looked *up* and *down*.
> ෨෨෨

Sometimes, <u>three or more</u> items are joined.

> **Example:**   Jason has keys, coins, and a comb in his pocket.

Place a comma after the items in a series that occur before *and*. Do no place a comma after **and/or** or after the *last item*.

> **Example:**   Do you want water, a soda, juice, or milk to drink?
>
> ෨෨෨෨෨෨෨෨෨෨෨෨

Directions: Join sentences.

> **Example:**   The farmer owns a cow.
> The farmer owns five goats.
> The farmer owns ten hens.

> <u>**The farmer owns a cow, five goats, and ten hens.**</u>

1. The chef made bread. The chef made a salad. The chef made a dessert.
    <u>**The chef made bread, a salad, and a dessert.**</u>

494

Two items can be joined by **and**. <u>They do not have to join the subject</u> of a sentence.

> **Examples:**   She *sang* and *whistled*.
>
> Mom buys *juice* and *water*.
>
> *He* and *I* are good friends.
>
> Her hair is *short* and *curly*.
>
> They looked *up* and *down*.
> ❧❧❧

Sometimes, <u>three or more</u> items are joined.

> **Example:**   Jason has keys, coins, and a comb in his pocket.

Place a comma after the items in a series that occur before *and*. Do no place a comma after **and/or** or after the *last item*.

> **Example:**   Do you want water, a soda, juice, or milk to drink?
> ❧❧❧❧❧❧❧❧❧❧❧❧

Directions: Join sentences.

> **Example:**   The farmer owns a cow.
> The farmer owns five goats.
> The farmer owns ten hens.

> ## <u>The farmer owns a cow, five goats, and ten hens.</u>

1. The chef made bread. The chef made a salad. The chef made a dessert.

_____

_____

2. Bob is going to a baseball game.
   Tara is going to a baseball game.
   Luis is going to a baseball game, too.

   __**Bob, Tara, and Luis are going to a baseball game.**__

   _____

3. A girl stood.
   She waved.
   She cheered.

   __**A girl stood, waved, and cheered.**__

   _____

4. I want to hike with Kim.
   I want to hike with Josh.
   I want to hike with Emily, also.

   __**I want to hike with Kim, Josh, and Emily.**__

   _____

5. Jana's grandma sends her cards.
   Jana's grandma sends her posters.
   Jana's grandma sends her pictures of tigers.

   __**Jana's grandma sends her cards, posters, and pictures of**__

   __**tigers.**__

6. An elephant stopped.
   An elephant tilted his head from side to side.
   An elephant lifted his trunk, also.

   __**An elephant stopped, tilted his head from side to side, and**__

   __**lifted his trunk.**__

496

2. Bob is going to a baseball game.
   ~~Tara is going to a baseball game.~~
   Luis is going to a baseball game, too.

   _____

   _____

3. A girl stood.
   She waved.
   She cheered.

   _____

   _____

4. I want to hike with Kim.
   I want to hike with Josh.
   I want to hike with Emily, also.

   _____

   _____

5. Jana's grandma sends her cards.
   Jana's grandma sends her posters.
   Jana's grandma sends her pictures of tigers.

   _____

   _____

6. An elephant stopped.
   An elephant tilted his head from side to side.
   An elephant lifted his trunk, also.

   _____

   _____

Two or more items can be joined by a conjunction. A conjunction is **and**, **or**, or **but**.

Examples: *Mike*, *Moe*, and *Mia* are triplets.   **(nouns-subject)**

The bug *flew* by, *buzzed*, and *landed*.   **(verbs)**

Give your books to *him* and *me*.   **(pronouns)**

Our teacher is *smart, funny*, and *strict*.   **(adjectives)**

The judge spoke *slowly, clearly, and kindly*.   **(adverbs)**

Place a comma when there are more than two items in a series.
Do not place a comma after *and/or/but* or after the *last item*.
🐦🐦🐦
Sometimes, the verb will change.

Examples: Cheese **is** on the table.
Fruit **is** on the table.
Bread **is** on the table.

Cheese, fruit, and bread are on the table.

Kit **owns** a scooter.
Parker **owns** a scooter.
Lisa **owns** a scooter.

Kit, Parker, and Lisa own a scooter.
🐦🐦🐦🐦🐦🐦🐦🐦🐦🐦🐦🐦

Directions: Join sentences.

1.   Movies are sold at the video store.
Games are sold at the video store.
Comics are sold at the video store.

Movies, games, and comics are sold at the video store.

_____

Two or more items can be joined by a conjunction. A conjunction is *and*, *or*, or *but*.

Examples: *Mike*, *Moe*, and *Mia* are triplets.   (nouns-subject)

The bug *flew* by, *buzzed*, and *landed*.   (verbs)

Give your books to *him* and *me*.   (pronouns)

Our teacher is *smart*, *funny*, and *strict*.   (adjectives)

The judge spoke *slowly*, *clearly*, and *kindly*.   (adverbs)

Place a comma when there are more than two items in a series.
Do not place a comma after *and/or/but* or after the *last item*.
ॐॐॐ

Sometimes, the verb will change.

Examples: Cheese **is** on the table.
Fruit **is** on the table.
Bread **is** on the table.

Cheese, fruit, and bread are on the table.

Kit **owns** a scooter.
Parker **owns** a scooter.
Lisa **owns** a scooter.

Kit, Parker, and Lisa own a scooter.
ॐॐॐॐॐॐॐॐॐॐॐ

Directions: Join sentences.

1.   Movies are sold at the video store.
Games are sold at the video store.
Comics are sold at the video store.

_____

_____

2. The man ordered fish.
   He ordered chips.
   He ordered lemonade.

   _____ **The man ordered fish, chips, and lemonade.** _____

   _____

3. Hannah has a goldfish.
   Her brother has a goldfish.
   Her sister has a goldfish, also.

   _____ **Hannah, her brother, and her sister have goldfish.** _____

   _____

4. The patient smiled.
   The patient opened his mouth.
   The patient stuck out his tongue.

   _____ **The patient smiled, opened his mouth, and stuck out his** _____

   _____ **tongue.** _____

5. Lana walks to her mailbox.
   Lana sometimes skips to her mailbox.
   Sometimes, Lana hops to her mailbox.

   _____ **Lana walks, hops, or skips to her mailbox.** _____

   _____

6. Tate walks with his mother to his baseball games.
   Tate sometimes walks with his dad to his baseball games.
   Tate sometimes walks with his sisters to his baseball games.

   _____ **Tate walks with his mother, dad, or sisters to his baseball** _____

   _____ **games.** _____

500

2. The man ordered fish.
   He ordered chips.
   He ordered lemonade.

   _____

   _____

3. Hannah has a goldfish.
   Her brother has a goldfish.
   Her sister has a goldfish, also.

   _____

   _____

4. The patient smiled.
   The patient opened his mouth.
   The patient stuck out his tongue.

   _____

   _____

5. Lana walks to her mailbox.
   Lana sometimes skips to her mailbox.
   Sometimes, Lana hops to her mailbox.

   _____

   _____

6. Tate walks with his mother to his baseball games.
   Tate sometimes walks with his dad to his baseball games.
   Tate sometimes walks with his sisters to his baseball games.

   _____

   _____

An appositive is a word or group of words that explains something in a sentence.

> **Example:**   We are looking for Banter.

Who is Banter? We don't know. Now look at the sentence with words that explain who Banter is. These words are called an **appositive**.

An appositive is placed <u>next to</u> the word it explains.

> **Example:**   We are looking for Banter, **his lost dog**.
>   **appositive**

An appositive is set off by commas.

> **Example:**   Miss Sue, **a teacher**, bikes to school.
>   ↑   ↑
>   We heard a noise, **a loud scream**.
>   ↑

೩೩೩೩೩೩೩೩೩೩೩೩

Directions: Place the appositive by the word it explains.

> **Example:**   They watched *Mary Poppins*.
>   *Mary Poppins* is their favorite musical.

<u>They watched *Mary Poppins, their favorite musical.*</u>

1. Sandy is a dentist.
    Sandy is their cousin.

    _____**Sandy,** *their cousin*, **is a dentist**._____

502

Date_____ **Appositives**

An appositive is a word or group of words that explains something in a sentence.

      Example: We are looking for Banter.

Who is Banter? We don't know. Now look at the sentence with words that explain who Banter is. These words are called an **appositive**.

An appositive is placed <u>next to</u> the word it explains.

      Example: We are looking for Banter, **his lost dog**.
                                         appositive

An appositive is set off by commas.

      Example: Miss Sue, **a teacher**, bikes to school.

                                We heard a noise, **a loud scream**.

৵৵৵৵৵৵৵৵৵৵৵৵

Directions: Place the appositive by the word it explains.

      Example: They watched *Mary Poppins*.
                         Mary Poppins is their favorite musical.

<u>**They watched *Mary Poppins, their favorite musical.***</u>

1. Sandy is a dentist.
     Sandy is their cousin.

     Sandy, _____**, is a dentist.**

2. Marty is a classmate.
    Marty won a writing contest.

    Marty, *a classmate,* won a writing contest.

3. I nearly stepped on a slug.
    A slug is a slimy animal.

    I nearly stepped on a slug, *a slimy animal.*

4. Iceland is near the Arctic Circle.
    Iceland is an island.

    Iceland, *an island,* is near the Arctic

    Circle.

5. Have you eaten a mango? Mango is a fruit grown in Hawaii.

    Have you eaten a mango, *a fruit grown in*

    Hawaii?

6. We saw mica at a rock show.
    Mica is a shiny mineral.

    We saw mica, *a shiny mineral,* at a rock

    show.

504

2. Marty is a classmate.
   Marty won a writing contest.

   Marty, **, won a writing** **contest.**

3. I nearly stepped on a slug.
   A slug is a slimy animal.

   I nearly stepped on a slug,

4. Iceland is near the Arctic Circle.
   Iceland is an island.

   Iceland, **, is near the Arctic** **Circle.**

5. Have you eaten a mango? Mango is a fruit grown in Hawaii.

   Have you eaten a mango,

6. We saw mica at a rock show.
   Mica is a shiny mineral.

   We saw mica, **, at a rock** **show.**

An appositive is a word or group of words that explains something in a sentence.

> **Example:**   Mike is coming to visit.

Who is Mike? We don't know. Now look at the sentence with words that explain who Mike is. These words are called an **appositive**.

> **Example:**   Mike, **my uncle**, is coming to visit.
> appositive

An appositive is placed <u>next to</u> the word it explains.

> **Example:**   I love Sassy, their cat.
> appositive

An appositive is set off by commas.

> **Example:**   Miss Pinky, **our pony**, was a gift.
> ↑   ↑

> Cass is going to Harney, **her hometown**.
> ↑

ॐ ॐ ॐ ॐ ॐ ॐ ॐ ॐ ॐ ॐ ॐ

Directions: Place the appositive by the word it explains.

> **Example:**   Gee is fun.
>   Gee is his grandmother.

__**Gee,**_____**, is fun**.__

__**Gee,** *his grandmother*, **is fun**.__

1. Jim left for college.
    Jim is my brother.

__**Jim,** *my brother*, **left for college**.__

506

Name________________________________ **Writing Sentences**

Date________________________________ **Appositives**

An appositive is a word or group of words that explains something in a sentence.

Example: Mike is coming to visit.

Who is Mike? We don't know. Now look at the sentence with words that explain who Mike is. These words are called an **appositive**.

Example: Mike, **my uncle**, is coming to visit.
appositive

An appositive is placed <u>next to</u> the word it explains.

Example: I love Sassy, their cat.
appositive

An appositive is set off by commas.

Example: Miss Pinky, **our pony**, was a gift.
↑ ↑

Cass is going to Harney, **her hometown.**
↑

Directions: Place the appositive by the word it explains.

Example: Gee is fun.
Gee is his grandmother.

Gee, ______________________, is fun.

Gee, *his grandmother*, **is fun.**

1. Jim left for college.
   Jim is my brother.

   Jim, ______________________, left for college.

2. Kimmy ran after her pet.
    Her pet is a goose.

    Kimmy ran after her pet, *a goose.*

3. That lady is pretty.
    That lady is my mother.

    That lady, *my mother,* **is pretty.**

4. Layla gave me a present.
    It was a yoyo.

    Layla gave me a present, *a yoyo.*

5. Mrs. Pope is a judge. Mrs. Pope took a vacation.

    Mrs. Pope, *a judge,* **took a vacation.**

6. He plays a fife.
    A fife is a musical instrument similar to a flute

    He plays a fife, *a musical instrument similar*

    to a flute.

7. The town built a new building.
    The building is a six-story hospital.

    The town built a new building, *a six-story*

    hospital.

508

2. Kimmy ran after her pet.
   Her pet is a goose.

   _____**Kimmy ran after her pet,**_____

3. That lady is pretty.
   That lady is my mother.

   _____**That lady,**_____**, is pretty**._____

4. Layla gave me a present.
   It was a yoyo.

   _____**Layla gave me a present,**_____

5. Mrs. Pope is a judge. Mrs. Pope took a vacation.

   _____**Mrs. Pope,**_____**, took a**_____

   _____**vacation**._____

6. He plays a fife.
   A fife is a musical instrument similar to a flute

   _____**He plays a fife,**_____

   _____

7. The town built a new building.
   The building is a six-story hospital.

   _____**The town built a new building,**_____

   _____

TO THE TEACHER:

The first 10 lessons (days) of **DAILY GRAMS: Guided Review Aiding Mastery Skills - Grade 3** appear on the ensuing pages. These are placed here for you and your students to experience the benefits of daily reviews.

Suggestions:

1. Make a copy for each student. Have students complete a *Daily Grams* review at the beginning of each English class. (This should take only a few minutes.) If you ask for volunteers to write the sentence combining on the board, it may take longer.

2. Ask students to read or write in journals until everyone is finished.

3. Using a transparency that you have made before class, go over the *Daily Grams* review. Be sure to solicit answers from students and discuss them. (The *Answer Key* is located after Day 10.)

4. Upon completion, move on to whatever you are doing in your regular lesson.

Daily Grams Workbooks are available for classroom use. They prove to be both time saving and cost effective.

510

CAPITALIZATION:

Capitalize the days of the week.

Example: Friday

1. we will go next tuesday.

PUNCTUATION:

Place a period after the abbreviation of titles with a name.

Example: Mrs. Soto

However, do not place a period after *Miss* in a title.

Example: Miss Cleek

2. Mr Jones

PARTS OF SPEECH: VERBS

Write the contraction:

3. is not - _____

PARTS OF SPEECH: NOUNS

A noun names a person, place, or thing.

Circle the noun that names a <u>thing</u> in this sentence.

4. The tree is growing.

SENTENCE COMBINING:

5. My sister is nice.

My sister is funny.

_____

_____

DAY 2

CAPITALIZATION:

    Capitalize a person's name.
    Capitalize initials.
    Capitalize a title used with a name.

        Example: Mr. Tony Loon

1.   does mrs. vargas live here?

PUNCTUATION:
    Place a comma between the number for the day and the year in a date.
        Example: March 1, 2002

  2. May 9 2015

PARTS OF SPEECH: **NOUNS**
    Plural means more than one. Most nouns add s to form the plural.

    Place a ✔ if the plural is formed by adding s:

3. A. _____ dog
     B. _____ skate
     C. _____ child

ALPHABETIZING:
    Write these words in alphabetical order:

4.   little   crayon   banana

        (1) _____
        (2) _____
        (3) _____

SENTENCE COMBINING:

5.   The lake is deep.
     The lake is wide.

_____

_____

512

CAPITALIZATION:

Capitalize the months of the year.

Example: January

1.   his birthday is in september.

PUNCTUATION:

2.   Miss Smith and Mrs Sims

PARTS OF SPEECH: NOUNS

A noun names a person, place, or thing.

Circle a noun that names a <u>place</u> in this sentence.

3.   I like the zoo.

SYNONYMS:

Synonyms are words with similar meanings.

Circle a synonym for *fast:*

4.   **fast:**   (a) slow   (b) tiresome   (c) rapid

SENTENCE COMBINING:

5.   A bee came close to me.

It was a bumble bee.

_____

_____

DAY 4

CAPITALIZATION:

Do not capitalize seasons of the year.

Examples: winter   autumn

1.   last summer i saw dr. little.

PUNCTUATION:

2.   May 8 1990

SUBJECT/VERB:

The subject of a sentence tells <u>who</u> or <u>what</u> the sentence is about.

Underline the subject once:

3.   That door is old.

SENTENCE TYPES:

A <u>statement</u> tells something.

A <u>question</u> asks something.

Name the type of sentence:

4.   We like ice cream. _____

SENTENCE COMBINING:

5.   The cat meowed

The cat purred.

_____

_____

514

CAPITALIZATION:

Capitalize the name of streets, roads, avenues, and other roadways.

Example: Hott Road

1.   he lives on cobb street.

PUNCTUATION:

Place a comma between the day of the week and the date.

Example: Friday, June 16, 2000

2. Saturday July 14 2001

PARTS OF SPEECH: VERBS:

Write the contraction:

3.   do not - _____

SUBJECT/VERB:

The subject of a sentence tells <u>who</u> or <u>what</u> the sentence is about.

Underline the subject once:

4.   Jenny is five years old.

SENTENCE COMBINING:

5.   A tree was planted.

The tree was a pine.

_____

_____

DAY 6

CAPITALIZATION:

Capitalize holidays and special days.

Examples: Memorial Day   Valentine's Day

1.   is easter on a sunday?

PUNCTUATION:

2.   Tuesday August 7

PARTS OF SPEECH: ADJECTIVES

Adjectives usually describe.

Circle the adjective that describes *shoes:*

3.   They took off muddy shoes.

PARTS OF SPEECH: VERBS

The verb must agree with the subject.
In present time - if the subject is singular (one), add s to the verb.

Example: My <u>mother</u> laugh**s** often.

Place two lines under the verb that agrees with the subject:

4.   This <u>apple</u> (taste, tastes) sour.

SENTENCE COMBINING:

5.   A baby laughs.

     A baby cries.

_____

_____

CAPITALIZATION:

1. we celebrate flag day* in june.

*name of a special day

PUNCTUATION:

Place a period at the end of a sentence that makes a statement.

Example: Her grandpa made lunch.

2. Dr Willis and I are friends

PARTS OF SPEECH: NOUNS

A noun names a person, place, or thing.

Circle the noun that names a <u>person</u>:

3. A fireman helped with a bake sale.

PARTS OF SPEECH: VERBS

The subject of a sentence tells <u>who</u> or <u>what</u> the sentence is about.

A verb tells what <u>is</u> (<u>was</u>) or what <u>happens</u> (<u>happened</u>) in a sentence.

Example: <u>She</u> <u>rubbed</u> her sore foot.

Underline the subject once and the verb twice:

4. The car skidded.

SENTENCE COMBINING:

5. A man came into the store.

The man was tall.

_____

_____

DAY 8

CAPITALIZATION:

> **Capitalize the name of a town or city.**
>
> > Example: Los Angeles

1.   has mario been to Nashville?

PUNCTUATION:

> **Place a question mark at the end of a sentence that asks a question.**
>
> > Example: Will you take me along with you?

2.   Who is going

PARTS OF SPEECH: ADJECTIVES

> **Adjectives usually describe.**
> **Circle the adjective.**

3.   Red flowers bloomed.

PARTS OF SPEECH: VERBS

> **Write the contraction:**

4.   A.   did not - _____

  B.   I am - _____

SENTENCE COMBINING:

5.   Nani's hair is blonde.

  Nani's hair is curly.

  _____

  _____

518

CAPITALIZATION:

Capitalize the name of a state or both letters of a state's postal code.

Examples: Alabama
AL

1.   has mr. b. j. smith arrived in michigan?

PUNCTUATION:

Place an exclamation point (!) after an interjection. An interjection is a word or words that show excitement.   Example: Oh!

Place an exclamation point at the end of a sentence that shows excitement.   Example: I did it!

2.   Yeah   We won

PARTS OF SPEECH: NOUNS

A noun names a person, place, or thing.

Circle a noun that names a <u>person</u>:

3.   A girl walked slowly.

PARTS OF SPEECH: VERBS

**The subject of a sentence tells <u>who</u> or <u>what</u> the sentence is about.
A verb tells what <u>is</u> (<u>was</u>) or <u>what happens</u> (<u>happened</u>) in a sentence.**

Example: <u>He</u> <u>has</u> two sisters.

Underline the subject once and the verb twice:

4.   My big toe hurts.

SENTENCE COMBINING:

5.   Karen stopped.
Karen sat down.

_____

_____

DAY 10

CAPITALIZATION:

1. we send cards on mother's day.

PUNCTUATION:
   Place an apostrophe (') + s after a person's name to show ownership.

   Example: Lisa's lunch

2. Tonys friend is Jose

PARTS OF SPEECH: VERBS

   Some verbs show action.

   Example: We **jumped** up and down.

   Some verbs help to make a statement.

   Example: Dad **is** tall.

   Place a ✔ if the verb is an action verb:

3. A. _____ He **shook** his rug.   C. _____ That dog **barks** at everyone.

   B. _____ You **are** funny.   D. _____ She **opened** her gate.

SENTENCE TYPES:

   A <u>statement</u> **tells something.**
   A <u>question</u> **asks something.**
   A <u>command</u> **tells you to do something.**

   Name the sentence type:

4. A.   Throw this away.   _____

   B.   Are you happy?   _____

SENTENCE COMBINING:

5. The boys threw a ball.
   The boys chased the ball.

   _____

   _____

520

Answers

NOTE: *AMV/RA* means *ANSWERS MAY VARY/REPRESENTATIVE ANSWERS.*

Day 1: 1. We, Tuesday   **2.** Mr. Jones   **3.** isn't   **4.** tree   **5.**
AMV/RA: My sister is nice and funny. My funny sister is nice.

Day 2: 1. Does, Mrs., Vargas   **2.** May 9, 2015   **3.** A. ✔ B. ✔
C. ___   **4.** (1) banana (2) crayon (3) little   **5.** AMV/RA: The lake is deep
and wide. The wide lake is deep.

Day 3: 1. His, September   **2.** Miss Smith and Mrs. Sims   **3.** zoo
4. (c) rapid   **5.** AMV/RA: A bumble bee came close to me.

Day 4: 1. Last, I, Dr., Little   **2.** May 8, 1990   **3.** door   **4.** statement*
5. AMV/RA: The cat meowed and purred.

*Note: The terms *declarative, interrogative, imperative,* and *exclamatory* will be
introduced later in this text.

Day 5: 1. He, Cobb, Street   **2.** Saturday, July 14, 2001   **3.** don't
4. Jenny   **5.** AMV/RA: A pine tree was planted.

Day 6: 1. Is, Easter, Sunday   **2.** Tuesday, August 7   **3.** muddy
4. tastes   **5.** AMV/RA: A baby laughs and cries. A baby laughs but also cries.

Day 7: 1. We, Flag, Day, June   **2.** Dr. Willis and I are friends.
3. fireman   **4.** car skidded   **5.** AMV/RA: A tall man came into the store.

Day 8: 1. Has, Mario, Nashville   **2.** Who is going?   **3.** Red (Red flowers)
4. A. didn't B. I'm   **5.** AMV/RA: Nani's hair is blonde and curly. Nani's
blonde hair is curly.

Day 9: 1. Has, Mr., B., J., Smith, Michigan   **2.** Yeah! We won!   **3.** girl
4. toe hurts   **5.** AMV/RA: Karen stopped and sat down.

Day 10: 1. We, Mother's, Day   **2.** Tony's friend is Jose.   **3.** A. ✔ B. ___
C. ✔ D. ✔   **4.** A. command B. question   **5.** AMV/RA: The boys
threw and chased a ball.

ASSESSMENT ANSWERS:

You may use your own point system.

A. Sentence Types: (4 points)

1. __C__   Put the cereal away.
2. __B__   Yeah! I'm finished!
3. __D__   Where's your dog?
4. __A__   Kim ate a few grapes.

A. declarative
B. exclamatory
C. imperative
D. interrogative

B. Capitalization: (11 points – ½ point each)
NOTE: If students capitalize a word that should not be capitalized, deduct a point.

1. **O**n **M**onday, **I** am going to **K**aw **L**ake near **P**onca **C**ity.

2. **J**ake asked, "**W**ho lives on **D**ale **L**ane?"

3. **D**ear **L**iz,

      Is **U**ncle **B**o driving to **L**ong **B**each on **M**emorial

    Day this spring?

                      Your buddy,
                      Tate

C. Punctuation: (7 points – ½ point each)
NOTE: If students insert additional punctuation, deduct a point.

1. Emily, may I help you**?**

2. No, we can**'**t leave before 4**:**00**.**

3. Yikes**!** I**'**m late**!**

4. We met Mr**.** J**.** Cobb on Dec**.** 24**,** 2004**.**

D. Subjects and Verbs: (8 points)
NOTE: Deleting prepositional phrases helps students to identify subject and verb. However, this was
not part of the instructions. Count 1 point for each correct subject and 1 for each correct verb.
Both parts of a compound must be identified in order to earn a point.

1. Our **aunt** **visits** ~~at the end of every summer~~.

2. ~~After lunch,~~ two **boys** **sat** ~~under a tree~~ and **talked**.

3. My **sister** and big **brother** **camp** ~~in a state park~~.

4. The **shed** ~~behind the big barn~~ **was struck** ~~by a car~~.

522

E. Contractions: (6 points)

1. are not - __**aren't**__   3. we are - __**we're**__   5. here is - __**here's**__

2. who is - __**who's**__   4. have not - __**haven't**__   6. were not - __**weren't**__

F. Subject-Verb Agreement: (6 points)

NOTE: Deleting prepositional phrases helps students to make subject and verb agree.
However, this was not part of the instructions. Count 1 point for a correct
subject and 1 for a correct verb.

1. ~~On the weekends~~, their **dad** (bake, **bakes**).

2. The **pastor** and his **wife** (plays, play) tennis.

3. **Farmers** ~~in that dry area~~ (**hope**, hopes) ~~for rain~~.

G. Irregular Verbs: (14 points)

NOTE: Count 1 point for the subject, 1 point for the correct helping verb(s), and 1 for each correct past
participle. The subject does not receive a point; it was used to help determine the verb phrase.

1. That **team has** (chose, **chosen**) uniforms.

2. **He must have** (**flown**, flew) home.

3. A **check could be** (wrote, **written**).

4. **Pears were** (ate, **eaten**) ~~for a snack~~.

5. **Have you** ever (saw, **seen**) a rattler?

6. The **river had** (rose, **risen**) two feet.

7. **Lanzo should have** (took, **taken**) his father's advice.

H. Tenses: (6 points)

NOTE: Count 1 point for subject *and* verb and 1 point for the correct tense.

1. __**PRESENT**__   Berry **tarts are** our dessert.

2. __**FUTURE**__   The **bell will ring** soon.

3. __**PAST**__   My **sister sneezed**.

I. Common and Proper Nouns: (4 points)

1. EMMA   2. **DOG**   3. **POODLE**   4. **CITY**

523

J. Singular and Plural Nouns: (8 points)

1. zebra - **zebras**   5. deer - **deer**
2. ruby - **rubies**   6. tray - **trays**
3. mix - **mixes**   7. watch - **watches**
4. child - **children**   8. calf - **calves**

K. Possessive Nouns: (6 points)

1. a drum that belongs to Ben - **Ben's drum**
2. a corral used by many horses - **horses' corral**
3. computer belonging to children - **children's computer**

L. Identifying Nouns: (4 points)
NOTE: If students circle a word that is not a noun, deduct a point.
1. We need to take this **shovel**, a sleeping **bag**, two **tents**, and some strong **rope**.

M. Conjunctions and Interjections: (2 points)
    Intj.
1. **Wow!** Jacy won!
                            Conj.
2. Give your ticket to my friend **or** me.

N. Identifying Adjectives: (6 points)
NOTE: If students circle a word that is not an adjective, deduct a point.
1. **Many dirty** rags lay on **the new** carpet.

2. We ordered **orange** juice and **French** toast.

O. Degrees of Adjectives: (6 points)

1. The second pail of water was (**sudsier**, sudsiest) than the first.

2. Of the five kittens, the gray one is (more playful, **most playful**).

3. My left foot is (**longer**, longest) than my right one.

P. Adverbs: (4 points)
NOTE: If students circle a word that is not an adverb, deduct a point.
1. One child stood **up quietly**.

524

2. Peter **always** goes **there** with his family.

Q. Degrees of Adverbs: (6 points)

1. Of the four friends, Tate swims (better, **best**).

2. Lisa rides her bike (oftener, **more often**) than her brother.

3. He held the second rope (**more tightly**, most tightly) than the first rope.

R. Pronouns: (12 points)

1. (**She**, Her) likes shepherd's pie.

2. Will a bellman take (we, **us**) to our room?

3. Jacy and (him, **he**) played checkers.

4. Today, (me and my friend, my friend and me, **my friend and I**) rode in a taxi.

5. These shells are for (**them**, they).

6. Mr. Bonds chose (we, **us**) to hand out programs.

S. Usage: (6 points)

1. I don't feel (good, **well**).

2. Marco doesn't know (nothing, **anything**) about it.

3. Do you want to go to the zoo to see (**an**, a) elephant?

4. The eagles soared high above (its, **their**) nest.

5. (Your, **You're**) a great skater!

T. Other Items: (6 points)

1. Circle the direct object: A boy threw a **stone** into the stream.

2. Circle the object of the preposition: That man in the dark blue **suit** is my uncle.

3. Write a regular verb: <u>**to stay** or **stay**</u>   (ANSWERS MAY VARY/REPRESENTATIVE ANSWER)

4. Write an irregular verb: <u>**to go** or **go**</u>   (ANSWERS MAY VARY/REPRESENTATIVE ANSWER)

NOTE ABOUT SCORING THE ASSESSMENT TEST:

You may want to ascribe a **percentage grade** to your test. **Don't let 140 points confuse you.** You may have a computer program to convert this. If you don't and want to use a percentage grade, two ideas have been provided.

a) You can divide the number of points scored by **140**.

For example: student score of 121 points (correct) divided by 140:

$$\frac{121}{140} \ = \ 87\% \quad \textit{(round up)}$$

b) Divide the student's score by 2.

$$\frac{121}{2} \ = \ 61 \quad \textit{(round up)}$$

Then, subtract that number from 70. $(70 - 61 = 9)$

Place your *Easy Grader* to 70. Go down the column to *9*. It should read 87%.

INDEX

CORRELATION of

Easy Grammar Workbook 3 with

Easy Grammar: Grade 3 teacher edition